SOCIETY OF WOMEN: A STUDY OF A WOMEN'S PRISON

SOCIETY OF WOMEN:
A STUDY OF A WOMEN'S PRISON

ROSE GIALLOMBARDO
NEW YORK UNIVERSITY

JOHN WILEY & SONS, INC.
NEW YORK   LONDON   SYDNEY

Copyright © 1966 by John Wiley & Sons, Inc.

Library of Congress Catalog Card Number: 66-14132
Printed in the United States of America

TO MY MOTHER AND FATHER

PREFACE

This book is an exploratory study of an adult prison for women. My purpose is to examine the prison from a sociological perspective, that is, as a system of roles and functions and to make comparisons with the literature on the male prison in order to increase our understanding of the prison structure within its larger societal context.

To analyze a community as a system of roles and functions is by no means an easy task. For the careful observer, the continuity of events is the important aspect. It is necessary, therefore, to examine the structure over a considerable length of time. The data for this study were gathered over a period of one year from July 1962 to July 1963, at the Federal Reformatory for Women, Alderson, West Virginia. In this connection, I am deeply in debt to James V. Bennett, former Director of Federal Prisons, who recognized the need for a comprehensive scientific study of the adult female prison and approved the project. His splendid cooperation made it possible for me to examine all aspects of the Alderson prison in considerable detail. Keen appreciation is also expressed to John C. Galvin and Benjamin Frank who helped in several important ways.

Needless to say, this study would not have been possible without the collective cooperation of the Alderson inmates who granted me the privilege of their hospitality and confidence.

Were I to discharge my responsibility to acknowledge members of the Alderson prison staff who cooperated in the research, it would be necessary for me to include almost every member of the staff. For obvious reasons, this is not feasible. I can only say that their cooperation was indispensable. However, there are several staff members to whom I owe special thanks and to whom

I would like to acknowledge my appreciation in print. Miss Gladys V. Bowman, Warden of the Federal Reformatory for Women, and Mrs. Virginia MacGlaughlin cooperated in every phase of the research. In addition, my many long conversations with them were extremely helpful in aiding me to understand the prison. I also owe thanks to Mrs. Helen England and her staff of lieutenants who cheerfully assumed the arduous task of scheduling all correctional officers to designated classrooms during working hours, so that I could conveniently administer a questionnaire.

Financial assistance from several sources made the study possible and is hereby gratefully acknowledged. A Public Affairs Grant and a fellowship from Northwestern University helped to support me while I was doing the field work and writing up the results. A grant from the Arts and Sciences Research Fund of New York University provided secretarial and clerical assistance.

I am indebted to Paul J. Bohannan and Raymond W. Mack who were close to the research from the beginning and whose enthusiasm helped immensely. I am especially grateful to Paul Bohannan, who provided much guidance during the period that I was doing the field work. In addition, he generously devoted considerable time to a critical and valuable examination of the manuscript. My greatest personal debt is to Richard D. Schwartz who directed the research from the planning stage through every phase of the study. I had the benefit of his advice and exacting criticism on every facet of the work, and he provided an unfailing source of encouragement. Erwin O. Smigel and Stanton Wheeler have been kind enough to read the entire manuscript, and I offer them my thanks.

An editorial problem should be brought to the attention of the reader. All the names of individuals used are fictitious. If any inmate or staff member at the prison had the same name as any which I used, it is coincidental.

Rose Giallombardo

New York City
December 1965

CONTENTS

CONTENTS

CHAPTER 1 ANALYSIS OF THE PROBLEM

Since Clemmer's classic work on the prison community was published in 1940, more and more attention has been focused on the prison as an object of scientific study. However, a review of the literature reveals the anomaly that the voluminous and rich work in the field has been confined—except in rare instances—exclusively to the study of male prisons and the singular adjustment problems of male prisoners.

The female prison community has been overlooked; it merits study, as does any other complex organization, in order to add to the growing body of theory on group behavior. The purpose of this study, then, is to fill this gap by examining in an exploratory way the structure of a women's prison as an organization of roles and functions, in order to increase our understanding of its numerous variables and complex interactions. My interest in social organization leads me to place emphasis upon relationships and interdependence in the processes of social interaction, upon the interpersonal and intergroup relations which are important in any study of social organization.[1] As a result, this research aims first of all to penetrate deeply into the social life of the female prison community [2] and to uncover the significance of its activities, from the standpoint of its members, for the informal and the formal structure of the organization. The dynamics of the inmate social role-playing and an inquiry into the processes of acquiring various types of inmate roles will be investigated.

A crucial area for further research lies in the comparison of organizations with differing social structures. I think the comparison of male and female prison communities is a good place to begin. The prison, a social setting, provides the researcher with an ideal social laboratory in which to test existing sociological theories. The comparability of prisons everywhere and the extreme conditions to which the prison aggregate must adapt offer a remarkable opportunity to determine the conditions under which certain behavioral patterns emerge.

The second objective of the study is to compare the findings of the female prison community with relevant literature on the social system of the male prison in order to determine what is common and what is variable. This research is a pioneering effort to establish a point of departure in this direction, underscoring the assumption that a comparative approach may provide additional understanding or raise significant questions about the nature of the two communities.

REVIEW OF CORE LITERATURE ON FEMALE PRISONER

The literature on women's prisons and the female prisoner is long on impressions and short on empirical data. A sizable portion may be subsumed under these general headings: first, articles which are programmatic in nature;[3] second, autobiographical accounts of released inmates;[4] third, historical accounts;[5] fourth, sensational exposés;[6] and, finally, attempts to establish the extent of the criminality of women.[7]

Unfortunately, the scientific description and analysis of the female prison and female prisoner have been overlooked. Rare exceptions may be noted. Kellor[8] studied the mentality of female offenders. As early as 1900, she reported a marked difference in the degree of mental defectiveness between prostitutes and other female offenders, the former being more defective than the latter. In a study of women after confinement, the Gluecks reported that in only 15.2 percent of the cases was the reformatory experience effective in curbing their delinquencies. In 84.8 percent of the cases, the prison experience did not succeed in preventing recidivism.[9]

Murtagh and Harris'[10] brief descriptive account of facilities for prostitutes in the New York House of Detention calls attention to the loyalty among the inmates. The authors suggest that the loyalty exists because "prison is the great leveler."[11]

A fictionalized autobiographical version of one woman's experience in the same prison describes an interesting kinship pattern which existed among Negro inmates. Several "family groups" were said to exist. These "family groups" were headed by a grandmother and grandfather, and included a father and mother, many children and grandchildren, aunts and uncles, as well as cousins, nieces, and nephews. The positions of grandmother, grandfather, mother, and father were held by individuals who "had gone together for some time." Incestuous relationships were said to pose problems for the group and to cause shifts in titles and family positions.[12] Murtagh and Harris, however, make no mention of this social phenomenon.

Margaret Otis describes homosexual practices between Negro and white delinquent girls in an institution in one of the Eastern states and maintains that difference in color takes the place of difference in sex.[13] Affairs are initiated by both Negro and white girls. Sexual significance, jealousies, states of martyrdom are prevalent in the relationship. Fifteen years later, in a different location and in another institution, Ford described similar conditions.[14] The Negro-white relationships, martyr feelings, sexual significance, and jealousies have been seen to persist. Participation in homosexuality is a voluntary matter; force is never brought to bear. "Friend" is the term applied to one engaged in homosexuality. Interestingly enough, no attempt is made to limit oneself to one "friend." The relationship between the two individuals is usually that of husband and wife. That is, in the notes they pass one person assumes the role of husband and the other of wife. However, the assumed role is not always the same for concurrent or subsequent "friendships." This would seem to suggest that these girls, besides lacking "fidelity," are also occupying dominant and submissive roles with respect to the same behavior.

Thus we see that both writers found homosexuality to be present in these institutions for female juveniles. Although much of the contact among inmates was said to consist solely of note passing between "friends," there was evidence of physical contact. By and large, the relationships appear to be characterized by egalitarianism.

There has been a clear lack of empirical work focused upon

the social organization of the female prison. An exception is the work of Harper.[15] Harper's analysis of a deviant role, i.e., the role of the "fringer," makes the point that these inmates achieved distinction because they did not confine themselves to either of the two "factions" into which the author found the staff and inmates to be divided. Each faction developed a power structure with a hierarchical arrangement in which a staff member was the leader. The author states that the staff leaders of the two factions had strong political support outside the institution, but we do not know how it was possible for the leaders to organize the inmates into the two factions.

Moreover, the fringer includes *both* staff members and inmates, and it is a very infrequent role. According to the author, there were nine individuals occupying the role of fringer in the social structure—three staff members and six white inmates. The inmate population averaged 180 inmates and the staff was made up of approximately 25 employees. Excluded in the factions were county inmates who had relatively short sentences and who made up approximately 23 percent of the inmate population. We do not know, however, the kinds of social relationships that developed among the county inmates or among the inmates in the two factions. In addition, the fringer role is a gross category. The author subdivides the nine fringers into three types: "newcomers," "betrayers," and "disorganized personality types." The last category, however, excludes staff members.

It is apparent that this study leaves many questions unanswered. The staff leaders of the two factions had strong political support outside the institution, yet neither had sufficient power to destroy the other faction. How was it possible for the leader of each faction to organize the inmates into separate factions? Were there any "betrayers" or "disorganized personality" types among the county inmates? If so, would this cast them into a fringer role? Were recidivists cast into the fringer role at the outset of their incarceration, or did their prior prison experience make it possible for them to move promptly into one of the factions?

Certainly it seems plausible to surmise that the limited range of the communication network between the factions may have been a factor in providing for the structural position of the fringers. That is to say, if there had been a high degree of communication between all links in the network, the factions might have held more attraction to the fringers than did their own individualistic roles. It would be interesting to know whether subsequent consolidation diminished the role of the fringer on both levels of the prison organization and their freedom to persist in a marginal status.

SOCIAL SYSTEM OF THE MALE PRISONER: THEORETICAL CONSIDERATIONS

Scholars generally agree on the nature of the inmate culture and social organization of the male prison. The most important features include (1) a sharp cleavage between the staff and the inmates and a normative order subscribed to by the inmates that opposes staff values and emphasizes loyalty to fellow inmates; (2) an inmate world which, although not a "war of all against all," is, nevertheless, notable for violence, struggles for power, and involvement in illicit activities; (3) social roles related to the inmate normative system that outline the prison community as a system of action. This informal social differentiation is reflected in a number of argot roles and provides evidence of the dominant values operative in the inmate culture.

The emergence of the inmate social system in the male prison is explained by current functional theory.[16] Inmate society is what it is because it reflects a response to the conditions of imprisonment. The inmate social system emerges as a response to the *deprivations* of imprisonment; namely, material goods and services; the constant surveillance of the guard; the attack on one's self-esteem; the deprivation of heterosexual activities; the loss of liberty; and the deprivation of security. It is argued that although the prisoner cannot completely eliminate the pains of imprisonment, a cohesive inmate system which has group allegiance as its dominant value provides the inmate with a meaningful reference group that may either reinstate the inmate's self-image or neutralize the deleterious effects of its loss.

Certainly this is an intrinsically reasonable explanation. But however persuasive this argument may be, it is extremely difficult to ascertain the validity of the conclusions because the external culture remains a constant in these researches. The male prison community has been viewed as a cultural island; the walls and bars are seen as a natural Rubicon which effectively shut out the outside world. This may well be the case, but, clearly, the problem calls for comparative analysis. Other factors may be operative.

The scattered but fascinating strands of data available on the female prison community, although they do not provide us with any definitive conclusions about the nature of the female prison community, are, nevertheless, extremely provocative. We are led to entertain the hypothesis that the informal group organization developed in the female prison differs markedly in structure from that which has been described in the male prison. If this is so, then the current functional account of the genesis of the inmate social system is inadequate as currently conceptualized because the informal organization of the female prison assumes characteristics of the external system which are absent in the male prison.

Let us, for the moment, assume that the difference between the two communities is, indeed, a real one and ask: Why is this so? How can we account for the variation in the two structures?

ARCHITECTURE AND GROUP FORMATION

The argument may be raised that differences in group formation may be due to spatial proximity of individuals and the general architectural features of living arrangements.

The architecture of the male prison has been historically oriented upon the general belief that the male criminal is aggressive and dangerous. On this subject, Rutherford B. Hayes declared in 1886:

A prison structure should represent strength and durability, as it is a building not for a day but for the future, as well as for the present. There should be no weak points in construction, inviting the crafty to deeds of daring and hazard, in order to regain liberty.[17]

In order to protect the members of society, it has been necessary to reduce the male criminal to a weak, dependent, and helpless status in the prison environment.

Whereas male criminals are usually feared as dangerous men in the eyes of society, the disgraced and dishonored woman has always been considered pathetic. This view has its roots in the fact that women's most frequent offenses were violations of the normative code with respect to sex and drunkenness. Moreover, women who committed criminal offenses tended to be regarded as erring and misguided creatures who needed protection and help rather than as dangerous criminals from whom the members of society should be protected.

The movement in the middle of the nineteenth century to separate the two sexes in prison reflected this protective attitude. This incentive originated in the minds of two women from the Society of Friends, Sarah Smith and Rhoda M. Coffin, who in 1869 were appointed to a committee on prison visitation by that church. While on this tour of inspection, they found "the state of morals in our southern prisons in such a deplorable condition that they felt constrained to seek some relief for the unfortunate women confined there. . . ." [18] Secular leaders founded correctional programs for women to express their deep piety and faith, and their own great need to serve other human beings as an expression of their religious convictions. The missionary zeal with which these early leaders approached their work is admirably illustrated in the following:

> We must work for regeneration, the cleansing of the evil mind, the quickening of the dead heart, the building up of fine ideals. In short, we must bring the poor sin-stained soul to feel the touch of the Divine hand. [19]

Reformation, in short, meant something quite different for women than for men. "Treatment" for women meant instilling in them certain standards of sexual morality and sobriety and preparing them for their duties as mothers and homemakers. Such goals, of course, have important consequences for the formal organization of the prison. If the task of the formal organization is to train women to occupy roles in society as mothers and homemakers, this can best be accomplished under conditions which approach home life. The organization of women's prisons was designed to accomplish this task, and the recruitment of personnel was directly related to this goal. Matrons were expected to have knowledge of the essentials of housekeeping, including laundry and cooking, good table manners, and general courtesies.

In the ideal case, women's prisons sought to surround their inmates with many of the so-called good influences: small home-like residences, individual rooms, attractive clothing to develop self-respect, educational classes, and recreation. In addition, the view that criminal women were sinful and misguided had much to do with the development of a benevolent maternal orientation of the staff toward their charges. The reduction of women to a weak, dependent, and helpless status was brought about by more subtle means than by the gun or the high wall.

But what, then, may be said of the informal social organization? What roles and value systems do small aggregates of individuals living in small residences have? Do residential arrangements in any appreciable way facilitate or deter the emergence of informal groupings? Can we reasonably expect that the form of social relationships is due to differences in architectural features?

Evidence of the significance of architectural features as a determinant of group formation has been marshaled by Festinger, Schachter, and Back.[20] They conducted a study of group membership in a housing project built by the Massachusetts Institute of Technology for occupancy by married veteran students. The units were assigned to the couples in the order in which their names appeared on the waiting list, so the couples had no choice in selection. The authors found that distance, arrangement of sidewalks, mailboxes, stairways, and location of the housing unit on a U-shaped court were important determinants of the persons with whom the individual made friends. Thus friendships tended to form most frequently between individuals who were next-door neighbors, or between those individuals whose houses faced each other. It was noted that friendships developed less frequently between individuals who were separated by one house. As the distance between houses increased, the number of friendships decreased.

The same study investigated the development of social groups in an adjoining project that was also maintained by MIT for married veteran students. This project consisted of thirteen two-floor apartment buildings with ten apartments in each building. In this project the authors found the same types of effects of architecture on friendship formation.

Other evidence points to the same conclusion. In the suburban housing project studied by Whyte,[21] physical design was a determinant of group membership. Here groups formed along and across streets, and these patterns persisted and remained unchanged, even when couples moved out of the area. There was a fierce togetherness in neighborly contacts; neighbors ran in and out of homes, often without even knocking.

The foregoing studies point out that people who move into an area where they have few or no previous contacts in the community are likely to develop friendships on the basis of brief contacts. The conclusions seem to bear out Homan's hypothesis: The more frequently persons interact with one another, the stronger their sentiments of friendship for one another are apt to be.

Ecological distance coupled with functional design of physical structures, then, have been shown as important determinants of which persons will most likely become friends. Firth's finding [22] is particularly relevant here, however, because it alerts us to the hazard of supposing that physical proximity is the whole story. The problem of group formation may involve vastly more complex factors than ecological distance, the fortuitous arrangement of streets, stairwells, and the like. In his investigation of kinship in a working class borough in South London, Firth's remarks about friendship are revealing. Here, as in the Festinger et al. study, a large block of flats were observed. (There were usually five flats on each landing.) The residents had a connecting link in that they all had a common relationship to the landlord Trust and an opportunity to share common club house facilities and bath houses. In addition, cooperative arrangements to clean communal facilities such as lavatory and tap-and-sink, brought the residents on each landing together. But Firth found that many of the residents claimed they maintained very little relationship with their neighbors. "We keep ourselves to ourselves, and then we can't get into trouble" was a frequent comment. As far as close relationships were concerned, it was explained that: "The individual flat remains the dweller's castle, outer doors to flats are usually shut, and there is little free-and-easy visiting of one another's premises. On the stairs, if the door is ajar and you happen to look in, they ask you what the b—— h—— you are looking at!" [23]

In this study it was found that kinship ties outside the household are important for social relations. Although this importance lies partly in the exchange of services, the major function of kinship ties is companionship. The following quotation explicates partially the values that are operative for maintaining social distance:

(Mrs. W.) said that in the winter of 1946 when she was short of coal, it was very handy to have her relatives living nearby and to be able to borrow from them, she returning the favour when the need arose. She pointed out that some of the H.B.B. residents had coal lockers, but others did not, and it made it very difficult for these to put by reserves of coal for the winter. When asked if it would not have been more convenient to have borrowed coal from one of her neighbours in the Buildings, she said that she always preferred to "turn to her own" and not to strangers.[24]

Firth points out that frequency of contact and intimacy of social relations between kin are not necessarily a function of geographical proximity.

It is difficult to state conclusively whether the formation of social groups in prison is unrelated to architecture. Ecological distance is perhaps an important variable in determining which individuals are likely to have more contacts with one another. Beyond that it is difficult to draw any definitive conclusions because the studies of male prisons have been made in maximum security prisons.

Unless individuals are forceably isolated from one another, as in the system which flourished in the nineteenth century, the argument that architectural features determine the *form* that the structure of the inmate system assumes does not seem logical for this reason: Whether three men share a cell in tier 2 of cellblock 3 or whether these same three men are housed in a dormitory in a cottage is not crucial. Assuming that interaction is possible among individuals, what does command our attention is how these interactions are patterned into stable social relations, and why the informal social organization assumes a particular form in the male institution and another in the female prison under similar conditions of existence.

It is quite true, of course, that severe constraints on communication and interaction would probably prevent the formation of a solitary inmate culture. But such constraints on behavior would be equally effective in small residences as in the cellblock arrangement.

Two important observations bearing on our problem were made independently by Shih and T'ien in industrial settings during the period when China was undergoing rapid social change. We will deal with these studies in detail because, although the workers were not prisoners, the conditions for survival for the Chinese male and female workers exhibited some similarities to the prison setting. In each plant the sexes were isolated, and both male and female workers were drawn from the same society. Moreover, although the residential arrangements for the male and female workers were similar in both plants, the informal social system which emerged among the female workers was notably absent in the industrial plant staffed by male workers.

In the plant studied by Shih,[25] management not only provided the workers with subsidies in the form of money, but also provided direct practical utilities to raise the standard of living and lighten the worker's expenses. These amenities took the form of housing accommodations and a mess hall. A small amount of money for board was deducted from the worker's pay. This amount did not cover the actual cost of the food, and the difference was made up by management.

Three dormitories were provided for the men. (The skilled workers who had families with them were provided with apartments.) The first dormitory consisted of two large bedrooms, each with eighteen double-decker beds; the second dormitory was about the same size and had the same physical arrangement; the third dormitory had no partition inside, but was merely one large room with tiers of thirty-two double-decker beds arranged in four sections.[26]

Shih points out that morale among the workers was very low precisely because management failed to establish a sense of personal relationship with the worker. The men, who came from an old preindustrial culture, were accustomed to face-to-face relationships in neighborhoods where everyone knew one another as "uncle" or "brother," and the failure of management to meet their expectations of informal interaction caused much antagonism.

With this background, let us now turn to a study made during the same period but concerned with the female worker. Ju-K'ang T'ien carried out an investigation of female labor in a cotton mill.[27] At the time of the investigation there were 634 female workers in the factory. (Practically all of the workers in the factory were women.) Of this number, 90 percent were unmarried girls. In this factory, as in the one described by Shih, dormitory facilities were provided by management for the women. An outstanding feature which the investigator noted about the women, however, was that they formed "imaginary" kinship groups. T'ien states that he was told of the existence of several such family groupings, one of which consisted of twelve workers who had no common kinship relations or place of birth. The family name was "Pine Tree Which Lasts Forever." The family composition is described as follows:

"Father" is away in the army. The "mother" is a former worker named Ch'en who left the factory some time ago, and is now considered "dead." The present mother is a "step-mother" (a worker named Hu). She and a "second uncle" (worker named Liu) are the heads of the family. In addition, there are two "aunts" who are absent from the factory. There are seven "sons" and two "daughters." Of the seven "sons" four have left and entered other "families" as "sons-in-law" (according to the matrilocal pattern). One of the remaining "sons" (worker named Chang) "married" a worker named Chow. Another "married" a worker named Ho. The third one is not yet "married" but is in love with a "girl." The two "daughters" are waiting to be "married" to "sons-in-law" who have come to live in the "family" (in the matrilocal pattern).[28]

It is unfortunate that T'ien merely outlines the composition of the family group but does not describe the interrelationships among the members occupying the different positions. It may be deduced, however, that features of the traditional Chinese family seem to have been incorporated into the structure. For example, the "mother" who left the factory is considered "dead" and has been replaced by a "stepmother" rather than by another "mother." This is probably based on the belief in the unbroken continuity of the Chinese family with its ancestors and in the bond between generations.

Significantly, the kinship structures which developed among the female industrial workers did not emerge among the male workers, although the lack of personal relationships between worker and management was felt keenly by both male and female workers. It is to be noted, also, that both male and female workers were housed in dormitories, and interaction among the workers was not restricted in any sense.

One major difference between the two forms of organization was that the female workers had to obtain permission in order to leave the factory during nonworking hours. That they had to ask was a source of irritation among the women, but since no evidence was stated to the contrary, we assume that this was a formality only and that the women were free to leave once they obtained permission.

The author states that the girls came to the factory chiefly as a means of escape from an unsatisfactory family environment in which their families were "broken up." He accounts for the presence of the "imaginary" families by stating that the "family" shows that "girls and women who come out of a miserable environment need most of all not a factory which can give them a fixed opportunity of work and self-support, but the warmth of a family to relax in. When a real family is not attainable," he concludes, "a substitute 'family' is perhaps the most natural outcome." [29]

At the time the study was carried out, there was no tradition in China of women breadwinners working away from home. The normal role of the Chinese woman is that of wife and mother, and it is in this role that she obtains status.

These two studies do not indicate that housing arrangements affected the relationships that were formed, although the situation in many ways parallels the prison case, i.e., the isolation of the sexes (and the traditional role of women as homemakers).

Unless evidence to the contrary is found, we have no *a priori* reason to suppose that the "pains of imprisonment" will be felt less keenly by female prisoners than by males. The foregoing studies show that we cannot account for the formation of group structures in terms of architectural differences. Architectural arrangements may set up some limiting features, but the answer to the problem is not likely to be found here.

It seems plausible to hypothesize that general features of American society are brought into the prison and function largely to determine the direction and focus of the inmate social system. If this is so, an excellent way to tackle the problem of the emergence of inmate society and culture is to examine the extent to which cultural expectations of differential sex roles in the same society are reflected in the response made by participants in the prison social structure.

CULTURAL EXPECTATIONS OF MALE AND FEMALE ROLES

The unisexual character of prison structures provides the sociologist with a unique social laboratory in which to test cultural definitions of male and female roles and to observe the extent to which such cultural definitions persist and find expression in patterned social relationships.

But are sex roles so sharply differentiated in American society that we would expect wide variations in behavior patterns to be found in the two prison communities? There are a number of areas in which American society differentiates male and female roles. In contrast to the male, who is expected to prepare for an occupational role, and whose prestige rank is established by the nature of his life work, the female's life goal is achieved mainly through marriage and child rearing. Although the "career woman" is an important social type,[30] the percentage of women who pursue uninterrupted careers is very small in our society. So long as women bear children, there must be some social arrangement to ensure that the functions of nurturing and training the child during the period of dependency are fulfilled.

Although many married women at one time or another do work outside the home for which they earn a salary, marriage and family are the primary goals for most American women. Indeed, despite the marked increase in the number of married women in the labor market, the worker role of women continues to be regarded by society as secondary to the traditional role of women as mothers and homemakers. Moreover, we find that the jobs usually held by women are concentrated typically in occupations closely allied to homemaking roles. Thus, we find women working as waitresses, domestic servants, librarians, teachers, hairdressers, nurses, social workers, and the like.

And we may point to other areas in which American culture tends further to differentiate the male and female roles. It does not discourage a public display of affection between two women, such as using terms of endearment, embracing, holding hands, and kissing. Such behavior on the part of the male, however, would be immediately defined as homosexual.

Moreover, women are said to be more dependent, more emotional, less aggressive, and less prone to violence than men. It is said that women generally show less initiative in openly defying authority, whereas men have been defined as independent, violent, aggressive, and the like. This *generalized popular culture* persists for women on another level—the woman-to-woman popular culture. Here the mass media perpetuate the stereotype that a "woman's worst enemy is another woman." Because the female is oriented to the marriage market, it is argued that she tends to see other women as rivals.[31] This view finds its significance underscored in the highly stylized type of the best friend "betrayed." A similar theme is operative when we find that working women state preferences for male supervisors rather than female supervisors.

The point is that on a common-sense level, perhaps, such attitudes persist in the prison environment, and they may have unanticipated consequences for the female inmate social system and for the structure of social relationships formed by the inmates. To the extent that the generalized popular culture persists, we would hypothesize a situation of *calculated solidarity* obtaining among the inmates. Calculated solidarity is defined as a social unity based not on automatic conformity to a set of common social norms perceived to be morally binding, but rather on a unity which is subject to constant interpretation by the inmate as she perceives each situation from the point of view of her own interests. Common responsibility in any particular situation, then, exists only to the extent that the individual perceives her own interests to be served. Although Malinowski has cogently pointed out that automatic conformity does not exist empirically,[32] we may conceive of automatic conformity and lawlessness as ideal types with the prison approximating calculated solidarity.

We would expect that an individual's behavior would be shaped by his relationships with other people and groups, by the normative structure which constrains the interacting members to relate their behavior to the membership group in which they are contemporaneously acting. The state of interdependence which is the stuff out of which a primary group is made is eloquently expressed by Whitehead:

A single tree by itself is dependent upon all the adverse chances of shifting circumstances. You may obtain individual specimens of fine trees . . . in exceptional circumstances. . . . In nature the normal way in which trees flourish is by their association in a forest. Each tree may lose something of its individual perfection of growth, but they mutually assist each other in preserving the conditions of survival. . . . A forest is the triumph of the organization of mutually dependent species.[33]

Unless the formal organization can supply the inmates with all of their wants, inmates must turn to one another for the satisfaction of needs that are attractive and agreeable to them, and that cannot be fulfilled by the formal organization. "Every organism," said Whitehead, "requires an environment of friends, partly to shield it from violent changes and partly to supply it with wants." [34] Clemmer's finding is relevant here. In response to questionnaire items, 70 percent of his subjects concluded that "friendships in prison result from the mutual help which man can give man rather than because of some admired trait." [35]

But if the popular culture on the woman-to-woman level is imported into the prison environment, we would expect that violations resulting in tabooed behavior may not be so severely punished, or may be overlooked, because the very nature of the case implies that expectations of behavior cannot be consistent. Possible latent dysfunctions of the popular culture, then, would be to neutralize deviant acts and, perhaps, to atomize the female community into small units.

Cultural expectations of male and female roles, therefore,

diverge along several crucial axes: first, orientation of life goals; second, acceptability of public expressions of affection displayed toward a member of the same sex; third, passivity and aggression; and fourth, perception of member of the same sex with respect to the popular culture. Because of these features of American society, we suggest that if we find the members of two social subsystems in an organization facing similar conditions for survival in the social environment, but the structure of social relationships and the sentiments attached to them exhibit significant differences in each system, then the reason may be found in the cultural definitions ascribed to the roles held by the members in the society from which they were drawn.

NOTES

1. For a cogent discussion, see especially: Scott A. Greer, *Social Organization,* New York: Random House, Inc., 1955; Charles H. Cooley, *Social Organization,* New York: Charles Scribner's Sons, 1913, Chap. 3 for the original statement of a primary group; George C. Homans, *The Human Group,* New York: Harcourt, Brace and Company, 1950; Robin M. Williams, Jr., *American Society,* New York: Alfred A. Knopf, Revised Edition, 1960, Chap. 12; Philip Selznick, "Foundation of the Theory of Organization," *American Sociological Review,* Vol. 13, November, 1948, pp. 25–35.

2. Community is defined here according to MacIver's usage. "Wherever any group, small or large, live together in such a way that they share not this or that particular interest, but the basic conditions of a common life, we call that group a community. The mark of a community is that one's life *may* be lived wholly within it, that all of one's social relationships *may* be found within it." Robert M. MacIver, *Society,* New York: Farrar and Rinehart, 1937, p. 9. (Italics in original.)

3. The following are representative: Henrietta Addition, "Institutional Treatment of Women Offenders," *NPPA Journal,* Vol. 3, January, 1957, pp. 21–30; Emily Barringer et al., "Minimum Standards for the Prevention and Treatment of Venereal Diseases in Correctional Institutions," *National Committee on Prisons and Prison Labor,* New York, 1929; Zebulon R. Brockway, "American Reformatory Prison System," *American Journal of Sociology,* Vol. 15, 1910, pp. 454–477; Edith M. Burleigh, "New Use of a Clinic in a Woman's Reformatory,"

Survey, Vol. 31, 1913, p. 155; J. K. Codding et al., "Recreation for Women Prisoners," *Proceedings of the American Prison Association*, 1912, pp. 312–328; Janie M. Coggeshall and Alice D. Menken, "A Women's Reformatory in the Making, Minimum Standards," *Journal of Criminal Law and Criminology*, Vol. 23, January-February, 1933, pp. 819–828; Katherine Bement Davis, "The Laboratory and the Women's Reformatory," *Proceedings of the American Prison Association*, 1920, pp. 105–108; Mary Dewees, "The Training of the Delinquent Woman," *Proceedings of the American Prison Association*, 1922, pp. 82–90; Martha P. Falconer, "Reformatory Treatment," *Proceedings of the National Conference of Charities and Corrections*, 1919, pp. 253–256; Mary B. Harris, *I Knew Them in Prison*, New York: Viking, 1936; Jessie D. Hodder, "The Treatment of Delinquent Women," *Proceedings of the American Prison Association*, 1919, pp. 212–223; Eileen C. Potter, "Problems of Women in Penal and Correctional Institutions," *Journal of Criminal Law and Criminology*, Vol. 25, May-June, 1934, pp. 65–75; Dean Shepard and Eugene Zemans, *Prison Babies*, Chicago: John Howard Association, 1950; Katherine Sullivan, *Girls on Parole*, Cambridge: Houghton Mifflin Company, 1956; Lorraine O. Williams, "Short-Term Treatment of Women: An Experiment," *Federal Probation*, Vol. 21, September, 1957, pp. 42–51.

4. Helen Bryan, *Inside*, Boston: Houghton Mifflin Company, 1953; Kate O'Hare, *In Prison*, New York: Alfred A. Knopf, Inc., 1923.

5. Eugenia C. Lekkerkerker, *Reformatories for Women in the United States*, Batavia: J. B. Wolters, 1931; Helen W. Rogers, "A Digest of Laws Establishing Reformatories for Women," *Journal of Criminal Law and Criminology*, Vol. 13, November, 1922, pp. 382–437; Helen W. Rogers, "A History of the Movement to Establish a State Reformatory for Women in Connecticut," *Journal of Criminal Law and Criminology*, Vol. 19, February, 1929, pp. 518–541.

6. Creighton Brown Burnham, *Born Innocent*, Englewood Cliffs, N.J.: Prentice-Hall, 1958; Virginia Kellog, "Inside Women's Prisons," *Colliers*, Vol. 125, No. 22, June 3, 1950, pp. 15 and 37–41; Virginia McManus, *Not For Love*, New York: G. P. Putnam's Sons, 1960, pp. 216–265.

7. Cecil Bishop, *Women and Crime*, London: Chatto and Windus, Ltd., 1931; Frances A. Kellor, "Criminal Sociology—Criminality Among Women," *Arena*, Vol. 23, 1900, pp. 516–524; Otto Pollak, *The Criminality of Women*, New York: A. S. Barnes and Company, Inc., 1950; Stephan Schafer, "On the Proportions of the Criminality of Women," *Journal of Criminal Law and Criminology*, Vol. 39, May-June, 1948, pp. 77–78.

8. Frances A. Kellor, "Psychological and Environmental Study of Women Criminals," *American Journal of Sociology*, Vol. 5, 1900, pp. 527–543.

9. Sheldon and Eleanor T. Glueck, *Five Hundred Delinquent Women*, New York: Alfred A. Knopf, 1934, p. 253.

10. Judge John M. Murtagh and Sarah Harris, *Cast the First Stone*, New York: Cardinal, 1958, Chap. 15.

11. *Ibid.*, p. 244.

12. Virginia McManus, *Not For Love, op. cit.*, p. 234. An examination by Kosofsky and Ellis of illegal letters written by delinquent girls revealed that there were references to "families" in them. See Sidney Kosofsky and Albert Ellis, "Illegal Communication Among Institutionalized Female Delinquents," *The Journal of Social Psychology*, Vol. 48, August, 1958, pp. 156–157.

13. Margaret Otis, "A Perversion Not Commonly Noted," *Journal of Abnormal Psychology*, Vol. 8, June-July, 1913, pp. 112–114.

14. Charles A. Ford, "Homosexual Practices of Institutionalized Females," *Journal of Abnormal and Social Psychology*, Vol. 23, January-March, 1929, pp. 442–444.

15. Ida Harper, "The Role of the 'Fringer' in a State Prison for Women," *Social Forces*, Vol. 31, October, 1952, pp. 53–60.

16. Robert K. Merton, *Social Theory and Social Structure*, Glencoe: The Free Press, Revised Edition, 1957, pp. 50–55.

17. Address by Rutherford B. Hayes, *Proceedings of the National Prison Congress*, Atlanta, Ga., 1886, p. 44.

18. Sara F. Keely, "The Organization and Discipline of the Indiana Women's Prison," *Proceedings of the Annual Congress of the National Prison Association*, 1898, p. 275.

19. Maud Ballington Booth, "The Shadow of Prison," *Proceedings of the 58th Congress of the American Prison Association*, 1928, p. 206.

20. Leon Festinger, Stanley Schachter, and Kurt Back, *Social Pressures in Informal Groups: A Study of a Housing Project*, New York: Harper and Brothers, 1950.

21. William H. Whyte, Jr., *The Organization Man*, Garden City, N.Y.: Doubleday and Company, Inc., 1956.

22. Raymond Firth and Judith Djamour, "Kinship in a South Borough," in Raymond Firth, Editor, *Two Studies of Kinship in London*, University of London: The Athlone Press, 1956.

23. *Ibid.*, p. 34.

24. *Ibid.*, p. 36.

25. Kuo-Heng Shih, *China Enters the Machine Age,* Cambridge: Harvard University Press, 1944.

26. *Ibid.,* pp. 98–99.

27. Ju-K'ang T'ien, "Female Labor in a Cotton Mill," in Kuo-Heng Shih, *op. cit.,* pp. 178–195.

28. *Ibid.,* p. 186.

29. *Ibid.,* pp. 186–187.

30. Robin M. Williams, Jr., *American Society, op. cit.,* pp. 64–65.

31. Simone de Beauvoir, *The Second Sex,* New York: Bantam Books, 1961, Translated and Edited by H. M. Parshley, p. 514.

32. Bronislaw Malinowski, *Crime and Custom in Savage Society,* New York: Harcourt, Brace and Company, 1932. See especially Chapters 3, 4, and 5.

33. Alfred North Whitehead, *Science and the Modern World,* New York: New American Library, 1925, p. 207.

34. *Ibid.,* p. 206.

35. Donald Clemmer, *The Prison Community,* New York: Holt, Rinehart and Winston, 1958 (Reissue of the 1940 edition), p. 123.

CHAPTER 2 PHYSICAL STRUCTURE OF THE PRISON

THE SETTING

The Federal Reformatory for Women lies on a hilltop in the shadow of the foothills of the Alleghenies, about halfway between Cincinnati and Washington, D.C. It is set in a rural farming region remote from metropolitan and industrial areas.

The high wall typically associated with the male prison is nowhere to be seen. Instead, a series of wire fences topped with barbed wire enclose the approximately five hundred acres of farm, pasture, and woodlands which make up the prison grounds. The unobtrusive wire fences, however, are buttressed by the lines of low mountain ranges which cut sharply against the horizon. The outlines are irregular; the contours continually change, depending upon the season of the year, the time of day, the weather, and the psychic disposition of the inmate viewing them. But at all times, the mountains form a remarkably compact natural wall around the prison and in many ways present a more formidable obstacle to freedom than a man-built fortress. Here, as in all prisons, inmates attempt to escape. Inmates have scaled the fences, but none has evaded capture for more than a few hours.

II

There were a number of important reasons for selecting the present site for the prison. First, it was the geographical center of the criminal population at that time; second, it was easily accessible to Washington for officials and visitors; third,

21

it had good climate, railway facilities, water, and available land for expansion; and, finally, a two-hundred-acre tract of land was donated by the town of Alderson in which the prison is located, and the adjacent three-hundred-acre farm was available for purchase at $48,000. The present plant consists of some fifty-eight buildings; the buildings and roads are valued at approximately $2,700,000.

The Federal Reformatory for Women was completed in 1927. Prior to its erection, women convicted in the Federal courts were lodged in jails, county workhouses, state prisons, and reformatories, or wherever the Department of Justice could find an institution to house and board them. The crowded conditions and lack of any rehabilitation program for these prisoners were so bad that a number of women's organizations throughout the country petitioned Congress in 1923 to erect a modern institution for women to remedy the injustices being done to women sentenced in the Federal courts. One of the first organizations to espouse the case was The Woman's Christian Temperance Union.[1] The first appropriation for the erection of housing units was made on March 4, 1925.

In keeping with the principles of the state reformatories for women and girls, the cottages were built to house thirty inmates. Each cottage was operated as an independent unit with complete kitchen equipment, dining room, living room, library, and individual rooms for every inmate. Moreover, living quarters for officers were provided in each cottage. In each unit the population led separate but integrated existences. The two major reasons for stressing this centripetal form of social organization were pointed out in Chapter 1: (1) it was felt that the break-up of inmate population into small housekeeping units provided the most efficient means to obtain skills in homemaking; and (2) it was believed that a domestic atmosphere was essential in making institutional life less painful for women.

As the criminal population increased over the years, however, the problem of adding housing space was solved by converting the officer's quarters and some of the dining rooms into dormitories. At the time of the study, for example, only four food service cottages were operating, and they prepared meals for the entire population. And in the near future, these food services will be discontinued because a central dining room was in the building stage during the tenure of the study and nearing completion when the study ended.

III

INMATE LIVING QUARTERS

The sixteen cottages which constitute the living units for the inmates are grouped around two quadrangles on two levels. (See Figure 1.) The upper level has an altitude of 1600 feet. A dairy cottage is located about a mile from the two main campuses.[2] The red brick cottages are two stories high, and the architecture is modified Georgian Colonial. The windows are covered with steel screens, with the exception of those of the two cottages that serve as maximum security units, which are equipped with bars.

With buildings arranged on two levels, groves of trees, shrubs, and artistic arrangement of flowers, the physical appearance does not suggest a prison. Indeed, the general appearance viewed on the short trip from the gate to the visiting room leads individuals (sometimes with patent relief) to exclaim soon after departure: "It wasn't what I expected. It looks like a college or a hospital." Inmates also comment on the physical appearance, but they are likely to have more to say. Below is an expression uttered by an inmate who was serving a sentence for her third criminal offense. It is fair to say that it is typical of the sentiment expressed by the general inmate population.

"When I came through the gate, I said to myself: "This is a prison?" All the trees and flowers—I couldn't believe it. It looked like a college with the buildings, the trees, and all the flowers. But after you're here a while—and it don't take too long—you know it's a prison. Yeah, that's what it is—a prison! All this beauty—the trees you see—that's just the outside. That's what the visitors see when they give them the Gold Coast tour. All they see is the outside. You have to go *inside* to see what it's like. It's just another penitentiary—a place to do time. But don't let them kid you that this is a college campus.

Perceptions of the *inside* or prison world vary greatly, of course, not only in terms of individual personality factors, but

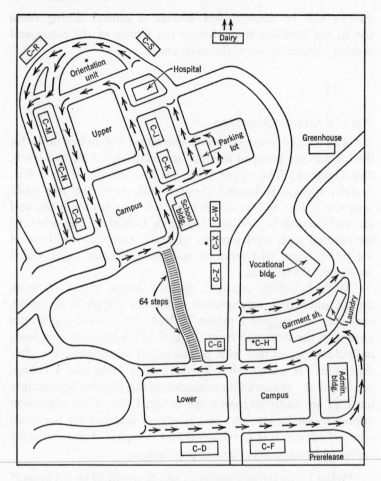

FIGURE 1   SITE PLAN OF THE PRISON. (* = food service cottages.)

also according to whether or not one has been previously incarcerated. For the recidivist who has been incarcerated three or four times, there is little at Alderson that is fundamentally new, and it may indeed be "just another place to do time." This is not to suggest, however, that all neophytes and recidivists perceive the prison world differently. The perceptions are apt to be influenced by the capacity of the individual to make a painless adjustment to the prison world promptly, and this factor is to a large extent dependent upon the capacity of the informal group to make its activities appear not only singularly attractive, but also absolutely indispensable to the successful consummation of a prison sentence.

There are, as we shall see later, many ways to "do time" in prison. All that need be pointed out now, however, is that the twin features of extreme isolation and the inevitability of concrete objectified time become translated by the inmates as determinants of social relations and normative behavior first, and subsequently, as the justification for the inclusion or exclusion of elements of civil society which impinge on the inmate's psychological suspension of self in the prison world.

The cottages which play such an important part of the prison world vary little in physical characteristics and general atmosphere. The visitor entering a cottage passes through a wide door into a short reception hall. This tiny vestibule opens into a long hall that runs the length of the building, connecting the living room at one end and a dining room or dormitory at the other. To the right of the entrance is the office of the correctional officer. The one staircase leading to the second floor is to the left. Almost directly facing the entrance is a small laundry room with two outmoded washtubs which service the entire cottage. An ironing board is usually to be found here, and its twin stands in the hall. Always in demand, these inadequate facilities produce many fights among the inmates.

The one radio for general cottage use is located against the wall near the laundry room.[3] A small group of inmates may always be seen huddled around it, seated in wooden rockers while knitting. The music, which blares forth loudly and which may be heard in the far reaches of the cottage, easily drowns out the rhythmic clicking of knitting needles but competes with the leaden repetitious repartee and the loud laughter of the inmates as they mill about the hall: going to and from the living room, visiting in one another's rooms on the first floor, or washing and ironing personal clothing.

The single rooms and dormitories for the inmates are located off the long hall on both floors. The transom over the door permits some cross ventilation, but when summer temperatures rise, these rooms seem to shrink considerably in size and become very stuffy. The furniture, which consists of a single movable bed, a locker, an enamel-covered night jar, a wooden rocker and chair, a low dresser, a dressing table and mirror, must be arranged according to institutional regulations. Inmates are also provided with a white cotton spread and curtains, as well as with a small cotton woven rag rug. The result is that each room looks strangely like all the others, despite the attempts made by inmates to individualize their surroundings by tacking old sheeting, begged or stolen material around the dressing table, and by displaying other handiwork in the form of pillows, chair pads, and the like. There are no closets in these rooms, and the clothing hung on the back of the doors contributes to the congested appearance of the rooms.

The majority of the inmates, however, spend most of their nonworking hours in the living room. Here the television set dominates the room, as witnessed by the row upon row of chairs and couches lined up facing it. An overturned pillow here and there on choice viewing seats is often perceived by the new cottage member as a mark of carelessness, but the harsh words and threats which follow attempted occupancy attest to the power structure which operates in each cottage, and the inmate "learns the hard way." Indeed, the way she handles herself in this situation frequently determines the treatment she will receive by other cottage members while she remains in that particular cottage.

A feature of the prison over which the inmate has no control is overcrowding. Each cottage houses approximately forty-five to fifty-five inmates,[4] and because the cramped single rooms cannot take up the overflow of incoming inmates, the dormitories are apt to become more and more crowded. Some women do find prison life easier in a dormitory in the company of others, but the lack of privacy is extremely painful for many. The physical proximity with Negroes is also quite distressing for many white inmates; especially acute is the fear of contamination [5] from the communal use of bathing and toilet facilities. As one white southern inmate put it: "It was hard to use the rest room, the shower and to eat with them. In the beginning I wiped off the toilet seat, and in the shower I would let the water run a long time before I used it. I did this the first week, and then they began to talk to me and I realized they were as sensible as I am—that they're like anyone else, and besides I was afraid they'd knock me in the head. You have to accept Negroes because you live with them twenty-four hours a day."

Even when interaction is acutely painful, toleration becomes expedient in prison; rare is the individual who can function autonomously in the prison environment. When one is living outside a prison, one never expects a single membership group to have relevance for all of one's needs. In civil society, when a particular group proves unsatisfying, one is free to leave it and join another. The unique aspect of prison life, however, is that inmates cannot do this. Under such circumstances, isolation can be very painful, as humans achieve satisfactory living only by interdependence with others.

The cottages are bleakly Spartan. But the dirt and unmistakeable odor compounded of toilet buckets and men who bathe infrequently which is said to characterize the male prison cannot be said to be a feature of the cottages at Alderson. Rather the pungent odor of floor wax always hangs heavily in the air. The ability to maintain a clean cottage is considered to be one of the marks of a good officer, and is a measure of how well she can "control" the group; she is ever alert, therefore, to see that inmates complete their cottage assignments. The cottages are clean and provide the inmate with adequate physical living conditions, but the net effect of the cottage atmosphere is cheerless and austere.

NOTES

1. In addition to The Woman's Christian Temperance Union, the following organizations and clubs petitioned Congress in 1923: American Association of University Women; American Federation of Teachers; American Home Economics Association; American Social Hygiene Association; Bureau of Home Economics; Daughters of the American Revolution; Democratic National Committee; General Federation of Women's Clubs; Girls' Friendly League; Lumen Femina,

W. T. A.; National Committee for Mental Hygiene; National Committee on Prisons and Prison Labor; National Congress of Mothers and Parent Teacher Associations; National Council of Jewish Women; National Council of Women; National Federation of Business and Professional Women's Clubs; National Women's Trade Union League; Republican National Committee; Women's City Club, Washington, D.C.

2. The two levels are called campuses, lower and upper campuses respectively. The staff refers to the prison as the "prison," "reservation," "res," or the "institution." The term reformatory is never used. Inmates do not use the latter term either, but they do use the aforementioned terms as well as "penitentiary."

3. Transistor radios were placed on sale in the commissary unit during the week of May 13, 1963. Prior to this time inmates were not permitted to own radios. The prices were $19.95 and $21.95. Sales had to be approved by the officials, and purchases were contingent upon accumulated savings, or purchase price sent in by one of the approved correspondents. When the study ended, approximately 100 radios had been sold.

4. The pre-release unit does not usually have more than ten inmates.

5. Types of contaminative exposures have been discussed by Erving Goffman, *Asylums*, Garden City, N.Y.: Doubleday and Company, Inc., 1961. See especially pp. 25–35.

CHAPTER 3   CHARACTERISTICS OF THE STAFF

More than any other employee, the correctional officer is the staff member who, from the standpoint of the inmates, has the most important continuous contact with them. The social isolation, however, has made it difficult to hire well-qualified personnel. Indeed, so serious is the recruitment problem that before interviewing potential officers, the captain invariably made the comment, "I'll be happy just to have a warm body." In fact, the isolation of the institution has consequences for recruiting personnel in all units of the organization. Serious problems in filling positions in the education department are also a concomitant of the geographical location. Moreover, the vocational skills necessary in arts and crafts are not easily found in the nearby community.

In addition to creating the personnel recruitment problem for the above-mentioned posts, the isolation of the institution from urban community resources has repercussions on other operations of the prison. An excerpt from a retiring physician's final report makes this point:

It is difficult to imagine the sense of isolation felt by the medical staff at Alderson especially when one doctor is here alone. . . . The most urgent need for this institution is a psychiatrist. Unlike the male institution, we have no alternate place to send disturbed inmates, and unless they are severely disturbed so as to require transfer to St. Elizabeth's, we must handle our own psychiatric and psychological treatment. The present staff is certainly willing to do this, but we feel unable to do a really adequate job of it because of lack of psychiatric training and a lack of the large amount of time required for such therapy.[1]

Five years later, when this study was in progress, the officials of the prison stated the same needs and problems.

In short, the isolation of the prison has serious repercussions for recruiting qualified staff personnel and for obtaining diagnostic services, which are resources typically centered in the urban community. In addition, the remoteness eliminates the possibility of inmates participating in community activities. (The presence of narcotic addicts poses special problems, but this point cannot be discussed here.)

II

The correctional officer begins employment at a starting salary of $5035. At the end of the probationary year, she may be promoted to the next grade, that is, from junior officer to senior officer at a salary of $5540. The appointment becomes a "career" appointment after an initial three-year period which is termed "career conditional." Within each grade level, however, periodic step increases are earned as long as the employee maintains an acceptable level of performance. Other salary increases are dependent upon being raised to another grade level and/or promotion in rank. Correctional officers are also provided with uniforms, and their blouses are laundered free of charge in the prison laundry. All staff members have the use of the staff dining room at a charge of 35 cents per meal.

Although the starting salary of $5035 is attractive to newcomers, it is not enough to counteract the limitations imposed by the geographical location, and as a rule, out-of-staters do not stay. The isolation and the inadequate housing facilities in the community are apt to pose severe hardships for the out-of-stater. Less than twenty employees live in staff housing, and these units are usually occupied by employees in the upper administrative posts, many of whom are subject to call around the clock, or may be needed in the event of an emergency. The posts of duty must be filled, however, and because the training period extends over many months, the officials are apt to prefer hiring local women, as they maintain that these women will probably remain on the job longer.

Moreover, in an area where employment opportunities are not only scarce, but many persons are unemployed, the out-of-stater who comes to "stay permanently" is apt to be made to feel unwelcome by fellow officers. As one out-of-stater explained: "We tend to get the cold shoulder from the others. They look at us and say, 'Why did she come here? My cousin or sister could have her job.' And that's another thing that you learn the hard way—everybody's related." The estrangement felt by the out-of-stater is especially keen during the beginning stages of the probationary period. During this time, many officers "cover up" the mistakes of another officer to "give them a break," although it is the responsibility of each officer to check the cottage and to report any infractions of rules committed by the officer who preceded her. Mutal aid, however, is usually more likely to be extended to locals than it is to the out-of-stater.

The emphasis on the impersonal nature of security rules is administratively important because it functions to decrease employee unity in an area which would have serious consequences if personnel became careless in the performance of their official duties. If carried out faithfully, "reporting" as a formal procedure of checking after another officer ideally has several important consequences: (1) it ensures bureaucratic efficiency by disrupting the social cohesion of the officers as a group; and (2) it provides one of the bases for evaluation of work performance.

There is wide divergence from the ideal, however, and the underlying motivations for deviance are far from simple. Officers are bound together by ties of many kinds: those of friendship and, in some instances, kinship; those of class and geographical location. In addition, cottage correctional officers are bound together by their common role of officer and by its attendant difficulties.

Officers complained that they thought the procedure of "reporting on another officer" should be eliminated. An important reason for this stems from the fact that violations are not perceived to be *intentional*, but rather as the natural outcome of a work routine so bound up with a minutiae of detail that it is inevitable that an officer will occasionally forget some things. This shared ideology that "anyone can forget," and the fact that reported violations are on public view in the lieutenants' office, so that anyone caring to take the time to look may note information concerning accused and accuser alike, tend to neutralize the extent to which this rule secures compliance.

Some officers, for example, maintained that they systematically refrained from reporting "little things" such as cigarette butts found in an ash tray but reported infractions constituting a clear risk to security. Other officers used discretion, reserving positive sanctions for friends. Then again, other officers preferred to overlook all infractions, setting matters right themselves, reporting neither formally nor informally. And, finally, a tiny minority denied the social cohesion of the officers by reporting every violation across the board; that is, by acting in the role of "stone cop" in connection with officers' activities. This type tends to be ostracized by other officers.

III

THE MALE OFFICER

Unless specifically noted, all future discussion will be confined to the female correctional officer. But a few words about the male correctional officer and his place in the organization are necessary. There are ten male correctional officers. In an almost exclusively female organization, the male officer has, as it were, nowhere to go, since he cannot rise in the staff hierarchy. He functions in an important role, however. His duties are many and varied: he supervises the gate at all times, delivers medical and other items to the cottages, makes trips to town for mail and other supplies, and assists at day and night patrol duty when needed. But more important, the male officer symbolizes brute force without benefit of a gun to the inmates. The female officer never exerts any physical force in her dealings with inmates unless she is physically attacked and acts in self-defense. When an inmate "refuses to listen to reason," the officer calls a lieutenant. If the lieutenant fails to secure compliance, two male officers are called and it is they who use physical force if necessary in escorting (in the company of a female lieutenant) a recalcitrant inmate to seclusion. Consequently, the male officer represents a negative symbol for the inmates, and he is never looked upon by them as a meaningful sex object.

THE HOMOGENEITY OF THE COTTAGE OFFICERS

The distinct homogeneous composition of the correctional officers with respect to certain social characteristics may be seen to be a peculiar function of the geographical location of the prison. There are a total of 102 correctional officers who work the three 8-hour shifts of duty.[2] As a group, they range in age from 25 to 69 years. The mean age is 43.3. The complete distribution appears in Table 1.

There are seven Negro female officers, and the ten male officers are white. Five of the officers are Catholic, and the others are Protestant, predominantly of the Baptist sect.

All but eleven officers are drawn from a 35-mile radius of the prison. As indicated in Table 2, almost all of the officers have a background of farm and rural life. For purposes of contrast, most inmates are drawn from urban areas. This is important because, as we shall see shortly, it has some bearing on inmate-staff relationships.

TABLE 1   CURRENT AGE OF CORRECTIONAL OFFICERS

Age (years)	Number	Percent
25–29	3	3.3
30–34	13	14.4
35–39	10	11.1
40–44	25	27.8
45–49	19	21.1
50–54	12	13.3
55–59	7	7.8
60–64	–	–
65–69	1	1.1
Total	90	99.9

TABLE 2   RESIDENCE DURING CHILDHOOD YEARS
REPORTED BY CORRECTIONAL
OFFICERS

Place of Residence	(N = 90) Percent
Rural—lived on a farm	56.7
Village—up to about 2,500 population	22.2
Town—over 2,500 to 5,000 population	13.3
Town—over 5,000 to 30,000 population	2.2
City—over 30,000 to 100,000 population	3.3
Metropolis—over 100,000 population	2.2
Total	99.9

Most of the officers are married, and the next largest category is made up of women who are divorced. Less than 10 percent of the officers are single, which is not surprising given the location of the prison. Although the distribution in Table 3 does not include the male officers, it should be noted that all of the male officers are married.

Many of the married officers have been drawn to prison

TABLE 3   MARITAL STATUS OF
CORRECTIONAL OFFICERS

Marital Status	Number (females)	Percent
Married	51	63.8
Divorced	12	15.0
Separated	4	5.0
Single	6	7.5
Widow	7	8.7
Total	80	100.0

work mainly because their husbands have been unable to provide for them economically; they want to assist their children in obtaining a college education or to provide their families with amenities they otherwise could not afford. Their husbands are intermittently employed in unskilled and semiskilled jobs, and as small farmers. In addition, many of them frequently take on odd jobs such as painting and carpentry work. As shown in Table 4, thirty-nine officers, or 73.6 percent of all married officers, said they had gone into prison work to add to the family income. (Males reported lack of other job opportunities, and the ten male correctional officers are included in that category.)

With the exception of eleven officers, all have a previous history of employment. This employment falls mainly into the following categories: waitresses and restaurant workers, salesclerks, clerical workers, and nurse's aides. Eleven respondents had taught elementary school. Actually, these individuals com-

TABLE 4   MAIN REASON FOR GOING INTO PRISON WORK
REPORTED BY CORRECTIONAL OFFICERS BY
MARITAL STATUS

| | Marital Status | | | | | |
Main Reason	Married	Divorced	Separated	Single	Widow	Total
Supplement family income	39	7	3	–	3	52
Lack of other job opportunities	11	2	1	1	1	16
Good retirement program	3	1	–	1	1	6
To help people	4	2	–	–	1	7
For new experience	–	–	–	1	–	1
Enjoy prison work	3	–	–	1	1	5
Needed challenge	–	–	–	1	–	1
Good salary	–	–	–	1	–	1
To fill leisure time	1	–	–	–	–	1
Total	61	12	4	6	7	90

pleted two years or less of college work, and their teaching was confined to rural southern grade schools.

Most of the officers completed high school, and a few have recently prepared for and passed a high school equivalency test. The precise picture of educational attainment is shown in Table 5. The educational level of parents reported in Table 6 is considerably lower: the difference in generations is strikingly reflected in the higher educational attainment of the officers at the high school level. The great majority of the officers listed father's occupations as farming or farming supplemented by part-time jobs.

From the limited data on hand, it seems safe to infer that the correctional officers as a group have come from rural working class homes. By way of summary, then, along the commonly accepted sociological stratifications of class, economic status, age, education, and marital status, officers exhibit marked homogeneity.

The fact that the officers are drawn almost exclusively from rural areas and have sought employment to help supplement the family income does not escape the notice of the inmates and has important consequences for interaction between inmates and officers. Inmates look upon the officers as women who are not there primarily to "help" them, but, rather, work solely for the income. Moreover, the limited educational background and nonprofessional status of the officer in the organization tend to reinforce the image of the officers as lacking in expertise and prestige. Inmates tend to perceive them as persons who are incapable of understanding the complexities of problems related to urban living.

Thus officers become defined as people who "know nothing," people who "can't *do* anything." The female correctional worker is a "keyturner" in the same way that the male guard is a "screw." Inmates disparage the staff in general and officers in particular as women who "have never lived," "know nothing of life," because they are "West Virginia hillbillies." The assessment of the officers by the inmates is neatly summed up in the statement: "The best of them are nothing." How well the officer performs her role depends, of course, on many factors, and we must now begin to examine these factors in detail in Chapter 4.

TABLE 5 EDUCATIONAL LEVEL OF CORRECTIONAL OFFICERS

Highest Grade Completed	Number	Percent
Completed grade school	3	3.3
Some high school	4	4.4
Passed high school equivalency test	16	17.8
High school graduate	48	53.3
Two years college or less	16	17.8
College graduate	2	2.2
Some graduate school	1	1.1
Total	90	99.9

TABLE 6 EDUCATIONAL LEVEL OF PARENTS AS REPORTED BY CORRECTIONAL OFFICERS

Highest Grade Completed	Mother		Father	
	Number	Percent	Number	Percent
Not known	–	–	1	1.1
None	2	2.2	1	1.1
Some grade school	17	18.9	26	28.9
Completed grade school	44	48.9	34	37.8
Some high school	10	11.1	12	13.3
Completed high school	14	15.6	8	8.9
Some college	2	2.2	7	7.8
Completed college	–	–	–	–
Graduate or professional school	1	1.1	1	1.1
Total	90	100.0	90	100.0

NOTES

1. Official files, Warden's Report to Advisory Board Meeting, 1958.

2. There are ten male officers. Data were collected from ninety correctional officers. The remaining officers were either on leave or ill when the questionnaires were administered. One officer could not be provided with a relief officer at the post of duty.

CHAPTER 4 ORGANIZATION OF THE STAFF AND RELATIONS WITH INMATES

The role performance of the correctional officer depends in the final analysis on the goals of the organization, the degree to which the officer accepts the organizationally defined goals, and on her ability to function in accordance with role expectations.

What are the goals of the prison? In the probationary training manual for new officers, the section on the warden's address to new officers includes the following assertion:

It doesn't take a book to explain the philosophy of the Federal Bureau of Prisons. It recognizes, without deviation, that it is responsible to carry out the orders of the court to hold prisoners in custody but paramount in its thinking is the fact that each individual prisoner is a human being who has the right to be treated with decency and given a fair chance to change her thinking and attitude toward the weaknesses which brought her to prison so that she may return to the community better equipped to take up her responsibilities.[1]

For the moment we shall concern ourselves with the content pertaining to custody. The correctional officer in particular carries a heavy burden in accomplishing the goal of custody, and custody is an integral part of her training. The concern was expressed by the captain at a Probationer's Meeting in this way: "Custody is our business—that's what we're here for and we do what we can with treatment." [2] It should not be assumed from this statement that "treatment" is being relegated to second place. It merely states that there is specialization of function, and that the major part of the officer's responsibility *is* custody, despite exhortations to the contrary. Much of her day is taken up with custodial duties, so that available time to delegate to the treatment function is limited. In the concern with custody, the captain pointed out the necessity "to be informed on what is going on."

Captain. Sometimes you don't know what it is, but you *know* there's *something* in the air. You don't know what it is, but it's something! And they always give themselves away. Maybe there's nothing today—nothing tomorrow, but soon it will be something.

Officer on Probation. Should we report it if we don't know what it is?

Captain. Tell the lieutenant that you feel there's something—you don't know what it is, but it's something you feel is in the air. And then watch for something to come out.

This brief exchange illustrates the *poised certainty* of the staff for action which is to occur at an indefinite future time: the tendency to doubt the trustworthiness of appearances; to have every action with inmates colored with doubt, mistrust, and the suspicion of something unreliable or menacing as an experienced future reality.

The emphasis placed on the officer's role as a custodial one was further attributed to the sources of authority believed to inhere in the role. The captain said: "The symbol of your authority is the keys you carry. The keys you carry, and your blue uniform. . . ."

Despite this emphasis on custody, however, the officer has been charged with other duties. The officer had traditionally fulfilled her organizational function by emphasizing her formal position and her authority. Recent emphasis on broadening the base of custodial functions by including treatment functions created serious problems for the correctional officers; their work became more complex and their duties were often seen to be conflicting and contradictory.

The role of the foreman is perhaps the best analogy to the officer's role. Although she is the lowest-level worker in the prison bureaucracy, she is a manager of inmates; she in turn is managed by a number of layered ranks from above who often have inconsistent expectations.

ADMINISTRATIVE CHANGES

In the so-called treatment-oriented prison, every effort is made to relate the treatment resources of the institution, such as educational, vocational, counseling, medical, and psychiatric services, as well as parole planning, to the specific needs of the individual. Such realization of treatment potential obviously depends upon overcoming such handicaps as inappropriate or overcrowded physical plants and a lack of professional services.

With the change of wardens in July 1961, certain policy changes moved the program from a suppressive emphasis in the direction of an integrated therapeutic milieu. Another important change took place in the role of associate warden-treatment, hereafter called associate warden (T). The superintendent of the garment shop was moved to fill the post of associate warden (T). The incumbent of this role had formerly moved to the superintendency from the custodial ranks.

Introduction of the new program was accompanied by a permissive attitude by the officials toward the behavior of the inmates, as it was felt that inmates needed opportunity for self-expression and "acting out." The immediate major changes were concerned with the extension of so-called privileges for the inmates; with the notion that the inmates were to assume more responsibility for their behavior by making more decisions for themselves; and with the broadening of the officer's treatment role to include "counseling" of inmates. Officers were to "understand" inmates and to help them with their problems.

These changes took shape in several ways. First, the smoking privilege was extended. Whereas smoking had been confined to the living room or to the inmate's quarters, the new smoking regulations allowed an inmate to light up a cigarette anywhere, at any time, except in the few places that clearly constituted a fire hazard. Secondly, restriction of movement was relaxed. Inmates were not permitted to roam at will, but were allowed to enjoy the open campus on the quadrangle adjacent to their cottage during nonworking daylight hours and on Saturdays. Sunday, however, remained a "quiet" day—the sole major activity was church services. During the afternoon, inmates who did not retire to the living room were locked in their rooms from one to four o'clock.

Another major change eliminated custodial escort for inmates en route to movies, church services, and other activities. The new program made it possible for them to go in an unescorted cottage group; the custodial function was fulfilled by a correctional officer checking off the names of the inmates from a list as they filed through the door at their place of destination. Moreover, inmates were now permitted at all activities to sit anywhere they chose, rather than with their cottage group, as had been the policy under the old administration.

This added freedom of movement and the liberal seating arrangements had important consequences for the inmate social system. Contact with other inmates was greatly facilitated. As a result, making of new acquaintances, reinforcement of old ties, bartering and other economic activities, commitments for homosexual alliances, and cottage changes were all greatly eased.

As part of the treatment emphasis, the warden declared in the fall of 1962 that henceforth the inmates were to be referred to as "residents." This was a clear indication that official emphasis was on the view that inmates were "clients" in need of non-punitive treatment services. For some of the old-timers, this was a threatening state of affairs. After the meeting where this change in policy was made known, one officer said to the observer with some indignation: "I've been here over twenty years, and they've always been inmates. Now they're *residents*. What next?" And she shook her head in disbelief.

By and large this added emphasis on treatment was greeted by the officers with derisive laughter and many jokes tinged with bitterness. The general opinion was that the officer would "end up by being a *servant* to the inmates." But socialization is at best always a slow process. It is not surprising, therefore, that the new reference term did not take hold immediately on all levels of the hierarchy. Officials and officers alike continued to use the old reference term almost exclusively, although sometimes in private conversations they would say quite pointedly— RES'idents. At meetings attended by the writer, officials would often start out by referring to inmates as "residents" quite self-consciously and would soon lapse into the habitual use of the old reference term. This inconsistency was also noted in official records. Official orders which were retyped to remove the word "inmates" indicated a lack of consistency, although they bore the official "approval" signature or initials.

The rate of integration of this item may have been slow because the officials did not use the new treatment term and because negative sanctions were not imposed to order behavior when the old term continued to be used.

Perhaps the change in policy with respect to homosexuality was the most difficult adjustment for most of the officers to make. A permissive but ambivalent pose was assumed by the administrators in connection with homosexual behavior. Unless found in bed together, inmates could no longer be charged with homosexual behavior. For inmates found in bed together, however, a term in the seclusion unit and a penalty of loss of days were imposed. A cottage change for at least one of the inmates usually followed as a matter of course, but both inmates were placed on the same campus. The reason for this residential arrangement was explained by the associate warden (T): "I put them on the same campus or next door to one another, so they can see each other and talk," because "for many of these people, this is the only way they can relate to one another."

We may contrast with this the policies of the former administration in this regard and the role expectations of the correctional officers in handling this behavior as they are spelled out in the minutes of the Correctional Officer's Meeting, January 21, 1959.

(An official) stated we have had rumors lately in several cottages of girls misbehaving,[3] and have received these rumors from other inmates who dislike this behavior. She realized that an officer does not want to report suspicions, but when an officer notices two girls showing an exclusive preference for one another and intuitively recognizes this type of situation developing she should write a note to the Captain stating only that these girls are constantly with each other. Also we should all watch out for any girl or girls who seem to run interference by delaying the officer when she is going about the cottage duties or when she starts to go from one floor to another. This may be to keep the officer busy so that she will not observe misbehavior. We should be especially alert to protect the younger inmates from affairs of this kind with older, more experienced inmates. It is hoped that by reporting the affair at an incipient stage, it might be possible to prevent further development by moving one or both women.[4]

The present attitude of tolerant resignation was difficult because it conflicted with the values and attitudes held by the officers with respect to homosexual behavior. A measure of these attitudes is provided by two items on a questionnaire. There was wide consensus to the item: "Homosexuality is a sin against nature and God." Of the 90 officers, 28.9 percent agreed strongly, 44.4 percent agreed, and 10 percent agreed slightly with the item, bringing the total agreement to 83.3 percent. In addition, the responses to the item, "The best way to handle homosexuality in prison," are revealing. Only 10 percent of the officers favored a "permissive and relaxed attitude about it." Ten percent said that inmates should be punished "that get involved in this way"; and 66.7 percent advocated "supervision and surveillance of inmates so that inmates do not engage in homosexual practices." Such attitudes, which conflict with the prevailing official norm of the prison administrators, indicate the persistence of individual attitudes and value orientations even when a definition of the situation and of the expected role behavior has changed. Although this situation contributed to the low morale of many of the officers, it should not be assumed that all officers held this view.

Indeed, some officers expressed amusement at many of the symbols of homosexual behavior, particularly those aspects which constituted a strain toward legitimacy of present behavior with roles formerly held in the outside community. "Kites" or love letters no longer found their way into the inmate's dossier, and homosexual behavior having its inception in the prison no longer constituted relevant information for the decision-making process. Instead, these kites were often the source of a moment of humor among two or three officers. Others expressed gratitude that the inmate social organization was so efficient that they would not have to process this form of behavior formally. "After you've been in a cottage a short time, you know who the ones are that are involved in homosexuality, but we don't put any labels unless you see them in bed. They're willing to 'pin' for each other, so you don't find many, and if they respect you so that you don't see anything, what more can you ask?"

In the treatment-centered prison, individual judgment and discretion are the means used for rehabilitation of inmates. With the new counseling emphasis, decision-making was decentralized in order that officers would handle inmates according to individual needs and personalities and reward them on an informal basis.

The difficulties for the officers stemmed in part from the fact that the administrative directives required her to use "judgment" and "discretion" in handling all problems with inmates and cottage concerns, but these vague frames of reference were not accompanied by specific techniques of implementation.

The officers felt insecure in carrying out counseling functions because they lacked expertise. "I don't feel confident to counsel with inmates," was a comment frequently made. This lack of confidence was further supported by comments from officials. The associate warden (T) expressed the opinion that officers weren't "ready" for such "elaborate programs as counseling." Indeed, on several occasions she volunteered the information that officers were "good only to lock and unlock doors, count, and to pass out toilet paper."

Furthermore, counseling placed the officer in a dilemma. Presumably counseling gives the officer considerable discretion in reporting violations. As part of her new role expectations, she is to assume the responsibility of handling minor infractions, rather than referring them to the Adjustment Board. However, she cannot enforce all rules to the letter. If she did, she would be rated as a "weak" officer unable to "manage" the group. Both in training and in the evaluation of an officer's worth, it was pointed out earlier that custodial considerations are foremost. Furthermore, the officer cannot admit that she tolerates certain rule infractions or she runs the risk of being accused by inmates of playing "favoritism" and not being "fair."

The new institutional emphasis stimulated frustration and discouragement among the cottage officers. Especially frustrating was their feeling that they were not supported or "backed up" in their disciplinary measures by the officials and were made to look like "damn fools" before the inmates. For example, a negative sanction imposed by an officer might arouse the loud demands of the irate inmate to "call the lieutenant." Often the lieutenant, after speaking to the inmate, would decrease the penalty and would so inform the officer. From the standpoint of the officer, the new state of affairs was seen as a loss of status in the eyes of the inmates and as a clear indication that the power which had once been legitimately hers by virtue of her position in the bureaucracy had now been diffused to custodial officials and the associate warden (T).

The inmates, on the other hand, perceived this course of events as "favoritism" and as whimsical behavior to be expected from staff, behavior to which adjustments and accommodations must be and were made.

The following examples written by cottage officers indicate the areas of concern expressed throughout the year.

Officer A. In our present state of no-discipline, no regard for rules nor regulations—no respect for the administrators of our institution, how can we ever hope to rehabilitate, and equip an inmate to go back into Society to live, work, and respect a fellowman? How many employers would retain an employee that would stamp his or her foot—curse and scream because a rule or regulation had been introduced to them as a vital part of an organization? How can an officer command respect, when no backing is in evidence, after an inmate once learns that in actuality all rules are so flexible that they will not only *bend* satisfactorily but break—all they have to do is to curse, scream and threaten their own life? Could this possibly be Rehabilitation? [5]

Officer B. Certainly we need to treat all humans with respect and kindness. However, we also need to command and receive respect at the same time. We need a strong administration—by this I mean—a fair set of impartial rules and regulations minus the petty small ones. All officers need to be able to *know* what the rules are and be able to say *yes* or *no* to one without fear of being ——— [illegible] and made to look foolish when trying to carry out an important rule—vital to a group of perhaps 40–50. Too often one inmate is allowed to absolutely disregard all rules. How then, can the other 49 be made to regard them? We need consistency—communication—and certainly a better feeling of comradeship among officers and supervisors. How can an officer perform her best, when her own morale is at zero? How can we expect people under our supervision to want to be above engaging in homo-sexuality, when we are not only hardly allowed to forbid it, but actually throw them together when we *know* it is not a healthy relationship? [6]

Officer C. It seems to me that somebody's idea of "allowing the inmates to express themselves" and "make their own decisions" has about gotten out of hand. A certain amount of this is good but, as with anything else, can be carried too far. They are not being taught self-discipline or self-control but they are being taught to rant and rave and curse in order to get what they want. This will not work when they are free and trying to hold a place in society. It makes the work of an officer very difficult when she tries to enforce a rule or discipline an inmate and receives no backing or assistance from the administration. The officer is not always correct, by any means, but in the presence of an inmate she should be, even if she is called in and shown where she is wrong later, but, certainly, not in an inmate's presence or her disciplinary just ignored. Most of these inmates have already molded their way of life. They do not appreciate and take advantage of the new "treatment." The more we give, the more they take. I believe a *firm* hand along with the "new treatment" is most necessary in this institution. Things have come to a point where the officer is almost a servant to the inmates. The work is becoming more difficult each day. There is no consistency with the rules and regulations. The communication system for the administration and the officers and the inmates is very poor. The officers have become very unsure of themselves. We are told: part of us, to pick up black slacks and turn them in, then we see inmates wearing them on the campus and to ball games. No one seems to know what is legal and what is not. Again, I say we are not equipped for an "individual treat-ment" program. There will have to be more consistency before the institution can successfully operate. [7]

In the previous program, correctional officers were required to be custodians, supervisors, and housekeepers. These interre-lated roles, emphasizing the functions of detention, surveillance, and the upkeep of the cottage, were generally consistent with one another in terms of the purposes they were supposed to achieve. In the new program, with its emphasis on freedom and understanding, the correctional officers were to counsel and to use friendliness and firmness to secure compliance from the in-mates. This meant that they had to accept some expressions of aggressive behavior which might be distasteful to them. Their confusion was further intensified because they were expected to control some forms of aggression by suppression just as they had in the earlier program.

The strain under which the cottage officers functioned was reflected in their silence at correctional meetings. They had questions about the program but refrained from raising them; they feared that questions would point up their seeming ignorance, or that expressions of opinion would be construed as being critical of the program and would result in "pulling the graveyard shift," or in an undesirable or difficult post.

The grumblings of the disgruntled officers reached such a high point after the first of the year, however, that early in May a meeting on discipline and control to restore equilibrium by reasserting custodial principles and concepts was held. What follows is an officer's account and reactions:

"I was so impressed with what Mrs. ——— (Captain) said that I think it should be written out and given to every inmate," she said. When asked what the meeting was about, she continued: "Mrs. ——— talked about discipline and control. She said that the *officer* is running the cottage. Not her, or the lieutenant, but the officer: And if we tell a girl to do something, *she is to do it.* And if we call a lieutenant, the lieutenant is to follow our instructions, and not the other way around. I'm glad she said what she did, because we just weren't sure how far we could go. When we ask an inmate to do something, or we give her a six o'clock lock, and she calls for the lieutenant, the lieutenant is supposed to back us up. I hope they follow through on it, because it makes it very hard in the cottage, when you give a girl a six o'clock lock, the girl calls a lieutenant, and the lieutenant says to forget the lock. It makes you look like a God damned fool.

If the inmate does not do what the officer says, that is a seclusion offense. The lieutenant is to take them to seclusion. It was always my understanding that that was a seclusion offense, but they never followed through on it. An inmate would refuse to do something, and you call the lieutenant to take them to seclusion. She comes to the cottage, talks to the inmate, and the next thing you know she says: 'Give her a six o'clock lock.' When this happens a few times, you get so you just close your eyes to a few things, and don't bother calling. I had a situation that happened the other week. I saw a girl come back from the dining room, and I could see that she had something under her coat that she was holding with her arm. I knew it had to be a pot of coffee, it couldn't be anything else. I asked the girl to give me the pot of coffee. She said: 'I don't have a pot of coffee.' I said: 'I know you've got it, and let me see it. I want that pot of coffee.' She said: 'I don't have a pot of coffee and I'm not showing you a mother ——' thing.' I went to the office to call the lieutenant, and the inmate went to her room. While I was on the phone, she came to me and said: 'Here, this is all I had.' It was two pieces of toast and jelly. I knew she wouldn't hold two slices of toast under her arm. When the lieutenant came, she talked to the inmate, and she told me to give her a six o'clock lock. From what Mrs. —— said today, though, it should have been a seclusion offense." [8]

When asked how the other officers felt about the meeting, she said, "There was no time to ask questions because everyone had to go right on duty, but Mrs. —— (an old timer) at the close of the meeting said real loud, AMEN,"—which seemed to express the sentiments of all the officers.

Such attempts to restore custodial control and re-evaluate custodial values of discipline and order occurred whenever exceptional circumstances arose. As soon as some semblance of order and equilibrium was perceived in the system, the treatment goal was once more held out as legitimate.

The participating members of any organization must be trained to respond to the values, symbols, and objectives of the organization in such a way that the individual's actions will sustain the organizational objective. The ease with which the resolution of organizational problems was conceived by tightening custodial elements may be seen as a consequence of the fact that the promotion of treatment personnel through the custodial ranks elevated the functional approach to the institution of custody and security via overlapping identification with former custodial roles and values. Goals, then, tend to be unstable when they are not clearly defined and when the individual participants in charge of their implementation are committed to other values.

We have pointed out that in the new treatment program correctional officers still continued their custodial security functions, but had difficulty integrating their custodial and treatment roles. How can we explain this? Without making any assumptions that custody and treatment are *necessarily* antithetical, let us begin by raising the question: How well can the officer accomplish the combined goal of custody and rehabilitation within the present structure? As a preliminary step to understanding the officer's role, we turn to an examination of the cottage schedule. The cottage schedule or "blueprint" provides in capsule form some of the organizational expectations of the officer and the areas of operation which receive greatest emphasis, which presumably may be inferred in terms of actual time allocated to these functions.

THE COTTAGE SCHEDULE

The daily routine of the correctional officers varies somewhat on Sundays and holidays and during certain seasons of the year, generally with respect to count procedures and scheduled activities. During July and August, baseball games are held on some Sunday afternoons when it does not rain. In addition, on holidays such as Christmas and Easter, special entertainment such as a musical program may be put on by the inmates—or a dance may be held. Such events are infrequent, however, and do little to relieve the monotony of the prison world.

The post orders, which the officer is expected to have complete knowledge of, are preceded by the following comments.

The following schedules for cottage work are provided as guides to assist the officer in organizing her work so as to accomplish in a systematic way the many details which must be handled, to provide uniformity in the work and to eliminate confusion among the inmates. No schedule will cover every situation which might develop in a cottage. For this reason officers must exercise sound judgment in handling unusual situations that develop which might require deviations from the schedule. But in no case should any of the requirements set forth in the schedule be eliminated or overlooked. Circumstances requiring deviations from the schedule should be reported to the supervisor. Officers will be held responsible at all times for the custody of inmates assigned to them.

COTTAGE SCHEDULE—WEEKDAYS

Shift 6:00 A.M. *to* 2:00 P.M.
6:00 A.M.
   Report to roll call, get keys from control room officer in exchange for chit, check folder and go to cottage.

Check log book for pertinent information. Unlock inside doors to laundry room and living room. Keep outside doors locked.

6:15 A.M.

Unlock inmates. Issue before-meals medicine. Under no circumstances should more than one inmate be in the office when the medicine cabinet is unlocked.

6:30 A.M.

Telephone count to control room.

6:40 A.M.

Issue supplies. Breakfast time will be as scheduled. Take count in accordance with count regulations. Lock outside doors when leaving for breakfast. Everyone will return to cottage after breakfast unless specific instructions are issued to the contrary. Issue after-meals medicine at one time. Miscellaneous duties.

7:45 A.M.

Check girls out to work when whistle blows. Notify control office of any emergency illness.

Spot check inmate rooms and communal areas of cottage. Enter pertinent information regarding inmates in log book. Call control center and report inmates remaining in cottage. Give names of women in a locked status and having days off.

At approximately 7:45 A.M. on Saturdays, follow laundry regulations.

8:00 A.M.

Officer assumes duties listed under specific duties. (Supervise custodians in cottage.)

12:00 Noon

Point out deficiences in cleaning noted at morning check to women who must improve room conditions or cottage areas assigned. (If cottage eats early, deficiencies may be pointed out and corrected after meal.)

12:10 P.M.

Take count as soon as women are in the cottage. Telephone count to control center. Dinner time will be as scheduled.

If it is necessary to permit an inmate to go to the basement for some purpose, the officer should unlock the door involved and require the inmate to return immediately after completing errand and then lock the door. By keeping the basement doors locked a custody hazard is eliminated.

Lock outside doors when leaving cottage for meal and return after meal with all inmates to cottage unless specific instructions are given. For example, when cottage group eats at last serving, inmates are sometimes required to go directly to work so as to be there at 8:00 A.M. or 1:00 P.M. The exact time will depend upon eating schedule.

General office period. Issue interview slips.

12:45 P.M.

Release women for work when whistle blows and check them out. Make quick check of rooms. Log pertinent information for officer coming on duty on afternoon shift and for other officers who might check cottage.

1:00 P.M.

Begin afternoon work according to post duties.

2:00 P.M.

Take keys, reports, and other papers to the Control Center. Keys must be handed to Control Officer who will return your chit to you.

Note: Follow regulations in furnishing names of inmates who are to attend unscheduled activities and make other specific reports as required.

Shift: 1:00 P.M. to 9:30 P.M.

1:30 P.M.

Report to roll call, get keys from control room officer in exchange for chit, check folder, and begin post duties as assigned.

If it is necessary to permit an inmate to go to the basement for some purpose, the officer should unlock the door involved and require the inmate to return immediately after completing errand and then lock the door. By keeping the basement doors locked, a custody hazard is eliminated.

5:10 P.M.

Take count as soon as inmates are in. Telephone count to control center.

Interview women upon request or otherwise as desirable and as time permits. Make general check of cottage.

5:30 P.M.

Supper time will be as scheduled. Return with inmates to cottage after supper. Make sure all of your inmates have returned with you.

Release women who wish to go to open playground. They will sign the Playground Roster for playground.

Issue after-supper medicine at one time only. Under no circumstances should more than one inmate be in the office when the medicine cabinet is unlocked. See that ladders, rugs or tools are not left outside cottage; that clothing has been taken from line.

Interview women as time permits. Turn on porch lights when it is getting dark. Keep in mind that you are responsible for the behavior of girls on second floor and make unexpected checks of cottage between 6:00 P.M. and 7:00 P.M. when inmates are at large. At approximately 6:30 Friday evenings follow laundry regulations.

6:55 P.M.

Release women for 7:00 P.M. classes.

7:00 P.M.

Lock women who want to go to their rooms. Supervise inmates in the living room.

Officers may permit a few women to have laundry privileges but the number must not exceed the number that can work comfortably at one time. Arrangements for this must be made in advance and such women should get their laundry ready at 7:00 P.M. as officer locks other women in their rooms. Laundry time, if given, must be carefully allotted on a basis fair to all. The names of the inmates and time allotted should be posted in advance on the bulletin board. Each woman using laundry must leave it in good condition. The officer should check for compliance with rules.

Twilight

Check women in from Open Playground and lock outside doors.

7:55 P.M.

Check women out for 8:00 P. M. classes.

8:00 P.M.

Lock women who want to go to their rooms. Check women in from 7:00 P.M. classes.

9:00 P.M.

Require inmates to empty ashtrays and arrange living room furniture in proper place and see that living room is reasonably tidy.

Excuse everyone from living room; permit bathroom privileges. Issue prescribed bedtime medicine at one time.[9] Under no circumstances should more than one inmate be in the office when the medicine cabinet is unlocked.

Permit toilet privileges to girls locked in earlier at own request.

9:05 P.M.

Check girls in from 8:00 P.M. classes. Take count when locking inmates. Look in on those locked earlier.

9:15 P.M.

All inmates' rooms should be locked. Telephone count to control center. Make notations in log book and pertinent facts sheet. Make out daily count and sick call notices in accordance with regulations.

At convenient time permit inmates who are locked for disciplinary reasons to empty toilet jars.

9:30 P.M.

Officers will be held responsible to see that before going off duty all doors are locked, that screens to living room and dormitories are securely fastened. The small lamp on the table on the first floor opposite the entrance door should be left lighted.

Take keys, daily counts, reports and other papers to control center. Keys must be handed to control officer who will return your chit.

Note: Follow regulations in furnishing names of inmates who are to attend unscheduled activities and make other specific reports as required.

10:00 P.M.

Control center will signal "lights out" by telephone.

This long detailed schedule by no means covers all the officer's duties. There are numerous housekeeping duties which must be carried out seasonally; for example, lawn furniture must be brought from the attic, scrubbed, and repairs must be requested if necessary; the attic must be cleaned; and the cottages must be checked for any "stray" linens which may have accumulated.

It is apparent that such detailed rules—in the best tradition of Weberian bureaucracy—are an attempt to create social conditions which constrain the members of an organization in the performance of duties so as to accomplish the organizational goals. An examination of this schedule makes it entirely clear that the majority of the officer's time is officially allocated to custodial and housekeeping duties, and "interviewing" of inmates is sandwiched between these functions. "Our greatest problem," summed up one officer at the end of the study, "is that we have too many things to think about and to do. We don't have the time to devote to individual problems. Custody alone is a great undertaking, and to be aware of where each girl is and at the same time to get meals out on time, take care of mail, medicine, check rooms, keep up the cottage, be on the alert for any trouble that might be brewing, see that inmates get out to classes on time, etc. On the whole, it is just a rat race—going as hard as you can and doing the best you can."

Certainly a cursory inspection of the cottage schedule, considering that each cottage contains a population of approximately forty-five to fifty-five women, might indeed lead one to suppose that the correctional officer would be deterred from accomplishing the counseling function solely because of lack of time. One might logically conclude that additional personnel would provide the solution. Although it is quite true that the time element is important, this factor alone does not explain the situation. We must still ask why the correctional officer spends so much of her time during the day and in the evenings, as well as on weekends, in her office alone.

Actually the problem of the officer's functioning in a so-called counseling role is vastly more complex, and an examination of official publications such as cottage outlines can be very misleading in explaining reciprocal role relationships.

We speak of roles as being reciprocal or complementary. The behavior specified for each role helps to make social interaction an orderly and reliable process. By this is meant that a role is a set of expectations, rights, and obligations. And these rights are defined with respect to any particular role as circumscribed by the obligation of others to respect them.

The process of "counseling" requires a reciprocal relationship of mutual trust between the counselor and counselee. But counseling components of individualized treatment resist integration into the present social structure, because the inmate social system precludes the quality of mutual interaction between officer and inmate which this process requires to be effective. Contacts with officers and, indeed, with other staff personnel in general are expected to be limited to matters of urgent business and to be transacted with swift dispatch. Like the "snitchers" and "squares," who are the pariahs of the prison community, officers in turn are "to be fed with a long-handled spoon." Exceptions are made for professional personnel such as psychiatrists and psychologists.

The inmate normative system specifies that the officer should be given "respect," for it is understood that the officer "has a job to do." But "respect" in this context means quite simply: Render unto Caesar that which is Caesar's. These duties and obligations fall into the realm of custodial functions: namely, getting into line for count when the bell rings, walking to the dining room in an orderly manner, etc. But treatment roles, however limited in scope, have not been delegated to the officers by the inmates as part of this reciprocal role relationship. In short, the integration of treatment and custodial goals in the role of the nonprofessional staff member requires acceptance by the inmate body of the legitimacy of the interaction patterns which are essential for a relationship of mutual trust between counselor and client. We turn our attention in Chapter 5 to an examination of other goals of the formal organization which further complicate the integration of treatment functions in the prison.

NOTES

1. Official publication: Correctional Officer's Probationary Training, Warden's address, p. 5.

2. Probationer's Meeting, held July 27, 1962. Notes were taken by the investigator at the meeting.

3. "Misbehaving" refers to homosexuality. The staff also referred to homosexuality with such terms as "involved," "emotionally involved," "close relationship," and "playing house," as well as "couples" and "the he-shes." The term "homosexuality" was also used.

4. Official files, Lieutenants and Correctional Officer's Meeting, Alderson.

5. Italics in the original.

6. Italics in the original.

7. Italics in the original.

8. Italicized words indicate change in inflection.

9. Medicine is always dispensed in the evening between 8:30 and 9:00.

CHAPTER 5   TREATMENT GOAL AND THE PRIMACY OF MAINTENANCE

The goals of an organization provide a meaningful basis for understanding differences in organizational behavior. The prison as a social system has in some respects extraordinary characteristics, because society assigns the prison many divergent and often conflicting functions with little regard as to whether these functions can be simultaneously integrated into a coherent pattern of action in the prison social structure. The incompatibility of these functions is made clear when an attempt to expand a treatment segment is perceived to disrupt the equilibrium of the system at the maintenance level.

We noted in Chapter 4 the consequences of conflicting custody and treatment orientations for the role of the correctional officer and for other staff members. In this chapter we present further evidence to demonstrate that formal organizations that attempt to maximize both punishment and treatment-oriented goals will be characterized by internal conflict. Now we view the problem more generally by focusing on the division of labor in the prison community. The task imposed upon the prison to strive toward a self-sustaining community generates pressures for functional autonomy at the level of maintenance structures when the expansion of treatment subunits threatens to disrupt the equilibrium of the system.[1] When the treatment goal begins to fragment custodial and maintenance structures, there is a tendency for the conflicting goal to be modified. Thus, events aimed at expanding treatment functions result in shifting compromise on the treatment level, whereas custody, internal control, and economic self-sufficiency emerge as relatively more important in the prison's hierarchy of goal statuses.

In addition, the goal of economic self-sufficiency requires that the inmate community be mobilized into a work force. In order to accomplish this goal, official expectations dictate that inmates subordinate their own interests to the interests of the larger collectivity, that is, the prison.[2] This social definition of legitimate motivation is at variance with the female's cultural definition of self-orientation internalized in the larger community.[3] These divergent orientations serve as an important factor in increasing the relative social distance between the inmates and the staff.

II

With the rare exception of a few prison camps for men in the southern states, prisons no longer require any "hard labor." Nevertheless, the public still adheres to the principle that inmates should work—that is, they should put in a full day's work. This ideology holds equally for female criminals as it does for male criminals; cries of "coddling" and "country club" apply to the female prison as well as to the male prison. Yet why should criminals work in prison?

Many reasons have been advanced at one time or another to justify prison labor. The most important of these objectives have been: First, it is held that if unpleasant tasks, as punishment, are the lot of the convicted criminal, work will serve as a twin-barreled deterrent to crime, for the law-abiding citizen as well as for the convicted criminal. Secondly, it is argued that when the inmate is busy working, time passes more swiftly and the monotonous routine of a prison sentence is relieved. Third, work is legitimate in order to reduce the operating costs of the prison. Fourth, work is assigned to enable inmates to earn money for themselves and their dependents. Fifth, the notion of work is justified in order to teach prisoners skills and to develop good work habits. Here it is assumed that good work habits will carry over into other occupations and areas of life. Finally, work is advocated as treatment—that is, work is regarded as therapeutic in restoring a criminal to society as a useful law-abiding citizen.[4]

All of these objectives serve as a basis for assigning prisoners to work tasks by the Alderson prison officials. The specific objective(s) taken into account, however, depends upon the state of affairs with respect to personnel shortages in any particular department and the nature of the problem in connection with the inmate to be assigned. An escape risk, for example, will not be assigned to landscape or farm details, even though from a treatment standpoint a work assignment of this nature would be best for the inmate.

III

Treatment and training consist principally of employment and teaching good work habits. Although recreation, opportunities for religious activities, medical treatment, general education, and help through group therapy are also part of the treatment program, the most important part consists of work. (We must discount group therapy as a major treatment device because there were only twenty-four inmates enrolled in four groups.) In addition to the assumed therapeutic value of work, the work assignments are more than simply a means of keeping the women occupied, for they help to bring the prison closer to being self-sufficient, which is one of the prison's important goals. Indeed this goal is second only to custody and the maintenance of internal order.

Two fundamental problems, however, confront prison administrators with reference to the dual purpose of inmate prison labor. First, there is the problem of assigning prisoners to work tasks in the prison. Theoretically, of course, a treatment program centered about work training would require that the individual needs of the inmate be taken into account without consideration for the maintenance requirements of the prison. The skills or work knowledge acquired in prison would correspond to the inmate's release plans in connection with work. Moreover, indeterminate sentence laws and the widespread use of early parole as a method of release make it especially important that an integrated work training program be planned at the outset of an inmate's confinement. On the other hand, it is obvious that an orientation to provide for economic self-sufficiency makes it incumbent upon the prison officials to rely heavily on inmate labor. This has, as we shall see, important consequences for the planned routine of the inmates.

The high rank assigned to the goal of self-maintenance in the Alderson prison is evident by the fact that work is the only part of the treatment program which is compulsory for the inmates. The degree to which the prison officials are dependent upon inmate labor becomes clear when we examine the differentiation of work roles in the prison.

It was stated earlier that the correctional officers make up by far the greatest number of prison employees; but in addition to these workers, there are other administrative and specialized posts. The following tabulation shows the number of employees and their locations in the organization at the beginning of the

Number of Employees	Position
1	Warden
1	Assistant Warden (Business)
1	Assistant Warden (Treatment)
1	Captain
102	Correctional Officers
1	Chief-Classification and Parole
2	Parole Officers (Case Workers)
12	Federal Prison Industries
13	Culinary Department
2	Physicians
7	Nurses
1	Medical Assistant (Pharmacist)
1	Psychologist
1	Supervisor of Education
2	Academic Teachers
1	Supervisor of Vocational Training
2	Vocational Instructors
2	Chaplains
1	Agent Cashier
1	Purchasing Department
1	Personnel Department
12	Clerical Staff
4	Farm Service
24	Mechanical Service

study. With the exception of the top administrative and highly specialized posts, however, most of these posts are supervisory with respect to inmates' work assignments. These supervisors are responsible for the varied work functions performed by the inmates, which include much of the clerical work, sewing of inmate clothing, uniforms, hospital gowns, bed linens, bedspreads, slip covers, draperies, curtains, and other household items. In addition, most of the landscape and general ground maintenance, painting of inner and outer parts of buildings, and many other tasks are all done by the inmates. A complete breakdown of the work functions for the entire population is presented on page 62. It is typical of the breakdown to be found on any day of the year.

In short, the Alderson prison represents a community where full employment is a reality. The *Idle Men* discussed by Sykes, or the *Crank Gang* described by Clemmer do not have their counterpart here. How is full employment achieved? To keep a prisoner occupied, a task is created if necessary—even though such work may consist solely of altering worn garments from the clothing room, mending, cutting up scraps of material to be woven into rugs, creating special handiwork to serve as display items which may one day find their way into the hands of important visitors, serving as cottage "helper," and many other tasks of this nature. It is worth mentioning that almost half of the entire population is concentrated in such jobs as cooking, cottage maintenance, sewing household items for general prison use, weaving, doing farm and dairy work, landscaping, baking, and painting. It is questionable that the "training" programs as presently organized do in fact have a real market; it is more realistic to state that these programs serve the needs of the institution.

Some writers have pointed out that "made work" exists in the male prison, but the proportion of unemployed men would indicate that the degree to which it exists is considerably lower than in the female prison. How can we account for this difference? In the first place, the male is oriented to look upon work as a *meaningful* activity in career terms, and this fact is recognized by the prison officials. It is very doubtful indeed that the male prisoner would accept—without a display of Martian re-

Work Assignments	Number of Inmates
Office Workers	37
Mail Room	3
Photographer	1
School and Library	7
Home Economics Department	3
Shoe Repair Shop	2
Coding Department	7
Beauty Shop	4
Inside Cleaners: Cottages and Offices	77
Fix-It-Shop (Light Fixtures, etc.)	2
Dressmaking and Arts	35
Paint Group	6
Storehouse Department	11
Commissary Sales Unit	1
Weaving Department	22
Orientation Helpers	3
Clothing Room	3
Farm Workers	14
Dairy Workers	21
Truck Driver	1
Landscape Detail	16
Sanitation Detail	3
Greenhouse	1
Hospital Department	26
Garment Factory	141
Laundry	38
Bakers	12
Culinary Department: Cottage and Staff Food Services	110
Orientation Status	39
Unable to Work (Hospitalized-Chronic Illness)	4
Records not Obtained	3
Total	653

sistance—the many small tasks, particularly with needle and thread, that the female prisoner is apt to perform with efficiency and often with enthusiasm.

Here, it seems to me, we have a splendid example of the cultural unity which exists between the prison world and the larger community. It is apparent that much of the "busy work" in the prison designed to keep the female inmates occupied is not unlike many of the tasks that women perform in carrying out a homemaking role. As was pointed out earlier, the American female is not oriented to a career as a life goal. While it is true that she figures prominently in labor force statistics, employment is apt to be intermittent; the worker role is secondary to the homemaking role. Secondly, it is necessary to take into account the *generalized popular culture,* the cultural definition of the female as a relatively passive creature, and the tendency for women to show less initiative in openly defying authority. It is in light of the interrelationship of these factors that we can begin to understand the almost stoical acceptance of work by the female inmate regardless of the nature of the work.

To be sure, all elements of the inmate population are not enthusiastic about work. Like Reimer's inmate who cried out: "Why should I make bricks for Kansas?" [5] the Alderson prison, too, has an occasional inmate who will insist that the sentencing judge "gave time," and that the notion of work was not part of the bargain. Time, it is argued, can be "done standing on one's head," once one has gotten the "knack" of it. (Or, for that matter, "sitting down, doing nothing!") The apathy with which these inmates are apt to tackle their assigned tasks provides clear indication of their preference in the matter of prison labor. But such inmates are rare.

IV

Notwithstanding the acquiescence of the female inmate, when we examine the structure of prison labor we see in clear relief one of the basic conflicts between the inmates and the staff which contributes to the social distance between them; namely, the collectivity-orientation of the administrators—the belief that the inmates "owe" the institution a full day's work. Inmates, on the other hand, think that "Uncle Sam" owes *them* something, namely rehabilitation, but rehabilitation is not phrased in terms of work. A memo to a prison official reveals rather vividly the conflict in orientation.

Phyllis ——, Cottage —— was assigned to the Craft Shop, Dec. 2, 1962. From the day she reported to the Weaving Department, she has done nothing for the institution. Phyllis has talent that could be used in that Department, but has done nothing that has not been for her own personal use. . . . She sits and knits from eight o'clock to five o'clock making sweaters and socks and ignores the officers. All officers as well as myself have tried to reason with her to no avail. She is very definitely a bad influence on the other women . . . and I feel that a change of assignment would be of great benefit to the department.

An attempt on the part of an inmate to further her own interests in the prison situation clearly conflicts with official policy, as the structure of the situation specifies that the inmate subordinate her own interests to those of the larger collectivity. This is considered to be the legitimate outcome of a prison commitment. In a real sense, it might be said that the prison situation provides an example of an instance where the client is the "employee" rather than the employer.

In a study of any social group, a consideration of the reward system is important, because this structure reflects the values of the organization. What rewards does the official have at her disposal to inspire a full day's work? Theoretically, the officer has at her disposal a good work report, which presumably will eventually find expression in the recommendation of meritorious good time and service pay. With the exception of the two prison industries, inmates are not paid for labor unless they can qualify and are recommended for meritorious pay. In any case, for the first three or six months (depending upon the length of sentence) inmates are not eligible for either monetary compensation or meritorious good time. (Limited budgets also mean that claims will be delayed or ignored, even when legitimate.) It is not general policy to assign inmates to the industries directly from Classification. Moreover, according to the Standards of Eligibility, meritorious pay and time may not be granted when an inmate is engaged in a full-time educational or vocational training program, because it is maintained that participation in such programs cannot be considered as engagement in institution operations. (An exception is made for the inmate engaged in a full-time vocational program if in conjunction with her training the inmate is providing a significant service to the institution.) Such restrictions on the distribution of rewards are consistent with the collectivity orientation of the prison. We see the task of maintenance reflected in the structure of the reward system as an important organizational value.

The goal of economic self-sufficiency has consequences in other areas of operation. An inmate assigned to the industrial garment shop, for example, will discover that the cancellation of scheduled educational courses is a condition of employment. Confronted with such practical considerations as meeting a monthly production quota the superintendent, understandably, is apt to take a dim view of the inmate's participation in any activities which require absences from the job. Similarly, problems of meeting production quotas also function to stabilize work routines. Specialization of function promotes efficiency, and the proficiency developed by an inmate in operating one machine may be taken up by the formal organization, thereby limiting an inmate's experience to the operation of a single task. The collectivity orientation is also evident when experienced workers are kept on year after year because these inmates are productive and knowledgeable, while other inmates who desire or who are recommended for an industry job may be put off. This process holds equally for other positions as well.

To summarize briefly, the collectivity orientation of the prison and the goal of economic self-sufficiency generate pressures in the social structure which result in (1) delayed or permanent postponement of rewards for the inmate, (2) curtailment of the range of activities the inmate may participate in, and (3) limitations imposed upon the boundaries of work experience for the inmate.

The internal stress generated by incompatible goals exerts pressures upon some members of the organization to circumvent formal communication channels in order that information on departmental personnel needs be included in the process of administrative decision-making. A letter sent to a high-ranking member of the inmate adjustment board by a kitchen supervisor provides an example:

September 2, 1962

Mrs. ———— (Prison Official)

As you well know by now Maria Sanchez and Bessie Miles, Davis Hall Kitchen food service girls are in seclusion over an argument in the kitchen this a.m. over whose job it was to put the coffee on the food carts.

Maria was busy frying hot cakes and apparently told Bessie to do it and Bessie refused.

One thing led to another and Bessie called Maria a "snitcher" so Maria went after her with a fork in her hand and she had a piece of salt pork on it to grease the griddle. I don't know if she intended to use the fork on Bessie or not but it stuck Bessie making a ———— (illegible).[6]

I know both girls were at fault but I do feel that Maria was pushed into doing what she did.

Bessie is an excellent worker but loves to argue. She wants out of the kitchen, too.

I would like, if at all possible to have Maria back in the kitchen as soon as possible and Mrs. ———— if at all possible don't take her days and pay because Maria does so much work and works so hard. She helps Bessie in every way she can, along with everyone else in the kitchen.

I just don't have another girl in the kitchen to put in Maria's place and I feel she would be awfully hard to replace.

Of course, all this is just between us and I do not let the girls feel they can't be replaced. I try awfully and do try to give them credit for what they do but still let them know the work will be done without them.

When all of the arguing started, I was in the walk-in helping Isabel Ortega put things away and get started on her work. I couldn't get either girl to stop shouting long enough to find out what it was all about. I don't feel it would be good to send both girls back to the kitchen and I can replace a vegetable cook much easier than a main dish cook.

M. Curtis
Davis Hall Kitchen

Such requests enjoining the members of the disciplinary board to take into account the maintenance needs of the organization in disposing of disciplinary cases represent an attempt to preserve existing structures when that lack of intervention may cause severe hardship in the performance of organizational duties.

From the standpoint of the formal organization, then, there may be a decided advantage in not handling disciplinary cases on a standard disposition basis, as this would be dysfunctional for an organization committed to divergent goals. This is a case where a structure created to serve individualized treatment needs is converted to another function—a kind of *tolerance mechanism* in order to resist any structural stress which threatens to shift or disrupt the equilibrium of the system.

EFFECT OF COMPETING GOALS ON TREATMENT FUNCTION

While the goals set for the prison in recent years increasingly include treatment and rehabilitation, these goals are added to, but not expected to replace, the custodial function. The goal of economic self-maintenance, an ancillary to custody, further compounds the goal of treatment. As we noted earlier, there is an important connection between the social organization of the prison centered upon the work function and the administrative decisions made with respect to an inmate's prison routine. The kinds of processes that occur to maintain the status quo have been briefly sketched above.

In the performance of its custodial function and in the attempt to strive for economic self-sufficiency, the prison seriously imperils its treatment function: these are not complementary functions but, rather, competing goals. The essence of these opposing goals is a clash of interests, the nature of which is such that successful functioning on the part of one unit precludes the proper functioning of the other unit, except in the most superficial manner.

The general problem becomes apparent when an attempt is made to expand a treatment function. The points raised previously will become clear to the reader when we analyze an account of a meeting in which expansion of educational facilities for inmates was being communicated to several levels of staff personnel.

The captain opened the meeting by stating that the purpose was to talk about the educational program; she added that a number of people would speak, after which the group would be free to raise questions. What follows is a verbatim account of the proceedings.[7]

Warden. An educational program in an institution like ours, or any institution is very important. No more is the correctional officer looked upon as a jailor by society—as a guard with a key. More and more she is looked upon as a specialist. The public image of the correctional officer is changing and the State and Federal Governments are recognizing the changes in the status of correctional officers. People are no longer sent to institutions for punishment, but to learn new values and standards. Regardless of our job in the institution, we are teaching. It's the job of everyone to support the program so this can be done. This is done by developing good work habits on the part of the girls and by discipline. Now we get the people here who couldn't make it on the outside. The recidivists should not be given an assignment where they will be happy and comfortable, but we should place them where they can learn, develop and gain some insight, so when they are released they can contribute to some phase of society. The educational program is part of the program. We have a definite program of education. It is important that we support the education program, as the success of a correctional officer depends to some extent on the education department. Miss —— (Supervisor of Education) can't do a good job without the support of every officer—and the officers can't do a good job without the cooperation of Miss ——. Whether the assignment is vocational or academic, it is important that the inmate goes to the classes and is on time; this is an important part of the program for the inmates. The women must learn discipline, and education if it offers nothing else teaches self-discipline. We're all working toward the same goals, and that is to help these women achieve a certain success in their life. Educational achievement plays an important part in determining if a resident is ready for parole. It's necessary that we all cooperate.

Supervisor of Education. I don't have a written speech, but I guess you can always talk about your business. In setting up the education program, scheduling the inmates was difficult. The education program consists of classes on Tuesday through Friday for the youths and the inmates sentenced under the Juvenile Act, and any others that the Classification Committee decides should attend. In setting up the classes, we've tried to give the women as much as we can. We have classes set up to give basic studies. On Tuesday and Thursday evenings, classes will be given for inmates who work during the day, and also classes on Saturday for those who work in industries and have to work during the day. Youth classes are scheduled in the morning. We stress the importance of the women obtaining a high school equivalency diploma if they are in high school classes. Classes will be given by Miss ——— (civilian teacher) —high school and junior high school classes; and June Olcott (inmate teacher) will help with the lower level and intermediate classes. Miss Long (correctional officer) is going to teach the Laubach classes. (*Laughing*) This does not refer to music class, as has been assumed by some, but it's a basic course in language and sounds. The book was written by Frank T. Laubach, a missionary, who had a great deal of success with the natives, but I don't know where. The course consists of basic sounds of words and the course has a series of films. This course is for the inmates who are in grade 1–6, and the classes have been scheduled so there is not too much conflict. The purpose of the education program is for the inmates to obtain as much knowledge as they can.

Chief—Classification and Parole. It's written in the Law and Bureau policies that we make an evaluation of why these inmates got into trouble, and we have to set goals for them to accomplish. We have to make recommendations as to what the person will need before making parole. We give information concerning accomplishments to the Parole Board so they can make a decision on parole plans. We should make definite plans for these youths for vocational and educational classes—as well as for a job and quarters. At Classification, if the Committee assigns an inmate to classes, it's because we feel it's important—whether it's vocational or academic. It's important that the self-image of the inmates be changed—by and large they have a poor concept of themselves. We have to make them feel that they can succeed in something—whether it's completing a course or handling a job. They need encouragement in being made to feel that they can do the job. A little sympathy and understanding helps. Now it's true that all the research on the degree to which vocations learned in institutions are used outside indicates that very few inmates use them—that they go into other things. But they're important in that it shows the individual that she can actually learn something. The work habits they learn can be applied elsewhere. Cooperation on the part of you officers will mean extra work, I know. But it's our responsibility that these youths achieve these goals. School is part of our training program, and we have to see that these people get to these classes. You have a responsibility to encourage the inmates in their educational activities.

Associate Warden (T). I don't have anything to add really—except the importance. If we're going to get a treatment program under-way, everyone will have to cooperate. The correctional officers will have to cooperate with the education department—we're not just jailors with keys. The success of the program will depend upon the attitude of the officer—to encourage them to attend classes and to support the classes.

At this point the speech making ended, and the captain added that everyone should try to "understand" what the education staff was doing and to "support the program." The associate warden (business) and the superintendents of the culinary and mechanical departments, who were seated in the rear of the room, whispered to one another several times during the meeting. When the question period opened, the associate warden rose to his feet.

Associate Warden (B). We in Fiscal and Operations have a question. If you send all the main dish cooks off to school when you have to get out a meal, what are you going to do? (addressing himself to the supervisor of education): Miss ———, when did this program start and how many people will it affect?

Supervisor of Education. It started last Thursday. It will affect the youth cases and the juvenile cases—about 60 of those, and I don't know yet how many of the others. They haven't been assigned as yet.

Associate Warden (B). Last Thursday! Warden, I'm Associate Warden here, and this is the first time I've heard of it! People in Opera-tions would like to be in on things so we can plan. (To this remark, the superintendent of culinary service silently nodded agreement.)

Associate Warden (T.) (*Quickly*) Well, I'm inclined to agree with Jim. I suppose it would have been better to let you know and talk about it a little. And maybe I'm at fault a little here—but I see your point.

Warden: I'd like to answer here. You say you've never heard of it? We're not doing anything we haven't always done. There's nothing we're doing that we haven't done for the past five years. Were you not at the meeting with Mr. Smith?

Associate Warden (B). No, I was not.

Warden: Did you receive a copy of his report?

Associate Warden (B). Yes, I did.

Warden. Well, we're only doing what was recommended in that report. We're going along with it. We only received one copy, but we had a few made and a copy was sent to you. Since you did not say anything, we assumed that you would go along with it.

Correctional Officer. (*Interrupting*) Were rosters sent around? Some of the girls didn't know anything about it. And I had one that didn't want to go anymore. She said she was going to lock. She said to me, "I know my ABC's, and I don't want to go anymore." So I said to her, "I know you do, but you're like me. I know my ABC's too, but sometimes I murder the English language."

Associate Warden (T). (*Laughing*) I know—like, "It don't make no difference."

Supervisor of Education. Was that Barbara?

Correctional Officer. Yes.

Supervisor of Education. She said the same thing to Miss ——— (school teacher). You know they like to say they're taking high school courses. They don't like to think they're taking anything elementary. But Miss ——— asked her if she could pronounce all the words, and she said she couldn't.

(*Laughter from everyone in the room*)

Warden. They're like children—you know we've got to tell them how to spend their money—how to use their time wisely—

Lieutenant. (Addressing Supervisor of Education) Miss ———, were the girls called in and told what the course was about? I mean, did they know what was involved, and did they say they wanted to take it?—Because *we've had a time* the past two days.

Supervisor of Education. They were told.

Lieutenant. Were they just called on the telephone and told they were being assigned to the class, or was the course explained to them? And did they agree to take it, because *we've had a time* the past two days. And were rosters sent to the details? We've had complaints that no one seemed to know what it was all about.

Supervisor of Education. Assignment slips or rosters were sent. Yes, assignment slips.

Lieutenant. (*Persisting*) Were their names just put on the list? You know, if these girls don't want to take something, they won't unless they're interested. I tell you, *we've had a time* with all this.

Associate Warden (T). Well, I know it's not easy. After all, we're dealing with the failures. These people are unintelligent, emotionally unstable, and insecure. They're not interested. But after all, you've got to remember that a GS7 correctional officer gets more money than a person with a Ph.D. degree teaching in a public school, and if these people weren't here, we wouldn't have jobs. Sure, we're dealing with unintelligent, emotionally unstable people. But we're supposed to do something with these people. We're supposed to have a treatment program, and we can't have one without everyone's cooperation.

Associate Warden (B). Well, do they have to go during those hours? Couldn't the schedule be arranged differently?

Supervisor of Education. In the Laubach course, there are different levels, and they have to be shown in sequence.

Associate Warden (B). Couldn't some of these people go from three to five or at another time? Or in the evening? (Note: inmates who work in food service are off duty for a few hours in the afternoon.)

Supervisor of Education. Perhaps some shifts can be made as far as the courses are concerned. It will have to be worked out.

Warden. If you're really interested in an education, you'll go in the evening. After all, people outside take evening courses after work. And you officers take your course in the evening. And—I don't have to tell you about Abraham Lincoln.

Associate Warden (B). Now I don't want you to get the idea that we in Operations don't want to cooperate. (*His voice rose a little.*) But it's the sheer *magnitude* of it! I think it would have been better if the program had been presented to the group—and we could have discussed it a little—with all concerned. Then we could have arrived at something that would have satisfied everyone.

Chief—Classification and Parole. Well, we'll get the information of assignments to you. It's going to mean cooperation and extra work from all of you. If any of you have any crises that come up, why call, and we'll do what we can. Call us, but I don't mean for just anything, now.

At this point the meeting ended. The associate warden (business) walked over to the lieutenant who had spoken at the meeting and patted her on the back approvingly.

As indicated in the foregoing material, the possibility of arriving at a solution to the problem by a reorganization of units at the maintenance and custodial levels was not considered. The strain imposed by the expansion of treatment functions was clearly expected to be resolved by integration with the custodial and maintenance ends. The prison, faced with the practical concern of maintaining itself and the uncompromised claims of custodial security and internal order views the treatment goal as an ideal to hold out as legitimate only when the predominant tasks of maintenance, custody, and internal order are clearly in equilibrium.

Expansion of treatment functions mobilizes the maintenance and custodial forces to resist changes which will in any way jeopardize the successful performance of their functions. This strain for functional autonomy and resistance to encroachment is a concomitant of the basic conflict between these competing goals in the prison.

The tendency for treatment personnel to rationalize the success or failure of any treatment program on a particular role group—or on the putative traits of inmates—misses the crucial point. *The basic conflict between the competing goals of self-maintenance and custody on the one hand, and treatment on the other, is a structural weakness of prisons: Any disturbance in the equilibrium of the system results in reconciliation of competing purposes at the treatment level.* In the nature of the case, it could not be otherwise.

NOTES

1. For a detailed discussion of the problem of functional autonomy see Alvin W. Gouldner, "Reciprocity and Autonomy in Functional Theory," in L. Gross, Editor, *Symposium on Social Theory,* Evanston, Ill.: Row, Peterson and Company, 1959, pp. 241–270; and by the same author, "Organizational Analysis," in Robert K. Merton et al., Editors, *Sociology Today,* New York: Basic Books, Inc., 1959, pp. 400–428.

2. The distinction between collectivity and self-orientations is taken from Talcott Parsons, *The Social System,* Glencoe: The Free Press, 1951, pp. 60–61.

3. See Simone de Beauvoir, *op. cit.;* for a recent, more extended treatment for the American case, see Jules Henry, *Culture Against Man,* New York: Random House, 1963, pp. 61, 147–180.

4. For an extended treatment of prison labor, see Edwin H. Sutherland and Donald R. Cressey, *Principles of Criminology,* New York: J. B. Lippincott Company, Sixth Edition, 1960, Chap. 25; and Harry Elmer Barnes and Negley K. Teeters, *New Horizons in Crim-*

inology, Englewood Cliffs, N.J.: Prentice-Hall, Inc., 1959, pp. 522–542.

5. Hans Reimer, "Socialization in the Prison Community," *Proceedings of the American Prison Association,* 1937, p. 154.

6. A check of the disciplinary report for that month reported officially that she had struck the inmate with the fork.

7. Meeting held January 10, 1963.

CHAPTER 6 COMPETING GOALS, HETEROGENEITY, AND CLASSIFICATION

Central to the individualized treatment philosophy in the prison based on classification procedures is the assumption that each role in the formal organization should be integrated toward the goal of treatment according to the needs of the inmates. Theoretically, in a treatment program the individual needs of the inmates should be taken exclusively into account rather than programs and procedures that serve only the requirements of the institution.

There are admittedly many problems in trying to integrate a coherent treatment program in the prison system. We considered previously the critical problem of competing goals in the prison and how conflicting functions work against setting a consistent course of action. We saw that the treatment goal was held as legitimate only when the prison goals of custody, internal order, and maintenance units were clearly in equilibrium. Now, in order to shed further light on the difficulties of achieving the treatment goal in a prison structure committed to competing goals, we turn to an examination of the human material which has been processed through the courts into the Alderson prison.

The heterogeneity of the inmate population with respect to a number of variables around which the prison must organize its educational, vocational, avocational, and other treatment programs creates additional problems of structural integration. In fact, a heterogeneous inmate population in a single institution would present problems for setting up treatment programs under the best conditions. Such a population would require integration of extensive treatment facilities within the prison structure, and the task of mobilizing a trained staff is not a simple matter. Another area of concern (although this is not necessarily a function of heterogeneity) is that a broad treatment program geared to the individual needs of the inmates requires that they have great freedom of movement, and this would pose serious administrative problems, as safe custody is the primary goal set for the Alderson prison officials by the courts. But when a prison has economic self-sufficiency as a goal, treatment programs must of necessity be cautious attempts and are at best a palliative. In such a case, treatment structures designed to serve individual needs must either be abandoned altogether on an informal level or so modified in structure as to seriously abort formally stated aims.

II

Due to the lower commitment rates for females, the large reception centers or clinics used in many states for diagnosing male prisoners prior to transport to specialized institutions do not exist for female prisoners. The Federal Prison System for the male offender is geographically extensive and provides an integrated system of classified institutions so that individuals may be placed in the type of institution most appropriate to their particular offense and sentence. Because of the lower commitment rates for females, some states have not built separate prisons for females, but instead provide them with a separate wing or other space in the male prison. Other states have built women's reformatories, most of which are built along the cottage plan, as it is advocated that this physical design allows for any necessary differentiation of inmates within the system. The physical structure of the Alderson prison is built on the cottage plan, and accommodates a high percentage of all federal female adult criminals.

With the exception of the facilities provided for approximately two hundred women from the far western states at the Terminal Island Federal Prison in California, women convicted of federal crimes are usually designated to Alderson. As a result, the inmates at Alderson come from almost every state in the nation. The population of 653 inmates, for example, represented every state except Delaware, Maine, New Hampshire, Vermont, Montana, Nebraska, Utah, and Wyoming. Nine others were classified as transients, and fifteen as aliens. The latter were from Peru, Mexico, France, Canada, Cuba, Chile, the Bahamas, Puerto Rico, and Germany. Thus the prison is located many hundreds of miles from the family and friends of most of the inmates; therefore, the travel expense prevents many of the inmates from having visitors while in prison. Most women, as a matter of fact, serve their entire sentences without a visit from the outside world. In the year 1962, for example, an examination of the records revealed that seventy-nine inmates or about 12 percent of the inmate population received visits during the entire year. This means that except for interaction with other inmates, the only other human contact is with staff members. Although this lack of intrusion from the outside world facilitates an inmate's induction into the inmate social system, from a treatment standpoint, the social consequences may be quite costly.

Now the process by which the prison attempts to attain the objective of reformation through individualized treatment is presumed to be the program of *classification*.[1] Classification was originally designed as a special device to focus specifically upon inmate treatment needs, and to make possible a coordinated treatment program in the individual case. How is this accomplished? The inmate's formal education, vocational, and other treatment needs are diagnosed, and individual assignments are made on the basis of the diagnoses. The prevailing principles taken into consideration are usually the length of sentence (often, but not always, prior commitments are taken into account), age, and personal characteristics of the inmates.

It is apparent that classification presupposes—for an effective program—the existence of treatment facilities within the prison structure, if the process is to be worth more than the paper upon which the many voluminous reports are written. Although the formal framework for classification is "played out," as it were, by the Alderson prison officials, on an informal level they have chosen to abandon the program in practice because it is necessary to balance organizational structures such as custody and maintenance in planning an inmate's prison program. The meaning of this fact for the formal organization and for the inmate's prison routine will be our concern for the remainder of this chapter.

III

Prison administrators hardly begin with blank canvas and primary colors, even with the first offender. With the recidivist, however, there is good reason to suppose that the staff must face the additional task of peeling off layers of values and attitudes assimilated in other prison worlds as well as antisocial attitudes and values internalized in civil society.

Some writers argue that experiences in jail, training school, and the like are not identical to the prison experience, and therefore they maintain that such information should not be included in tabulating statistics for recidivism. I think this practice may be grossly misleading, however, because evidence suggests that the banishment of the individual from society into a correctional institution—whatever rubric it claims—is sufficient to bring about certain attitudes and values inimical toward society.[2] The experience of incarceration in jails, training schools, and the like exposes the individual to an inmate culture which is not unlike that found in the prison.[3]

For the purposes of the study, therefore, recidivism was defined as any prior commitment. Inmates whose records indicated that they had previously been incarcerated in other reformatories, prisons, jails, workhouses, and girls' correctional or training schools were all classified as recidivists. In these terms, an inmate who had served a thirty-day jail sentence was classified as a recidivist. According to this definition, on a selected day the records revealed that 52.1 percent had been previously jailed or imprisoned. A breakdown of the number of prior commitments appears in Table 7. Of the 312 first offenders, 60.6 percent were white, 38.1 percent were Negro, and 1.3 percent were Mongoloid. Of the total population, 15.3 percent were recidivists of the Alderson prison. Approximately half of the inmate population, in other words, had been previously incarcerated.

TABLE 7   NUMBER AND PERCENTAGE DISTRIBUTION OF THE
PRIOR COMMITMENT HISTORY OF INMATES BY RACE

Number of Commitments	Negro Number	Per- cent	White Number	Per- cent	Mon- goloid Number	Per- cent	Total	Per- cent
None	119	42.5	189	51.5	4	66.7	312	47.8
One	66	23.6	90	24.5	1	16.7	157	24.0
Two	39	13.9	45	12.3	–	–	84	12.9
Three	16	5.7	23	6.3	–	–	39	5.9
Four	15	5.4	12	3.3	–	–	27	4.1
Five or more	25	8.9	8	2.2	1	16.7	34	5.2
Total	280	100.0	367	99.1	6	100.1	653	99.9

Because recidivists constitute potent socializing agents, one of the fundamental problems which must be faced squarely by the prison administrator is whether to isolate them from the first offenders. The first offenders at the Alderson prison were scattered throughout the cottages and followed the same program as the other prisoners. Given the competing goals of the prison, it follows that to separate such a large group of inmates would pose serious administrative problems. For example, inmates assigned to work in food service are *ipso facto* assigned to live in a food service cottage regardless of age, personal character- istics, or prior criminality.

Recidivists are important because they bring with them the values they have assimilated in other institutions, tend to rein- force the values in interaction with other recidivists, and social- ize first offenders to these values. Secondly, the dispersal of in- mates throughout the prison system facilitates the induction of the first offenders into the inmate culture and social system. Thus, the possibility of positive identification with staff mem- bers and values is sharply reduced.

The question of whether prisoners should be isolated from one another no longer arises in connection with criminal offenses as far as classification of prisoners is concerned. A sharp distinction is made between male prisoners who are considered violent and dangerous regardless of the offense, and are said to require the bastille-type prison, and those who may be safely housed in minimum and medium security insitutions. As explained previously, whatever distinctions are made in the case of the female adult prisoner, females must be accommodated within the same institution. Maximum security units exist within a single institution, but they are few in number. Yet we do not find the same sharp distinctions made for the female prisoner in terms of passivity and aggression. This lack of distinction is not a result of the range of female criminality being sharply limited. On the contrary, the data in Table 8 reveal that the criminality

TABLE 8   OFFENSES OF INMATES CLASSIFIED ACCORDING TO TYPE OF CRIME

Type of Crime	Number	Percent
Bank robbery	12	1.8
Embezzlement	12	1.8
False impersonation	5	.8
White slave traffic	5	.8
Forgery	128	19.6
Narcotics	193	29.6
Kidnapping	4	.6
Income tax evasion	2	.3
Immigration violators	4	.6
Fraud	24	3.7
Liquor law violators	15	2.3
Larceny	204	31.2
Counterfeiting, possession or passing of counterfeit materials with intent to defraud	5	.8
D. C. cases	3	.5
Government reservation and territorial cases	12	1.8
Conspiracy	15	2.3
Miscellaneous	10	1.5
Total	653	100.0

of the Alderson inmate population includes a broad range of federal offenses.

Despite the broad range of offenses committed by the inmates, the distinctions based on violence (and, on an informal level, on criminal offense) usually made in the male prison by staff and inmates alike are rarely made in the case of the female inmate.

A few inmates were defined as unfit to mix with the general Alderson population and were housed in the maximum security cottages, mainly because they were perceived to be behavior problems. The behavior problems were a function of incarceration, and the inmates in question were often referred to as "troublemakers" and "psychotics." (All nonprofessional personnel in the prison tended to label all inmates defined as "troublemakers" as "psychotic.") Refusal to work, for example, would be just and sufficient reason to move an inmate to a maximum security unit. It is worth noting, however, that the two maximum security cottages were filled to capacity by other inmates who chose to live there mainly because they found living with a smaller group of inmates to be less hectic; it was clear that they did not require the closer supervision and greater restriction on freedom that living in these quarters entailed. In addition, under some circumstances an inmate may find it necessary to make a "Sonya"-like Siberian trek to be with a homosexual lover. There are, in other words, several reasons why an inmate may be housed, by choice or otherwise, in a maximum security unit.

The fundamental difference between the male and female prisons in this respect may be explained partially by the fact that there is a *principle of reduction* which operates in the case of the female prisoner—from the point of view of both the inmates and the staff. In the first place, cultural prescriptions of the female prisoner make a concerted effort to reduce all female offenders, on the basis of their common criminality, to the same generalized status of equality, *criminal,* in order to neutralize the generalized popular culture pertaining to women and thus to lay the groundwork for intensive interaction among the inmates in the prison.

On the staff level a similar reduction process operates due to the persistence of the societal-cultural definition of the nature of the female criminal. It will be recalled that historically society has looked upon the female criminal as a misguided, sinful, pathetic creature in need of protection and as a passive rather than an aggressive individual. And the Alderson staff tends to look upon the inmates as generally lacking in moral fibre—as being "weak," "like children," [4] as well as "selfish." This basal reduction eliminates the necessity to make sharp differentiations among inmates and makes it possible to handle them in large groups by the use of standardized routines.

For example, in the matter of differentiation, no distinctions are made by the Alderson officials on the basis of age, although there was great disparity in the ages of the inmates. As Table 9 indicates, the commitment age ranged from fifteen to sixty-seven years, with a mean of 32.2 and a median of 30.5.

TABLE 9 CURRENT AND COMMITMENT AGE
DISTRIBUTION OF INMATE
POPULATION

Age	Current Age Number	Commitment Age Number
15–19	29	53
20–24	121	132
25–29	114	129
30–34	132	114
35–39	103	89
40–44	63	67
45–49	38	27
50–54	23	16
55–59	15	13
60–64	9	7
65–69	5	6
70+	1	–
Total	653	653

The current ages of the prisoners ranged from sixteen to seventy. The mean age was 34.4 and the median was 30.8. Ultimately, of course, whether or not age is made a criterion for separating prisoners depends upon the goals of the organization. An organization committed to balancing custodial and maintenance goals against a broad scheme of differentiation which would disrupt the equilibrium of these units will be guided by convenience to the organization rather than by treatment needs indicated in the individual case.

In this context, it may be pointed out that the official in charge of classification proceedings always had a list of job "vacancies" which "had" to be filled. In other words, the function for which this structural device was created is aborted or compromised because the maintenance requirements of the organization are accorded priority. We observed earlier a similar process occurring in connection with the disposition of inmate rule infractions. In general, when convenience is the criterion used for assignment, a compromise with the treatment objective is made. In this regard, the former occupations of the inmates are particularly vulnerable to exploitation by the formal organization precisely because this experience fits so nicely the goals of the existing structure.

Although most of the information concerning occupational status obtained from the female prisoners at the time of entry is verified by a social history form filled out either by relatives, former employers, or is verified by information on presentence reports, these data must nevertheless be interpreted with extreme caution. In the first place, the stated occupational status of an inmate does not necessarily mean current occupation immediately prior to incarceration. For many inmates, as for other women in the labor force in the United States, employment is frequently intermittent to help supplement family income. At other times, an occupation is assumed prior to marriage, as a result of divorce, or because of separation. The information in Table 10, then, is an indication of the kinds of work experience which each inmate has had in the past. As might be expected, most of the inmates are represented in occupations closely allied with homemaking roles, as these have been historically filled by women. Approximately one-third of all inmates

TABLE 10   OCCUPATIONAL STATUS OF INMATE
POPULATION REPORTED AT TIME
OF ENTRY

Occupation Reported	Number	Percent
None	45	6.9
Housewife	55	8.4
Domestic laborer	72	11.0
Waitress and other phases of restaurant work	174	26.7
Hospital attendant	31	4.7
Beautician	11	1.7
Factory operator	66	10.1
Laundry worker	18	2.8
Seasonal farm laborer	10	1.5
Clerical worker	72	11.0
Salesclerk	25	3.8
Prostitute	15	2.3
Teacher	3	.5
Seamstress	6	.9
Elevator operator	9	1.4
Bank teller or executive	7	1.1
Owner—small business	12	1.8
Manager—small business	3	.5
Entertainer	6	.9
Florist's helper	2	.3
Telephone operator	2	.3
Stock room clerk	4	.6
Insurance sales	1	.2
Organist	1	.2
Interpreter	1	.2
Cab driver	1	.2
Garage worker	1	.2
Total	653	100.0

had worked in such service occupations as waitresses, hospital attendants, and beauticians. Of this group, 26.7 percent were waitresses. Eleven percent were engaged as domestic laborers and about the same number were engaged as factory operatives. The twelve women listed as owners of small business included proprietors of cafes, bars, restaurants, taverns, and grocery stores.

It is apparent that the former occupational experience of the inmates in the labor market, or their former roles as home-makers lend themselves very effectively to the efficient attainment of the prison's goal of economic self-sufficiency. As we saw in Chapter 3, the bulk of the inmates are assigned to tasks concerned with various forms of sewing, cooking, and cleaning. The organization of the prison around these major functions stems historically from the theory that women should be trained in the prison primarily as mothers and homemakers. As a consequence, vocational and other "educational" treatment programs were in turn generally coordinated about the necessary occupations of the prison. Vocational "training" in the female prison actually meant training in one of the maintenance functions of the institution; thus women, upon release, could work as service workers such as domestics and waitresses, or in the needle trades. Such occupations, as well as laundry work, were available to released inmates.

The Alderson prison was built along the pattern adopted by the best state institutions of the day, where it is said to have been demonstrated that home-like units and smaller kitchens provided opportunity for training in cooking, house decorations, table service, and all phases of homemaking. Consequently, formal instructions tended to supplement and illustrate the basic training in the cottages. This was consistent with the prevailing goal of the prison, namely, to train inmates for roles as mothers and homemakers; but this training goal was never allowed to interfere with what were considered to be the necessary occupations of the prison.

Society has been slow to change the vocational preparation of female prisoners, and the emphasis on kitchen and needle arts has persisted. A vocational program in the prison, however, is justifiable to the extent that the training may be used by the inmate in earning an adequate livelihood upon release.

More than likely, vocational *knowledge* rather than work "skills" and "good work habits" derived from prison labor will gain increasing importance in the future; evidence strongly suggests that the majority of female inmates must seek some form of employment when released. The marital status of the inmates indicated that 27.1 percent were single; 31.5 percent were married; 20.7 percent were separated; 16.4 percent were divorced; and slightly over 4 percent were widows. Even many of the married women will find it necessary to seek employment upon release.

It is interesting to note that the most recent figures on female labor in the United States seem to point in the direction of increasing concentration of women in the clerical field in the future. Although the occupations of women varied widely in the 1960 census, the largest concentrations were in the clerical field, which comprised about 7 million women. (The three other major categories comprised service workers such as waitresses, beauticians, and hospital attendants; and professional and technical employees such as teachers, nurses, accountants and librarians. These groupings number between 3 and 3.75 million each.) [5] The underrepresentation of inmates in the clerical field is due to their low level of educational attainment. It has been reported that the median full-time income of women who had graduated from elementary school but had not completed high school was $950 in 1961.[6] A major problem which confronts the prison administrator, of course, is the realistic planning of vocational knowledge, that is, knowledge which the inmate can actually put to use in earning a livelihood upon release. Although it is true that the labor market for women is changing in the United States, the stigma of a prison sentence would perhaps exclude employment in clerical jobs for released inmates.

But without the integration of extensive community resources, it seems to me that the task of integrating meaningful treatment functions in the prison will always be seriously hampered. For example, think what it would mean to provide individualized educational treatment for inmates. As shown in Table 11, approximately half of the inmate population, or 325 inmates, had eight years' schooling or less. There is no marked

TABLE 11   EDUCATIONAL LEVEL OF INMATES BY RACE AS
SHOWN ON CLASSIFICATION RECORDS

Highest Grade Completed	Negro Number	White Number	Mongoloid Number	Total
Grammar School				
None	–	6	–	6
One year	–	–	–	–
Two years	3	1	–	4
Three years	8	5	–	13
Four years	7	8	–	15
Five years	13	17	1	31
Six years	31	28	2	61
Seven years	25	40	1	66
Eight years	49	79	1	129
High School				
One year	55	46	–	101
Two years	34	46	1	81
Three years	26	20	–	46
Four years	22	50	–	72
College				
One year	1	13	–	14
Two years	3	3	–	6
Three years	–	–	–	–
Four years	2	4	–	6
Graduate School				
One year	1	1	–	2
Total	280	367	6	653

discrepancy in educational achievement between the Negro and white races: 49.6 percent of the Negro inmates attended grade school; 50.1 percent of the white inmates attended grade school. A higher portion of the Negroes attended high school: 47.9 percent as compared with 44 percent of the white inmates. Of these two groups, however, a higher proportion of the white inmates graduated from both grammar and high school. For example, 17.5 percent of the Negroes completed grammar school, whereas 21.5 percent of the whites completed eight grades. Similarly, 7.9 percent of the Negro inmate population completed high school, but 13.6 percent of the white group graduated from high school.

The question is frequently raised as to whether prisoners have the mental capacity to benefit from formal educational treatment facilities. If by "intelligent" is meant whatever it is that intelligence tests measure, then a breakdown of the actual full scale I.Q. scores as revealed by tests administered in the prison indicates that the inmates do not differ appreciably from the general population.

As Table 12 indicates, 13 percent of the inmate population scored below a score of 70, which is generally accepted as defective mental status. Negroes scored considerably lower in the extreme categories; but 51.2 percent of the white population and 45 percent of the Negro group fall into the average category. Approximately 50 percent of the total inmate population fall into this grouping. Combining the average and low average groups, the breakdown is 67.3 percent white and 67.9 percent

TABLE 12   I.Q. SCORE BREAKDOWN OF INMATE POPULATION BY RACE

Category	White	Per-cent	Negro	Per-cent	Mon-goloid	Per-cent	Total	Per-cent
Superior	20	5.4	4	1.4	–	–	24	3.7
High average	63	17.2	15	5.4	–	–	78	11.9
Average	188	51.2	126	45.0	4	66.7	318	48.7
Low average	59	16.1	64	22.9	–	–	123	18.8
Inferior	18	4.9	65	23.2	2	33.3	85	13.0
Not tested *	19	5.2	6	2.1	–	–	25	3.8
Total	367	100.0	280	100.0	6	100.0	653	99.9

* This constitutes an error of omission; it should not be thought that these inmates were illiterate.

Negro. For our purposes, the significant point is that according to the prison records, 13 percent of the inmate population may be classified as defective.[7] In other words, the problem lies not so much in the ability of the inmates but, rather, in *what* and *how* to teach, and what relative emphasis to place on social and academic education for treatment.

The problem of implementing broad treatment functions in the prison setting is, without doubt, complex. The inmates vary in previous education from a handful of college graduates to others who can speak little or no English, their ages range from fifteen to seventy, and they enter the prison on any day of the year.

In addition, the length of the sentences for the crimes varies widely—the range is from three months to life. The mean sentence without consideration for parole is 54 months. The complete distribution appears in Table 13.

In this heterogeneous and shifting population, then, the prison must organize a "school" presumably suited to the individual needs of the inmates and at the same time adapted into the necessary maintenance work of the prison.

As the societal goal for the prison progressively shifts from punishment to rehabilitation, the conflicting purposes stand out more sharply. The competing goals of the prison induce pres-

TABLE 13   LENGTH OF SENTENCES FOR
INMATE POPULATION

Sentence	Number	Percent
1 year or less	46	7.0
1 year, 1 day to 3 years	271	41.5
3 years, 1 day to 5 years	174	26.6
5 years, 1 day to 10 years	132	20.1
10 years, 1 day to 15 years	18	2.8
More than 15 years	11	1.7
Observation and study	1	.2
	653	99.9

sures toward goal displacement. Displacement of goals has been evidenced in the function of the classification process for the prison routine of the inmates as a consequence of overconcern with organizational stability.

It is apparent that criteria such as history of recidivism, educational attainment, length of sentence, and personal characteristics such as drug addiction do not fit neatly into the organizational scheme when assignment to work, quarters, and treatment activities must be based on convenience to the institution. For this reason, although such information as age, education, and former occupation is carefully noted on classification reports, it is not made an integral part of the classification process.

The lack of meaningful differentiation of individual characteristics makes it possible to perceive inmates as more alike than different and, thus, to handle them *en masse* with standardized routines.

We saw in Chapter 5 that in order to maintain the equilibrium of the system, treatment structures were modified or converted to other uses. Similarly, the mechanism of classification, however nobly its purpose is stated in official publications, serves as an administrative device to balance institutional manpower needs in the prison. Because of the competing goals of the prison and the priority placed upon maintenance and custodial needs of the institution, classification requires extensive compromise with these structures.

NOTES

1. Frank Loveland, "Classification in the Prison System," in Paul W. Tappan, Editor, *Contemporary Correction,* New York: Mc-Graw-Hill Book Company, Inc., 1951, pp. 92–101; Edwin H. Sutherland and Donald R. Cressey, *Principles of Criminology, op. cit.,* pp. 462–477.

2. See especially Sheldon and Eleanor Glueck, *Five Hundred Criminal Careers,* New York: Alfred A. Knopf, 1930. The authors followed the careers of delinquent graduates from one correctional school and found that over 75 percent of them subsequently engaged in criminal or delinquent behavior. More recently, it has been reported that 15 percent of admissions during the year 1956 had been at the same institution at one time or another and were returned either for commitment of a new offense or parole violation; see Children's Bureau,

Statistics on Public Institutions for Delinquent Children, 1956, Washington, D.C.: U.S. Department of Health, Education, and Welfare, 1956, p. 1. See also the follow-up analysis of community adjustment and deviant outcomes of the Hollymeade group by Howard W. Polsky, *Cottage Six,* New York: Russell Sage Foundation, 1962, pp. 183–185.

3. See the brilliant analysis by Howard W. Polsky, *ibid.* For an example of the adult prison, see Donald Clemmer, *The Prison Community, op. cit.,* especially pp. 298–315. More recently, Wheeler's findings indicate that conformity to conventional norms varies depending upon the stage of the inmate's career. It was observed that conformity to conventional norms was higher at the beginning and at the end of imprisonment than in the middle. However, despite the U-shaped pattern of change, there was a tendency for inmates to move away from conformity to conventional norms with each increment of prison experience. Thus, first offenders and recidivists exhibit the same pattern, but the recidivists exhibit lower conformity than the first offenders. Stanton Wheeler, "Social Organization in a Correctional Community," Unpublished Ph.D. Dissertation, University of Washington, 1958. See also Stanton Wheeler, "Socialization in Correctional Communities," *American Sociological Review,* Vol. 26, October 1961, pp. 696–712.

4. See Erving Goffman, "On the Characteristics of Total Institutions: Staff-Inmate Relations," in Donald R. Cressey, Editor, *The Prison, Studies in Institutional Organization and Change,* New York: Holt, Rinehart and Winston, Inc., 1961, p. 78.

5. *American Women,* Report of the President's Commission on the Status of Women, 1963; Washington, D.C.: U.S. Government Printing Office, 1963, p. 28.

6. *Ibid.,* p. 70.

7. For the reader interested in crime statistics, the 85 inmates classified as defectives were convicted of the following crimes: 1 case of false impersonation; 27 cases of forgery; 22 cases in connection with narcotics; 1 case of fraud; 2 cases in violation of the liquor law; 29 cases of larceny (postal theft accounts for 22 of the larceny cases); and 3 cases of murder.

CHAPTER 7 THE NATURE OF THE PRISON EXPERIENCE

The clipped head, a form of female degradation dating back to medieval inquisition, is no longer part of the repertoire of punishments which prison officials are prepared to inflict upon their female prisoners. And other former punishments such as restricted diets and solitary confinement are now rare in the modern prison. In general, society has made the lot of the female prisoner less harsh than that of the male prisoner; most female prisons, as we noted earlier, provide their inmates with many of the so-called "good" things.

Notwithstanding the "good" influences, however, it would be a mistake to assume that society does not intend the female prison to be a place of punishment. We must remember that in the adult court the primary focus has always been on punishment. And in a sense the primary focus on punishment poses a dilemma for the adult prison, given the conflicting goals society sets for it. As George Bernard Shaw has put it: "To punish a man you must injure him: to reform a man you must improve him: and men are not improved by injuries." Imprisonment is an injury to the individual: For one cannot gloss over the fact that the prison experience—whether one views it from the point of view of the male, or as we shall do shortly, from the point of view of the female—is enormously painful.

II

Sykes noted in his study of the Trenton prison that the pains of imprisonment for the modern prisoner are not rooted in physical brutality, but rather in attacks on the psychological level.[1] The "residue of apparently less acute hurts," he argues, such as the deprivation of liberty, goods, and services, heterosexual relations, autonomy, and security, "may indeed be the acceptable or unavoidable implications of imprisonment, but we must recognize the fact that they can be just as painful as the physical maltreatment which they have replaced."[2] Sykes recognizes that different prisoners perceive imprisonment somewhat differently and accord similar conditions "a different emphasis in their personal accounting." Nevertheless, he insists that the major fact is the "hard core of consensus" existing among the inmates: They agree that life in the maximum security prison is "depriving or frustrating in the extreme."[3]

What would constitute serious deprivations for women? Are the pains of imprisonment such that the structure of the female cultural system will parallel that of the male prison community? Actually it is difficult to state *exactly* at what level the effect of imprisonment upon the Alderson prison inmates is "depriving or frustrating in the *extreme*."[4] The perceptions of the Alderson inmates vary, depending upon the stage of the inmate's prison career; her former commitment history; and the relative ease with which she may adjust to the inmate social system; and, as we shall see in another chapter, the inmate social system plays a major part in the individual's adjustment to the prison world. Nevertheless, the evidence clearly suggests that prison life *is* depriving and frustrating for the Alderson inmates.

The loss of liberty and autonomy are among the most uniformly felt deprivations among the Alderson prison inmates. To the casual observer, the many restraints imposed upon the individual in the prison community are not always readily apparent. But the mere fact that the prisoner cannot leave the premises, for example, is an enormous restraint on personal freedom. In addition, the fact that communication with family members and friends is sharply limited to specified times and under specified conditions is also painfully restraining. Although the inmate is allowed five hours of visiting time each month, she finds it difficult to translate this regulation into reality because the distance from family and friends precludes face-to-face interaction for all but a few of the inmates. The Alderson inmates, then, are forced to rely almost exclusively upon letters as the major means of communication. Each inmate may include up to seven persons on an approved mailing list—each of whom may send one letter a week unless notified to the contrary by the inmate. Prison regulations, however, limit the number of outgoing letters to three per week, which the inmates view as a deprivation. This curb on letter writing functions to inhibit the spontaneity of the inmate's communication with members of the free community and serves as one link in a long chain of conditions which tend to weld the inmates into an inter-dependent community.

Yet, important as letters from family and friends are so that the inmate does not "feel like a complete outcast," it must be kept in mind that letters often bring unpleasant news. A partic-ularly frustrating aspect of imprisonment for the female inmate is that she is not in a position to control the course of events in the outside world: children may be neglected, for example; husbands may become unfaithful or may obtain a divorce; a loved one may die. To dwell persistently on events in the outside world is to run the risk of doing "hard time." Thus, important as letters from the outside world are to the inmate, the content— whether good news or bad news—requires some *management* on the part of the prisoner if she is to be successful in doing "easy time," a value stressed by the inmate culture. Therefore, the prisoner must learn—and here her sister prisoners are helpful —to suspend deep emotional involvement in outside events. She develops an immunity to emotional shock to events both within and without the prison gate for the term of her sentence.

Many other restraints in the prison world either may not be apparent or may appear to be relatively unimportant to the casual observer. Viewed in the aggregate, however, they amount to a very regimented way of life. For example, the inmate must appear in line and fall in twos for breakfast count and whenever else the bell is sounded. She leaves for work at the sound of a bell and returns to her cottage at the sound of a bell. Moreover, the route she takes is fixed by the prison regulations. If the inmate wishes to attend a scheduled function, she must "sign out" on a list. If she wishes to exercise on the field, she may do so at specified times but must "sign out." If an inmate wishes to speak to a staff member, she must "write an interview slip," and wait until she is called. If she is not successful on the first try, she has the privilege of writing another interview slip—and yet another interview slip—and must wait to be called. If she wishes to go to the clinic for "sick call," she must put her name on a list the evening before, and must wait until she is called. The inmate cannot be late for a meal. If she does not wish to sit in the living room in the evening, she must be locked in her room. She cannot use the telephone to communicate with her family. In short, "everything is planned for you," in the words of one inmate, "from the time you get up until the time you go to bed."

Such restraints on the inmate's freedom are keenly felt, and the transition from liberty to rigidly restricted movement must be made by the female inmate in order to survive psychically in the prison environment. In addition, what seems to be particularly frustrating for the Alderson inmate, as well as for the adult male inmate, is the total imposition of the many bureaucratic rules to control behavior; that is, the inmate is not only powerless to change the prison rules but cannot voice an opinion as to the legitimacy of a rule regardless of how irrational it may appear. Furthermore, and very important for the informal social system, the restricted ability to make choices in the prison imposes the status of childhood dependency on the inmate. This is bitterly resented and may unleash mental conflicts and arouse acute anxiety for the Alderson female.

Although standards of material living are relatively high in the United States, it is reasonable to suppose that the deprivation of goods and services is meaningful to the prisoner depending upon the circumstances of her private life in civil society. Whatever the situation may have been, however, denying the inmate ownership of personal goods in prison removes the last resource the inmate possesses to express individuality; therefore the abrupt removal of personal effects tends to destroy her self-image. The denial of personal goods is considered deeply depriving by the vast majority of prisoners.

The stripping process occurs shortly after the inmate's entrance into the prison; her personal clothing and other effects are carefully listed item by item in the presence of the inmate, packaged in sturdy brown wrapping paper, and mailed to family members or friends in civil society. In this single act, a kind of symbolic death of the individual takes place. And in the performance of this stripping and mortifying process,[5] the prisoner is brought to terms with society's rejection of the criminal.

No clothing may be kept by the inmates except girdles (if they are not the panty type), brassieres, and shoes of simple (relatively low-heeled) closed styles. Medals, simple style earrings, and wedding rings which are not studded with precious or semiprecious stones, as well as wrist watches valued under fifteen dollars may be kept by the inmate. To replace the inmate's personal clothing, a set of items referred to as the "standard outfit original issue" is distributed to the inmate while in orientation status. Substitutions for some of the items appearing on the list are made if the items of clothing are not available. A skirt and blouse, for example, may replace a dress. This initial issue is supplemented with other items after classification, according to the nature of the inmate's work assignment. (See Appendix E.)

The inmate is hard-pressed indeed not to view the prison issue of clothing as a punishment and as a deliberate attack on her self-image. In the first place, the clothing is fairly uniform; secondly, the clothing issued to the new inmate is often faded, certain to have been worn by generations of prisoners, and either sizes too large or sizes too small. Nevertheless, the inmate cannot cut any material in making alterations, as the same garments must service future generations of criminals who will in turn take hems up or down, seams in or out. The more attractive items of prison issue are always kept in the possession of inmates in the prison. Although clothing must be returned to the clothing room prior to an inmate's release, exchanges take place informally among inmates, and usually only worn items of clothing find their way back to the clothing room.

The mortifying process in connection with clothing perhaps reaches its apex for the inmates in the issue of the shapeless cotton petticoats and the brown or white cotton broadcloth panties that resemble men's boxer-type shorts far more than they do ladies' underwear. Yet the inmate cannot keep her own underwear, nor does she have the freedom to puchase any with the fifteen dollars per month she is permitted to spend for commissary. The items of clothing the inmates are allowed to keep upon entry—or which may be purchased if the inmate has funds— are the items already mentioned, such as shoes and brassieres, which are always in short supply, or girdles, which are not issued to the inmates. It should be noted that all these items may be sent to the inmate by an approved correspondent at six-month intervals. Since the purchases of these "staple" items are considered to be "privileges," the inmates conclude rightly or wrongly that society *wants* to punish them. Why else, they ask, would it be a "privilege" to buy the necessities, when the prison doesn't issue them?

When one recalls that it is always open season on women's fashions, one is not surprised to learn that the attack on the individual's self-image with reference to clothing is particularly acute for the female inmate. The effort of some of the inmates in the admission and orientation unit to individualize the prison issue by the simple handworking of a monogram on a collar, embroidery on a blouse, or strategic placement of pleats on a surplus WAC jacket in an attempt to make them "more like free world clothes," are all evidence of the subtlety of deprivation.

For this reason the occasional issue of a few yards of surplus material to the inmates is much welcomed, although there is no choice of color or fabric, simply because it gives the inmate an opportunity to own a garment styled and suited to her own taste and provides—within a very circumscribed range—variety, that very scarce commodity in the prison world.

It has been pointed out that the lack of heterosexual intercourse is frustrating and depriving for the male prisoner, and the evidence indicates that the same holds true for the great majority of the female prisoners. Most inmates have enjoyed the company of men outside, and sex constitutes a major problem of adjustment for almost every inmate. Women do not choose to live their lives entirely apart from men, and the necessity of doing so in prison is frustrating for the individual, and adjustment is imperative. The obvious exceptions to this, of course, are the homosexuals who have practiced homosexuality in the

free community. Approximately 5 percent of the inmate population falls into this category. For this group this aspect of
imprisonment is not depriving. In a sense, the imprisonment
of the homosexual—whether male or female—is ironic, for the
loss of liberty, except in a few countries, is always accompanied
by the denial of contact with the opposite sex to increase the
burden of punishment. The homosexual in prison, however, is
actually in a favored position because the competition from the
opposite sex has been excluded.

As a result of the problem engendered by the lack of heterosexual relations, interpersonal relations in connection with homosexuality play a major part in the lives of the Alderson inmates.
Cast in the context of a "marital" relationship, the homosexual
dyad is viewed by the inmates as a meaningful personal and
social relationship. From the mass of interview data it is clear,
however, that this mode of adjustment (with the exception of
homosexuals who practice homosexuality in the free community)
would be repugnant for most prisoners, but the uniqueness of
the situation compels the inmate to redefine and attach new
meanings to homosexual behavior within the prison structure.
homo— The evidence on homosexual relations in the Alderson
prison is consistent with that recently reported by Ward and
Kassebaum in their study of a California female prison; that is,
homosexual relations are established voluntarily between the
principals involved, with no physical coercion applied.[6] This
same pattern was observed in the previously cited study of juvenile institutions for girls. This lack of coercion differs markedly
from the male prison, where homosexuals or other inmates are
usually victimized or raped by "wolves" or by what are sometimes referred to as situational homosexuals. In the female prison,
as we shall see in detail shortly, the goal is to establish a homosexual *alliance* with a mutually compatible partner not only to
release sexual tension—as is the case with the male prisoner—but
also to cover a broad range of interpersonal behavior.

The lack of heterosexual relationships for the male prisoner is said to be depriving on two levels: (1) sexual frustration
in physiological terms generates anxiety concerning the inmate's
masculinity; and (2) the inmate's self-image is "in danger of

becoming half complete, fractured, a monochrome without the hues of reality," because the inmate is shut off from the world of women, and thus a significant half of his audience is denied him.[7]

ṭ The situation for the imprisoned female is even more serious. "(American) culture," writes Jules Henry, "gives women no firm role except an erotic one." [8] Parsons has discussed three broad categories of adjustment for the American female: (1) the "good companion" role, (2) the "glamor girl" role, and (3) the "domestic" role.[9] Thus, with the closing of the prison gate, the female prisoner finds herself cut off from the structure of American society conducive to the cultivation of a female role, from the avenue through which she achieves self-respect and status. ṭ

Whereas the loss of liberty, material goods, heterosexual activities, and autonomy are clearly perceived to be depriving and frustrating for the female inmate, the evidence does not suggest that the other major deprivation suffered by the male prisoner, namely, the loss of security, evokes quite the same degree of anxiety for the Alderson female inmates. Rather it would be more accurate to say that the loss of security occurs on another level of experience for the female inmate. For the male prisoner, Sykes argues that:

> The prisoner's loss of security arouses acute anxiety . . . not just because violent acts of aggression and exploitation occur but also because such behavior constantly calls into question the individual's ability to cope with it, in terms of his own inner resources, his courage, his "nerve." Can he stand up and take it? Will he prove to be tough enough? These uncertainties constitute an ego threat for the individual forced to live in prolonged intimacy with criminals, regardless of the nature or extent of his own criminality. . . .[10]

It is clear that the cultural definition of the female role and the popular culture on the woman-to-woman level preclude any expectations of strength or moral toughness on the part of the female inmate. Traits such as "courage," "nerve," and "toughness" are not meaningful concepts to the female and thus arouse no anxiety on her part. In the words of the inmates: "The hardest part of living in a prison is to live with other *women*."

The following are commonly expressed attitudes of the nature of women:

> You can't trust another woman.

> To live with other women is to live in a jungle. Women are vicious. But in a jungle you know when an animal is going to spring. With women you never know.

> Every woman is a sneaking, lying bitch.

> It's dog eat dog with women.

> I never tell another woman anything important—you can only go so far.

> If I don't get there first, someone else will.

> With women, you never really know.

It is not the constant fear of violence or sexual exploitation which creates a hardship for the Alderson prison inmates, as is often the case with the male prisoner, but rather it is the adjustment that living in close proximity with other women in general engenders, the strain involved in being in the forced company of others who are believed to be untrustworthy and capable of predatory tactics. There is a widely held belief that women stand ready to take advantage of one another, and one must remain alert to the possibility and must take the necessary precautions. In addition, there is enough differentiation among the inmates so that some women experience insecurity in adjusting to living in the company of others whom they consider to be socially inferior: some of the white women, as we pointed out in an earlier chapter, find living in close proximity with Negroes distasteful; others feel repulsion at having to associate with prostitutes, women who are untidy in their personal habits, or who use vulgar language.

The cultural orientation of the female in the terms we have been discussing begins at a very early age. Henry states that in American culture, by the time the schoolgirl is twelve she must validate herself as a female by proving that she can attract boys. Consequently, this discourages the formation of female groups and encourages the development of predatory interpersonal patterns of behavior among females, with gossip serving both as a potent weapon of defense and as a negative sanction. The boy, on the other hand, tests and validates his masculinity in the group. The group, therefore, is important to the male because it is the structure within which he proves his masculinity. In the male group, a concept such as "being fair" has meaning; this is not so among females. In contrast to the norm held by the boys, a "steady" is not taboo to the teen girl, even if he is her best friend's.[11] In this same connection, Simone de Beauvoir has said that the marriage market from one age period to another is very unstable for the female. Consequently, the process of acquiring a husband becomes an urgent matter, and this concern, she argues, is often destructive of feminine friendships. The young girl sees rivals rather than allies in her companions; thus she fears the attractiveness of other females.[12]

Another point, made by Henry, which is germane to this problem concerns group size:

. . . As they grow toward adolescence, girls do not need groups; as a matter of fact, for many of the things they do, more than two would be an obstacle. Boys flock; girls seldom get together in groups above four whereas for boys a group of four is almost useless. Boys are dependent upon masculine solidarity within a relatively large group. In boys' groups the emphasis is on masculine unity; in girls' cliques the purpose is to shut out other girls . . . girls do not have teams but cling closely to "best friends," fighting (using gossip as a weapon) to hold them against other girls who might steal them in order to make them *their* best friends. . . .[13]

Thus, because of differences in the orientation of sex roles in American society, the imprisoned female must come to terms with what she believes to be the predatory interpersonal pattern of females. She is apt to fear the consequences of aroused jealousy transformed into vitriolic verbal attacks from other women more than she fears the threat of physical violence. She suffers acute insecurity and anxiety in confronting and handling the frequent attacks of "penitentiary darby"—gossip which has no respect for truth or consequences and which takes place at all times and on all sides within the prison. The insecurity produced in the inmate by the ostracism by other inmates or by attacks on a more subtle level can be as threatening on a psychological level as are attacks of a more violent nature.

The need to assert or defend one's femininity in the same way that the male inmate must prove his masculinity in the group if his manhood is called into question clearly does not arise for the female inmate. This is because the female validates her femininity by proving she can attract men. This is not to say, however, that there is no violence in the Alderson prison. As a matter of fact, many fights take place among the inmates, but the real violence in the Alderson prison tends to occur in connection with a homosexual triangle. The great fear is not so much fear for one's life as fear of disfigurement—the fear that an inmate "out to get" another will use razor or scissors to disfigure the other's face. It is worthwhile noting that the prison officials issue scissors to each inmate; the blades are fairly blunt but, nevertheless, this indicates the widely held belief that women are nonaggressive types. Actually, much of the potential violence inherent in the prison homosexual relationship is sharply reduced, as we shall see in later chapters, because of the play of these forces: (1) the generally passive orientation of the female, and (2) the facility with which the inmate cultural system may redefine inmate relationships when structural changes occur in the social distance between the incumbents of strategic roles.

By way of summary, we may say that the conditions for survival in the prison social environment faced by the Alderson prison inmates are similar to those in the male prison environment. The pains of imprisonment, namely, the loss of freedom, withholding of material goods, loss of identity, autonomy, sexuality, security, and so on, are perceived as depriving and frustrating by the Alderson prison inmates. However, in some areas the deprivations of imprisonment are not quite as harsh for the Alderson inmate as for inmates in other prisons. The physical surroundings are certainly more pleasant; the cottages, although starkly simple, are clean, and provide the inmate with adequate physical living conditions; with some ingenuity and mutual aid, the inmates enjoy limited opportunity for variety in the matter of dress.[14] The list could doubtless be expanded.

III

Despite the contrasts mentioned, it would be a gross error indeed to suppose that a real difference exists between the male and female prison environment in the conditions for survival faced by both male and female inmates. The difference between the two communities—despite the mitigation of the pains of imprisonment—is clearly not in kind: that is the crucial point. The problems to be solved by the female inmates in the Alderson prison are the same as those which face the male inmate. These problems have their basis in the disorientation resulting from the abrupt termination of the individual's freedom: the lack of opportunity for heterosexual relations; the fracturing of every influence favorable to the cultivation of emotional reciprocity as a result of being cut off from family and friends; the attacks on the self through the humiliating experiences incidental to a prison commitment; the loss of autonomy and responsibility, to which life in a prison inevitably leads; and the lack of security, property, privacy, and so on.

In an attempt to cope with the major problems of institutional living, the male prisoner has evolved an informal social structure which provides a complex of clearly defined social roles for the prisoners and sets the limits of mutual accommodation. The inmate code clearly specifies the rules of behavior and the sanctions for violation. Furthermore, in the male prison the informal social differentiation is reflected in a number of argot roles and provides evidence of the value structure operative in the inmate culture.

Like the male prisoner, the female prisoner soon discovers that there are few escape routes in prison—psychological and physical withdrawal are not significant modes of adaptation to mitigate the pains of imprisonment. In contrast to the male prison, however, the evolution of an informal social structure in the female prison to withstand the deleterious effects of physical and social isolation is in many respects an attempt to *resist* the destructive effects of imprisonment by creating a *substitute universe*—a world in which the inmates may preserve an identity which is relevant to life outside the prison. In this structure, the inmates' orientation is quasi-collectivistic, depending upon where one stands in terms of homosexual or kin relationships; the degree of mutual aid and the expectation of solidarity decrease as one goes from nuclear members or proximal relationships to distal relationships. It is the character of this social environment to which we shall now turn.

NOTES

1. Gresham M. Sykes, *The Society of Captives,* Princeton, N.J.: The Princeton University Press, 1958.

2. *Ibid.,* p. 64.

3. *Ibid.,* p. 63.

4. *Ibid.,* italics added.

5. Stripping and mortifying practices are discussed in Erving Goffman, *Asylums, op. cit.;* see especially pp. 14–25.

6. David A. Ward and Gene G. Kassebaum, "Lesbian Liaisons," *Trans-action,* Vol. 1, January, 1964, p. 28. See also, "Homosexuality: A Mode of Adaptation in a Prison for Women," *Social Problems,* Vol. 12, Fall 1964, pp. 159–177. Ward and Kassebaum found little evidence of the differentiated social types or of inmate solidarity that is typical of the male prison.

7. Sykes, *op. cit.,* p. 72.

8. Henry, *op. cit.,* p. 61; also compare Margaret Park Redfield, "The American Family: Consensus and Freedom," *The American Journal of Sociology,* Vol. 52, November, 1946, p. 182. "Beyond the roles of glamor girl and nursemaid, the part to be played by women is but vaguely defined in our society."

9. Talcott Parsons, "Age and Sex in the Social Structure of the United States," *American Sociological Review,* Vol. 7, October, 1942, pp. 610–613.

10. Sykes, *op. cit.,* p. 78.

11. Henry, *op. cit.,* pp. 150–155.

12. de Beauvoir, *op. cit.,* p. 345.

13. Henry, *op. cit.,* pp. 150–151; italics in the original.

14. Yarn may be purchased at the commissary store. Knitted items such as socks and sweaters provide another means by which the loss of goods may be mitigated.

CHAPTER 8 THE SOCIAL ROLES

According to Samuel Strong, "Social types stand for what the members who live in . . . various social worlds believe to be critical and important." [1] Behavior patterns are precipitated by the special circumstances of the group's position in reference to "axes of life which are crucial lines of interest in the life of the group." [2] The orientation of the group to the differential social roles and the conditions under which these roles are held in esteem or condemnation may be taken as a measure of the meaning with which the behavior is held in the social life of the group. Theoretically, the importance of the social type lies in the fact that it is a classification of role patterns made by the participants themselves; the classification does not rely upon abstractions of actual behavior by the investigator.

Strong's method of isolating indigenous types, presented over two decades ago, has provided fruitful conceptual foundations for the classification of inmate role patterns in the male prison. Sykes, for example, reported a systematic structure of roles in the prison he studied which described the general behavior patterns of the entire inmate community as a system of action. In keeping with the inmates' designations, Sykes has labeled these classifications "argot" roles. [3]

In order to cope with the major problems of institutional living, the Alderson inmates have also labeled the reactions of prisoners according to the mode of responses exhibited by the inmate to the prison situation and the quality of the inmate's interaction with inmates and staff. These roles form the basic social structure of the prison community as a system of action. Nevertheless, they constitute only a partial description of the empirical state of affairs. As we pointed out in Chapter 7 the homosexual relationship in the form of a "marital" relationship as an adjustment to the pains of imprisonment forms an important structural unit in the inmate social system. But the dyad relationship, as Simmel pointed out long ago, is an inherently vulnerable structure. Moreover, in Chapter 1 it was seen that the importation of the popular culture into the prison community affected the nature of the social relationships obtaining among the inmates; namely, that these relationships would be characterized by calculated solidarity. Calculated solidarity was defined as a social unity based not on automatic conformity to a set of common social norms perceived to be morally binding but, rather, on a unity which is subject to constant interpretation by the inmate as she perceives each situation from the point of view of her own interests. Common responsibility in a particular situation, then, exists only to the extent that the individual perceives her own interests to be served.

By now it is abundantly clear that the self-orientation of the female begs the question: Given the calculated solidarity which obtains in the female community, how are the roles of the inmates integrated so that interaction between inmates is sustained over time? This problem for the social organization of the inmate social system will be the subject of subsequent chapters. But first it is necessary to describe the social roles formed by the Alderson inmates. In keeping with the theoretical orientation of Strong, and to facilitate comparison with the literature on the male prison, the social roles are described in the everyday language of the inmates.

II

SNITCHERS AND INMATE COPS OR LIEUTENANTS

Communication across caste lines is strictly forbidden in the Alderson prison except for matters of urgent business, and all such interaction is expected to be handled with swift dispatch. Indeed, to violate the ban placed on legitimate communication flowing from inmates and staff is considered to be a very serious matter. The Alderson inmates argue that no inmate should jeopardize the successful execution of activities based upon the common interests of the inmates in illegal functions to relieve the pains of imprisonment; secondly, supplying information to officials may result in the withdrawal of privileges or in other forms of punishment, thereby adding to the pains of imprisonment for the inmate.

In the Alderson prison, the role of the "snitcher" is the female counterpart to the "rat" in the male prison. To accuse an inmate of snitching is the most serious accusation one inmate may hurl at another, for it clearly signifies the division of loyalty between the staff and the inmates. The importance placed upon the "no snitching" norm is apparent; it covers every range of behavior and is put in the imperative to the new inmate or the deviant: "See and see nothing! Hear and hear nothing!"

Although the Alderson prisoners agree that inmates should never snitch or give any information concerning an inmate to the staff, the females' self-orientation and their tendency to see one another as rivals both function to decrease general expectations of rigid allegiance from one another. Consequently, the female inmate rarely expresses any surprise when she suspects another inmate of deviating from the norm prohibiting communication of inmate affairs across caste lines; she feels only a kind of bitterness that the status of inmate is not sufficient to bind and solidify the inmates completely into a cohesive group. The popular culture, then, in connection with the extent to which any female may be trusted, functions to neutralize many deviant acts in the prison. As a result, many deviant acts are overlooked or are not severely punished by the Alderson inmates.

Snitchers are distinguished by the Alderson inmates in terms of the frequency with which their deviant acts are performed. First, there is the occasional or sporadic snitcher: any prisoner, according to the Alderson inmates, may at one time or another engage in this type of snitching when it serves her interest. This type is frequently motivated by jealousy—of economic property in the form of contraband which is not accessible to all inmates, or of a homosexual affair, which she attempts to break up by reporting this information to prison officials.[4]

A second type of snitcher, referred to as the "good girls" by the officers, are those inmates who systematically keep the officers in the cottages informed on inmate activities. New officers, upon assuming a new post, learn of their identity from older officers, and these inmates constitute a bloc of informants that are shifted about from cottage to cottage by the officials. They are sometimes known to the inmate body because they tend to exceed the acceptable time limit set by the inmates when talking with officers. Not only are snitchers despised by the inmate body, but also the officers in turn are despised because they often act on the basis of information received by snitchers. In the eyes of the inmates this is clear evidence that the officer is not capable of doing her own job, and the fact that she relies upon other inmates for information contributes to the low esteem with which the officer is held.

In subclassification meetings, there is a tendency for the officials to give preferential treatment to requests made by such snitchers for job changes or other requests. These inmates are easily identified by the phrase: "She's been truthful with us." While it is true that from the point of view of the administrators the snitcher often performs a valuable service, there are times when information about illicit inmate activities places officials in a position where they must take action although they would prefer to preserve the status quo. This is especially true when deviance concerns valued inmate employees, where disciplinary action would clearly result in loss of job for the inmate and thereby interfere with production quotas, as, for example, in the industries. It is equally true of inmates placed in jobs that are referred to by the prison administrators as "key positions," as these inmates cannot be easily replaced because of their special education and training.

From the official standpoint, then, it is clear that all items of information supplied by snitchers are not welcome. Knowledge of illicit activities supplied by snitchers often forces the officials to display formal disapproval when they prefer to ignore such acts. (This is, of course, not the case when it concerns deviance such as the possession of glue, type cleaner, gasoline, and other noxious agents sometimes used by the inmates for sniffing purposes. Homemade hooch, the prison liquor, also falls into this category.) An example supplied from the field notes will serve to clarify the foregoing point and will reveal the process involved in the disposition of a "nuisance act," as well as the consequences for the formal and informal organization:

An inmate reported ·that an unsewn suit cut from cloth stolen from the garment shop was hidden on the second shelf in a closet of a small dormitory occupied by two inmates. Acting upon the information, the officer went directly to the spot where it had been reported the cutout cloth was hidden, found the material, and confiscated it. Although the officer removed the cloth, she did not, however, investigate any other area of the room, although by the admission of the inmate later to the investigator—and also as related by this inmate in her group therapy class—she had contraband hidden in every drawer, in the bed, as well as other parts of the closet. These areas remained undisturbed by the investigating officer. The inmate also stated that by innuendo the officials processing the case implied to one of the inmates in question that it was a "setup job." This inmate did not lose her industry job, although one of the conditions of continued employment in the garment shop is that inmates cannot be involved in disciplinary action.

By limiting investigation to the letter of the information supplied by informants in some instances, the staff in effect says that if the information had not been supplied by an inmate in the first place, the deviance would have been completely overlooked. Moreover, by not imposing negative sanctions, the inmate code that "anything goes in the penitentiary," that is, lawful behavior has no place in the prison world, receives at least quasi-official sanction and approval. Thus, the formal organization maintains deviant conduct in the inmate community in these important ways: (1) official nullification of deviant behavior by looking the other way when it is clearly open to view; and (2) investigation in pantomime with a telling lack of thoroughness when informed of deviant action. Such deviance-maintaining conduct is a structural adjustment to maintain the status quo when the processing of acts to their logical conclusion might seem frivolous from the point of view of the formal organization. The mechanism of social disapproval in connection with many deviant acts, therefore, is not sustained by the prison officials.

On the other hand, there are limits to official tolerance of deviation. At one point in the study, several inmates in the honor cottage (some of whom are office workers) began to walk about boldly wearing contraband clothing, with little fear of official disapproval. In this connection, it was brought out in a subclassification meeting that the top administrator had called the associate warden's attention to the fact that she thought some of the inmates in the honor cottage were looking "too chic" and feared that this state of affairs might arouse the jealousy of other inmates and cause trouble. Interestingly enough, the matter was not processed formally but, rather, it was handled very informally. Communication filtered from the top through several hierarchical levels and finally reached some of the inmates in the honor cottage who were informed of the warden's observation.

Anonymous snitching is a rare occurrence in the Alderson prison; the inmates are very candid about revealing their identity to the officials. In contrast to the male prison, however, we find that violation of the "no snitching" norm does not often result in violence. In the words of one prisoner: "A lot is said about what will be done if you catch a snitch, but you know women! They talk loud, draw a crowd, and that's as far as it goes. When it comes to a showdown, they chicken out." This does not mean, however, that negative sanctions are not imposed. Fights, "panning," and "signifying" are all modes of punishment to control behavior in the Alderson inmate community.

"Panning" is general derogatory gossip about an inmate when she is not physically present. "Signifying," on the other hand, is a more compelling negative sanction because the inmate is physically present. A group of inmates will discuss the deviant act in the inmate's presence, often in considerable detail with biting sarcasm, scorn, and mimicry. Although the inmate's name is not at any time mentioned, little doubt is left as to the inmate's identity. It is usually a very effective mode of social control.

An incident which took place in the dining room of the admission and orientation unit provides an illustration of signifying: For several days three inmates had expressed disapproval among themselves of an inmate co-worker in the pantry because she did not in their words "act right," that is, honor the egalitarian ethos of the inmates in the work situation. She had a reputation of being both a snitcher and an "inmate cop." (It must be kept in mind that there are many recidivists in the admission and orientation unit. Reaffirmation of the inmate code—and, when necessary, indoctrination to its values—takes place in this structure.) Because of the seating arrangements in the dining room, it became necessary for the offending inmate to join the other three inmates at the same table. The tables in the dining room are very close together, and the investigator seated at the next table could observe with ease the interaction taking place among the inmates. Mary is the offending inmate, and the others are Beth, Jean, and Carol. The following is taken from the observer's field notes.

Today, Mary was completely ostracized by the other inmates seated at the table. They overlooked her when handing plates of food to one another which made it necessary for Mary to ask. Only after she had made two or three requests was food given to her by the inmates, and this was done without glancing in her direction. Mary sat very straight in her chair, her face was flushed, and she pursed her lips constantly. She mouthed her food with a great deal of deliberation, looked straight ahead into space, and she wet and pursed her lips frequently. Carol, Beth, and Jean engaged in light banter among themselves, but excluded Mary completely. Occasionally they would catch each other's eyes, cock their heads in Mary's direction and in an exaggerated fashion, mimic Mary by holding spoons with small fingers held in a vertical position, and then very slowly move their hands almost simultaneously to mouths that opened very round. They would then all wet their lips, press them tightly together, and wink at one another.

About halfway through the meal:

Beth. Hey, what do you think of an inmate that thinks she's an officer. You know who I mean, don't you? You dig it? She likes to give another inmate orders like an officer. Say, don't she know she's got five numbers across her chest just like the rest of us?

Jean. Maybe she forgot. Maybe she thinks she's here for a vacation in the mountains. Yeah! Here for the season and not for a reason! (*Much laughter from Beth and Carol.*)

Carol. Any inmate that would treat another inmate like that, and always *rapping* to the officer, would turn their own mother in.

Beth. You *sure* you know who I mean? She's the one who walks around here with her head up and shaking from side to side—with her nose up like she's suffering or something. You know who I mean?

Carol and Jean. Yeah! Yeah!

Although both panning and signifying are extremely effective modes of social control among the prisoners, sanctions are not always so obvious. The fact that the prison is isolated of course makes the prisoners extremely interdependent for emotional reciprocity, and this in itself serves to check much continued deviant behavior. In the words of an inmate: "It's rough when the group ignores you." Inflection in one's voice, then, pretense that one has not seen another, and a turning of the head to avoid a greeting can be exquisite punishment in the prison community and can often be quite as devastating as the more pointed panning and signifying.

Inmates who violate the ban on communication are watched closely, and pertinent information concerning their activities is circulated quickly to other inmates. The snitcher, in short, is *persona non grata* in the prison community, and any common cause with her would in all certainty hurt one's reputation and close off interaction with the great majority of inmates. The snitcher is condemned by the Alderson inmates because she denies the cohesion of the inmate community and jeopardizes the successful execution of the many illegal activities that take place in the prison to mitigate the pains of imprisonment. And the fact that the snitcher is disloyal to the inmate group adds to the burden of imprisonment.

The behavior subsumed under "center man" in the male prison finds expression in the role of "inmate cop" or "lieutenant." "Inmate cops" are prisoners who are in a position of authority over other inmates because of a work assignment. In the process of executing their work function they issue orders to other inmates or report infractions of rules in connection with work. As one prisoner said contemptuously: "She tries to act just like an officer. She forgets that she came through that gate, and she's got five numbers across her chest just like the rest of us. She's an officer without a uniform, and she tries to tell another inmate what to do. They're always in the officer's face. . . ."

The prison experience is considered to be the "great equalizer" [5] and inmates resent taking orders from other inmates. In issuing orders to inmates, or in reporting infractions in the course of a job assignment, the inmate cop or lieutenant in effect takes the role of the officer and thereby violates an important tenet of the inmate code: she denies the egalitarian ethos of the inmates.

The caste division between the inmates and the staff is clearly revealed in the following exchange among several inmates at a group therapy session. Four inmates, a staff member, and the investigator were present. Inmate Barbara was hesitant about presenting her problem to the group for discussion, and did so only after a little coaxing from the other inmates. She is labeled as an inmate cop by the inmate community. Inmate Ruth, who acts as a socializing agent, is a graduate of several prisons.

Barbara. Now you tell me. Maybe it's me. Maybe it's the way I do things. I don't know. But I feel that when an officer tells me to do something, I should do it. It's part of my job. If I'm told to tell an inmate to go somewhere, I'll go out and tell one of the girls: "You're to go to the clinic." "You're to go to the Ad Building." And then I'll go back to the office. But the inmate never takes my word for it. I'll go back to the office, and I no sooner get there, then the girl I just talked to will come in and ask Lorraine (other inmate helper in office), "Am I supposed to go to the clinic?" Right after I finished telling her! Now I wouldn't just go out there and tell her to go, if I hadn't been told to tell her and yet she doesn't take my word for it. They don't believe me and they come and ask Lorraine. What I want to know is why they ask her. Why don't they take my word for it? I want you to tell me what I'm doing wrong.

(At this point the other inmates exchanged glances, but remained silent for several minutes. One inmate silently mouthed words, made a motion as if to speak, but held back. Finally, she spoke hesitantly.)

Betty. It's—It's the way you say it.
Ruth. (*Angrily*) Now wait a minute! You gotta remember one thing. You're an inmate just like the rest of us. Whose side are you gonna

be on—the inmates' side or the officers'? *There's them and there's us.* Hell, they really whip it on us in the Garment Shop. You gotta close your eyes to some things. *You're here to do time.* You're not here as an officer. Have you got any keys? You weren't sent here by the judge to do the officer's job. It's their job to find out things. That's why they get paid. You gotta give the girls a break.

Barbara. But if you have a job where you're supposed to do certain things, you should do them. I was that way when I worked outside. I always was that way outside, I've been a supervisor and I've always done my job and gotten along with everyone I worked with.

Ruth. If you wanta get along with the girls here, you gotta change your attitude. You can't expect the girls to like you if you're always going to the officer with every little thing—maybe get a girl in trouble. You gotta close your eyes to things—you don't see it.

Barbara. Well, I thought maybe the girls were riding me 'cause I'm new. But I really like my job. I want to do well and I want to keep it.

Ruth. Barbara, you know the girls are jealous of the inmates who get the good jobs—the hospital, the Ad Building, and the office jobs. And when the girls that get these jobs act uppity—well!

Barbara. I don't feel uppity. I don't feel no better than the other girls. It's just if my job is to report what girls are late for work, that's my job and I think I should do it.

Ruth. Now look, Barb. You got five numbers just like all of us. You're here doing time! Uncle Sam didn't send you up here as an officer. If reporting a girl means losing days! Girl, you gotta wise up. You on the inmates' side or the officers'? You can't be on both. It's either one or the other. It can't be both.

So far as expectations of loyalty and allegiance to the inmate code are concerned, no opportunity is lost to confirm inmate values, as evidenced by the fact that the foregoing took place in a group therapy class. Nor is this an isolated example. Indeed, the study revealed that one of the functions of the group therapy classes is to expose the staff to the inmate culture via informal inmate discussions. The values and norms of the inmate code are clearly revealed in this attempt to socialize a deviant into the behavior patterns consistent with the inmate culture.

When an inmate assumes a role other than one which is normatively consistent with inmate status, a frequent negative sanction imposed upon her is to ignore the orders issued by the inmate cop—a clear denial of the individual's existence. Thus, the inmate's assumed status is nullified by the fact that other inmates do not respond to requests made by her. Orders issued by inmate cops are overlooked in two ways: First, when the orders specify that an inmate's presence is desired in another part of the prison, confirmation of the order is sought from an inmate sympathetic to the inmate code or, if necessary, from the officer in charge; and, secondly, when the deviance of the inmate cop is restricted to the work situation in connection with increased output, the inmates simply continue working as if no one had spoken and whistle or hum loudly, thereby making it clear that such orders are not legitimized by the inmate community.

The inmate cop's disloyalty is despised not only because it is open to view, but also because it is often flaunted in the face of other inmates. Here is an open-and-shut case of identification with staff values, and the inmate cop's actions deny the solidarity of the inmate body and weaken the bonds of interdependence which bind them together. Moreover, the inmate cop is apt to rationalize her actions in terms of noncriminal values, which according to the inmate code have no place in the penitentiary. Unless this inmate can be persuaded to "see the light" through socialization into the inmate culture, she cannot be reasoned with or bought. In this sense she poses a real threat to the Alderson inmate community, because the inmate cop is an added bulwark to the staff's forces, and the fact that an inmate is adding to the pains of imprisonment by joining forces with the staff makes her doubly despised.

SQUARES AND JIVE BITCHES

Along with the snitchers and the inmate cops, the "squares" are truly the pariahs of the inmate community. "Square" is a derisive label pinned on inmates who are considered to be accidental criminals. The behavior of the square in the prison community clearly betrays her alien status; she is oriented to the prison administration and tends to possess "anti-criminal" loyalties. Degrees of "squareness" are recognized by the Alderson inmates ranging from the inmate who is thought to be "so square that she's a cube" to the inmate designated as "hip square." The "cube square" is very definitely oriented to societal values and the prison administration, whereas the "hip square" tends to sympathize with the inmate code and adheres to some of its principles, sometimes going so far as to "pin"—act as lookout—for other inmates. The distinguishing characteristic of the hip square, however, is that she does not engage in homosexual activity and is oriented to the administration and societal values. Her sympathy takes the form of stated tolerance for inmate activities. In the Alderson prison, anyone who does not engage in homosexual activities in one form or another is automatically labeled a square.

Not only are squares placed outside the mainstream of inmate activities, excluded and ostracized by the inmate population, but more important for the inmate social system, squares are pitied. It is said that squares "don't know any better," and further, it is widely believed that the square is not "woman enough" to commit a crime. "They're the kind of people who in the Free World don't know enough to come in out of the rain"; "They're suckers and fools—gullible without even knowing it." And herein lies the key for understanding the threat that the square poses for the inmate community. Like the inmate cop or lieutenant, the square tends to identify with the institutional officials. In the case of the square, however, association is considered to be doubly hazardous—for in her presumed gullibility the square may unwittingly divulge information to the officials. It is for this reason, as we noted earlier, that squares are apt to be "fed with a long-handled spoon,"—that is, information concerning inmate activities is carefully sifted and censored.

The deviance of the square is often the consequence of an artless simplicity and presumably leaves open the possibility that induction into the inmate culture may remedy the situation. (Indeed the pressures applied are so great that this frequently does occur.) The deviance of the "jive bitch," on the other hand, is a deliberate, calculated strategy to cause conflict. In short, the jive bitch is a troublemaker. The strategy often employed by the jive bitch involves a distortion of the facts, as for example, when she is interested in breaking up an established homosexual relationship: she will volunteer information about "kites" and illicit rendezvous to the injured party, who in many cases would prefer not to know on the theory that ignorance is bliss, and may goad the inmate into terminating an affair, which although perceived to be less than perfect, may be felt to be better than none.

The jive bitch succeeds in creating unrest among the inmates in several ways. In addition to presenting a deliberate distortion of facts to an injured party, she often tells inmates involved in a "couple" relationship different versions of the same situation in the hope that it will cause conflict between them. Moreover, the jive bitch cannot be trusted to keep her word when she gives it, indicating her disloyalty to the inmate group. Although inmates do not trust other women, it is normatively demanded that once you give your word to a prisoner, you should keep it, particularly in connection with matters concerning mutual aid. An example described by an inmate follows:

> You're out of cigarettes, and you go to a girl and say, "Look, I'm out of cigarettes, and I won't have any money until next week. When you go to Commissary, would you buy me a carton, and I'll pay you back next week?" She says, "Sure, baby, sure. I'll get them for you on Friday." When Friday comes, you go to her house to get the cigarettes and when you say, "Did you get the cigarettes?" she opens her mouth like she's surprised and maybe slaps her cheek and looks at you and says, "Oh, baby, I forgot all about it. I'm sorry, baby, honest!" That's a jive bitch 'cause she had no intention of getting you those cigarettes in the first place.

The jive bitch, in short, is an example *par excellence* of the woman-to-woman popular culture translated into role behavior. The fact that she cannot be depended upon weakens even the bonds of calculated solidarity which exist among the Alderson inmates.

RAP BUDDIES AND HOMEYS

In prison the popular culture on the woman-to-woman level is buttressed by the common criminality which in many ways binds the inmates together, for it is a widespread belief that "There's no honor among thieves." No inmate trusts another inmate completely ("You pick your people, and even then you only go so far"). Within these limitations, an inmate may single out another prisoner in the cottage or on the job as special friend. This individual is one with whom she can converse easily and assume reasonably that the conversation will be mutually binding as secret. Any two people who find one another compatible in this way may become "rap buddies" to one another. This relationship is dissolved if the expectations concerning the relationship are not honored by either of the incumbents of the rap buddy role; or, if the relationship flowers into one of deeper meaning, the inmates become a "couple" and assume the obligations relevant to this relationship.

The "homey" role, on the other hand, is probably as close to "blood" relationship as one finds in the Alderson female prison and holds a special place in the lexicon of the inmates. Technically speaking, even if conflict ensues between homeys, the relationship still holds. The homey is an inmate who is from another inmate's home town or nearby community. Homeys may or may not have known one another before incarceration; but in any case, within the prison these inmates become homeys to one another.

Contact is made as soon as the presence of a homey becomes known. This information is usually obtained by inmate orientation helpers or from inmate office workers. Inquiries as to whether a homey's needs have been met are immediately made: Cigarettes, soap, toothpaste, facial tissues, and any other commissary items which she needs in orientation will some how be routed to her. The special bond of reciprocity which is established between homeys is of a vastly different degree of intensity than that between rap buddies and is expected to cover a wide range of behavior. In the first place, it includes mutual aid. Homeys have the right to turn to one another when material need arises; and the further expectation exists that if the inmate can possibly do so, the merchandise is to be returned at a later date. No such obligation exists between rap buddies. Although superficially the rap buddy and homey roles may appear to be quite similar, the basis for allocation of these roles and functions is clearly quite different.

What is the basis for allocation of functions with respect to the homey role? Although a special relationship exists between homeys, significantly the homey relationship excludes homosexuality. Indeed, an inmate will express great indignation if the suggestion—however lightly veiled—is made that a homosexual relationship exists between her and a homey. "That's my homey. I wouldn't do that to her," certainly suggests the exploitative evaluation many inmates have of the homosexual alliance. But when we examine other aspects of the role, this explanation adds little to our understanding of the function the role plays in the lives of the Alderson inmates.

A significant aspect of the homey relationship is that inmates sharing this status address and refer to one another by the term "homey," emphasizing to the incumbents of the role and to the inmate community alike the nature of the special relationship involved. Indeed a novitiate who calls a homey by her given name is promptly corrected by other inmates. One may quite reasonably ask why mutual aid and mode of address are patterned between homeys and not, for example, between rap buddies. Does the answer lie in the fact that homeys are from the same geographical area? Given the self-orientation of the female, it is not very likely that this would be a plausible explanation. Actually the occupants of the homey role are buying insurance for the future. The extension of mutual cooperation between homeys insures both role occupants that the possibility will not arise that a homey will "read" her—that is, speak derogatorily of her prison behavior to anyone in civil society. Presumably, the inmate who resides in the same geographical area would most likely be in a favored position to do so.

The homey relationship is a splendid example of the refinement of social roles in the Alderson prison community that solve the special problems which stem from the cultural definition females have of one another.

CONNECTS AND BOOSTERS

Few legitimate channels are open to the Alderson inmates to improve their economic lot in the prison. It will be recalled that inmates are permitted to spend fifteen dollars per month at the commissary store. This is not a large sum, considering that it covers almost all purchases including cigarettes. (It is possible to make special withdrawals for yarn purchases which ease the hardship for a few inmates who have savings in the prison.) However, even the modest sum of fifteen dollars per month is beyond the reach of many inmates.

Packages and gifts other than money are not permitted. (Mention was made earlier that brassieres, girdles and shoes may be sent to an inmate by an approved correspondent.) The one exception to the gift regulation is the Christmas box not exceeding four pounds in weight which may be sent to the inmate by one of the regular correspondents. This package may contain candy and/or nutmeats. In addition, one nonfiction book subject to approval may be sent at Christmas.

Like the male prisoner, then, the Alderson inmate finds it necessary to exploit the environment to improve her material circumstances. She can steal from institutional supplies, and, as we shall see shortly, in the role of the "commissary hustler," she can manipulate other inmates through sexual exploitation. In Chapter 9 we shall see that some inmates entering into a couple relationship may also be motivated principally as a solution to the economic problem. Significantly, a role based upon aggressive physical tactics (such as the "gorilla," reported by Sykes, who takes what he wants from other inmates by force) does not emerge in the Alderson inmate community.

By contrast, in the Alderson prison the "connect" is any inmate with a "good job" who will cooperate in the procurement of scarce goods and information. A "good job" by inmate standards means placement in the prison organization where information and scarce goods are available. Connects are also those inmates who are in a position to negotiate with other inmates to obtain information or goods, that is, who act both as middleman and distributor. Thus this role includes the procurement of both goods and services.

In this connection, the inmates draw a sharp line between the connect, who often takes a dual role and the "booster," whose exploitation of the environment consists solely of stealing from official stores and who carries on a successful business enterprise. It should be made clear that stealing from the officials is universal at Alderson. Even inmates designated by sister inmates as squares and inmate cops declare they will sometimes take a pot of coffee out of the dining room "on principle." Inmates, however, make a clear distinction between the petty boosting which is engaged in by all inmates—say, a few teaspoonfuls of sugar placed in a napkin, a sandwich, and the like while in the dining room—and the stealing engaged in by the booster. Boosters in contrast to the petty thieves (or petty boosters) would steal a ham. The difference lies mainly in the source of supply, the regularity with which the goods may be procured, and the purpose for which the items are stolen. Items stolen sporadically for individual consumption tend to be classified under the category of petty boosting. The booster, however, is the inmate who is in a position to steal desired objects regularly and in fairly large quantities.

Now, in the male prison, regardless of the source of supply, giving and sharing is normatively demanded by the inmate code, especially if the materials have been stolen from the officials. The "pedlar" or "merchant" has been described as "A man so alienated from other prisoners, so selfish in his pursuit of material advantage, that he is willing to thrive on the misery of his companions. He places his own well-being above the well-being of the inmates as a whole. He does not share the goods in short supply but exploits, instead, the need of others." [6]

Significantly, the same behavior for which the "merchant" is despised in the male prison is praised by female inmates. To "get a good thing going," that is, to engage in a successful business enterprise is to be admired by the inmates, who say: "If you can get a little racket going, more power to you." And yet at the same time inmates rationalize many of their actions by saying, "If I don't get there first, someone else will," which clearly indicates their self-orientation.

No sharp line is made by the Alderson inmates between selling and giving except when it concerns members of the "family." And sharing among the members of the "family"—in the sense of outright giving—is normatively prescribed only under certain conditions: namely (1) when the staff has removed an inmate's privileges as a consequence of a disciplinary action; or (2) when an inmate is economically deprived. But it must be emphasized that sharing under these conditions is quite strictly regulated within the confines of the homosexual relationship and among other "family" members.

In a real sense, boosters are inmates who have "gotten there first," and for this feat there is admiration—albeit tinged with not a little envy. In addition, inmates tend to feel gratitude to the booster because they recognize that the booster's role involves a certain amount of risk. Whatever recompense is necessary to enjoy the pleasure of making a cup of coffee at odd hours of the day is thought to be well worth the price. The inmates will gladly exchange a carton of cigarettes for a pound of coffee,[7] and if this transaction can be carried out weekly, prison life is made more tolerable.

Who are the clients for the supply of illicit goods? All prisoners do not have an opportunity to enjoy these luxury items, regardless of their financial situation. Low-caste inmates, such as snitchers, squares, and inmate cops or lieutenants, of course, lie outside the boundary of legitimate giving. These inmates have deviated from the inmate code and therefore have alienated themselves from the privilege of sharing in the scarce goods that circulate about the prison. They are in the same position as "rats," "center men," "weaklings," and "fish" in the male prison.

Apart from the pariahs in the Alderson prison, mutual aid is greater near the locus of high intensity of emotional reciprocity as, for example, among family members. As intensity of emotional reciprocity decreases, mutual aid decreases proportionately. As we shall discuss shortly in detail, inmates are apt to give priority to the members of their prison family. All other inmates are defined as strangers in comparison to the family. And the links in the family progressively lose claim as the putative relationships become more distant.

PINNERS

Since complete elimination of detection is never possible in the performance of many illicit activities, the Alderson inmates find it necessary to minimize the risk of being detected by the prison officials. And for this reason the role of the "pinner" is a very crucial and important one: The pinner in the Alderson prison is a lookout. She is stationed as a sentry to prevent a surprise attack upon inmates engaging in illicit activities from all unauthorized persons, whether they be staff or inmates. With discovery always imminent and punishment certain, the pinner's role cannot be allocated to amateurs or to inmates whose loyalty is in doubt. The pinner must be an inmate who can be trusted, who can stand up under pressure, and who is "in the know." It is not unusual, therefore, that this function is often allocated to family members, particularly in connection with homosexual activities—sons and daughters often pin for parents, and parents in turn pin for sons and daughters.

Depending upon the task at hand, sometimes the inmates find it necessary to mobilize a team of pinners, each of whom must share the responsibility that the task be carried out successfully. Now although it is important that the pains of imprisonment be mitigated, it is also imperative that in the process of doing so, deviant actions do not result in disciplinary action which will increase the burden of punishment. The pinner, therefore, is a valued individual, as she imparts to the inmates a measure of reasonable security that their deviant performances will not result in loss of days or other forms of punishment.

THE HOMOSEXUAL CLUSTER: PENITENTIARY TURNOUTS, LESBIANS, FEMMES, STUD BROADS, TRICKS, COMMISSARY HUSTLERS, CHIPPIES, KICK PARTNERS, CHERRIES, PUNKS AND TURNABOUTS

The problems and concerns of the inmates in adjusting to deprivation of heterosexual relationships are revealed by the number of roles channelized into homosexual behavior. Moreover, the female inmates' *role refinement* of the categories in connection with homosexual activity illustrates its function as both a motivating force in their lives and as an organizing principle of social organization.

The inmates apply a number of labels to homosexual behavior depending upon the specific role assumed, the adeptness with which the assumed role is played, or the motivation for the behavior. Broadly speaking, the inmates differentiate between "penitentiary turnouts" and "lesbians." The "penitentiary turnout" resorts to homosexuality in the prison because heterosexual relationships are not available. The "lesbian" by contrast *prefers* homosexual relations in the free community, in this respect resembling the "fags" in the male prison. As with the male prisoner, this stated preference for homosexual relations defines in the eyes of the Alderson inmates the lesbian's behavior as a sexual perversion, as contrasted with the behavior of the penitentiary turnout, which may be viewed as a temporary adjustment to the prison situation. The lesbian, therefore, is labeled as a sick person by the inmates because her preference and selection of homosexual relations in a situation where choice is possible clearly constitutes a *true* perversion. It is only in the penitentiary world where men are unavailable that the values and norms regarding homosexual behavior are redefined by the inmates—and within the limits imposed by this definition—accepted as a temporary substitute for heterosexual relations.

The "femme" or "mommy" plays the female role in a homosexual relationship. The femme role is highly sought-after because most of the inmates want to continue to play the feminine role in a meaningful way in the prison. In the context of a "marital" relationship the femme continues to act out, as we shall see in Chapter 9, many of the functions assigned to the role of wife in civil society.

The complementary role to the femme is the "stud broad" or "daddy" who assumes the male role. The stud broad is accorded much prestige by other inmates for these reasons: First, the stud provides the prison with the male image; secondly, the role is considered to be a more difficult one for an inmate to assume and sustain over a period of time because it is thought to be "unnatural" for a female to assume the guises of the male. Indeed, an occasional inmate playing a stud role becomes carried away with "his" performance and attempts to transcend psychologically the immutability of anatomy and biological function. The subject of symbols of communication will be taken up in detail in Chapter 9. For the moment I would point out that the role is also considered to be a difficult one because studs not only assume certain external symbols of sex differentiation but are also expected to incorporate into role behavior the many social expectations of the male role.

When a stud and femme have established a homosexual alliance, they are said to be "makin' it" or to be "tight," that is, they are socially recognized as constituting a legitimate married pair. Although the ideal is to sustain this relationship, the stability of an alliance actually depends upon several factors. The part played by the jive bitch has already been noted, but the important structural problem of maintaining dyadic components must be deferred until Chapter 9. Sometimes the stud becomes so smitten with another stud that she "drops the belt"— she shifts from the male role to the female role. In the eyes of the inmates, the individual who "drops" immediately loses prestige. It is said, "Only a fool would do it. Hell, he had it made, and now he turns femme!" (Note that the masculine pronoun is used when referring to the "male" population in the prison.) In addition the inmates tend to view the inmate who "drops" with suspicion as it is looked upon as a sign of inherent weakness.

But perhaps a more important concern is that any decline in the sex ratio is vital to the inmates for the simple reason that the femme population outnumbers the stud population. Above all, the inmates want predictability in the prison world, and the restructuring of roles which takes place due to the process of "dropping the belt" threatens the structure of predictability by decreasing the stud population. "Competition," declare the inmates, "is very keen on the reservation."

Since one of the important goals in establishing a homosexual alliance is to strive for what is referred to as a "sincere" relationship, which means a stable relationship based upon romantic love, the "trick" is held in low esteem by the inmates because she allows herself to be exploited rather than to develop a relationship that is sincere. And the trick is exploited in a variety of ways—usually economically and as a source of labor. Any individual who allows herself to be exploited in this manner is considered "weak." Moreover, tricks are regarded as "suckers" and "fools" because they may be kept dangling with promises.

Who are the inmates who utilize exploitative tactics? The "commissary hustler" establishes a single homosexual alliance with an inmate living in the same cottage, but also establishes relationships with a number of inmates in other cottages for economic purposes. This is called "mating for commissary reasons," and any femme other than the inmate who lives in the stud's cottage is labeled as a trick in the relationship. The commissary hustler presents a commissary list to the tricks scattered throughout the prison, and they, in turn, supply the commissary hustler with needed material items. The function of all the tricks in this "polygynous" system is an economic one. The "wife" in the cottage takes precedence over all others. She shares in the bounty and usually knows of the existence of other femmes, i.e., tricks. Indeed, if the couple is in serious economic difficulty, she may suggest to her stud that this role be assumed. Or the stud may consult the femme in arriving at a decision to "work a few tricks."

So long as the "wife" shares the same household as the stud, the existence of other femmes (tricks) in the relationship is tolerable. As the inmates put it: "The nearest is the dearest, and the closest gets the mostest." In addition, it should be pointed out that the wife who lives in the same household as the stud also derives security from the public recognition of the relationship as legitimate. They are recognized as a couple. The additional wife (or wives) merely serves an economic function. One may ask why an inmate enters into a trick role. As pointed out previously, the stud population is outnumbered by the femme population, and competition for studs is very keen. Actually, each trick in this situation anticipates and plans for the day when the relationship will become a permanent one, and waits in hope for an invitation from the commissary hustler to move to "his" cottage. In other words, each trick anticipates displacing the cottage wife in the affections of the stud. And since the trick is, after all, an inmate with a commissary account, this might well occur. While it is more or less understood that she is to be invited, sometimes a trick may lose patience and forego prison etiquette by taking the initiative and moving to the stud's cottage. Such cottage moves present complicating triangular situations which often lead to violence.

The role of commissary hustler requires a certain amount of adroitness to be carried out successfully. The inmates at the Alderson prison argue that in the free community the commissary hustler would tend to exploit men, but since there are no men at the prison, she exploits women. Although there may be individual personality factors involved, there are structural features in the prison which precipitate this role. Not every inmate, as we pointed out earlier, is compensated for work, and the role of commissary hustler provides an avenue to take care of economic needs.

The dyad configuration cast into the framework of a marital relationship covers a wide range of behavioral expectations. The commissary hustler, although in some respects exploitative, nevertheless does maintain a stable and sincere relationship with the femme who shares the same cottage. However, when the individual exploits each situation with a partner for its unique possibilities, whether for sexual or material gratification, the inmate is said to occupy a "chippie" role. This role differs from the commissary hustler in a very important way. Although the commissary hustler actually establishes one sincere relationship and exploits other inmates in order to provide for the femme in the relationship, the chippie establishes no single relationship of this type. Chippies are said to be "makin' it," but not to be "in love" with any individual. The chippie is looked upon as the prison prostitute. The inmate who "chippies from one bed to another"—i.e., terminates affairs too quickly—is scorned by the inmates, and her behavior is held to be promiscuous. The ideal cultural pattern in the prison is to establish a permanent relationship: The chippie clearly deviates from the ideal pattern, as her affairs are characterized by their striking temporary quality.

The inmates distinguish clearly between homosexual activity that is of a promiscuous nature and that which is engaged in solely for sexual gratification. Although "kick partners" are also not said to be involved as "lovers," there is, nevertheless, a predictable permanence in their relationships, although the motivation for entering into the partnership is clearly understood to be solely for physical gratification. There is usually no economic exchange in this relationship, and the inmates involved exhibit no jealousy. An inmate is apt to enter such a relationship when she does not wish to assume the responsibilities that a more permanent tie would entail. The object of this relationship is to release sexual tension. Kick partners may also consist of a group of several women among whom partners are exchanged and who all maintain friendly relations. To the extent that kick partners are "discreet," their behavior is not looked down upon by the inmates.

Every society has a reserve of members from which potential mates may be obtained. When resources are limited, or culturally prescribed, mates may be drawn from other groups. In the Alderson prison, the kick partner may be drawn into a permanent tie. And the square may possibly in time "see the light" and enter into the inmate social organization. But one category of inmates in the prison, those labeled "cherries," constitute an uncommitted sizeable reserve for potential mates; they are inmates who have never been "turned out"—initiated into homosexual practices.

Although squares also do not engage in homosexual practices, the cherry is not a square. The difference is that the cherry simply has not been "turned out." Often they are young and first offenders, and they are usually initiated by older women. Cherries in this context are "hep" individuals, i.e., they know what the score is from the point of view of the prisoners, but for one reason or another have not engaged in homosexuality. Sometimes a short sentence may be the reason for her preference not to become emotionally involved; or she may decide that this mode of adjustment may not be desirable.

One who assumes a false part or assumes a character other than the real one is despised for his hypocrisy both within and without the prison gates. Within the Alderson prison, the "punk" is despised for pretense and deceit. In the male prison, the "punk" is an inmate who plays the submissive part because he is coerced into doing so. In this respect, "punks" differ from "fags," who it is said are "born" not "made." In a sense fags resemble the lesbians for the inmates say that they are "born that way," or that "something happened to them in their childhood." In the Alderson prison, the punk is so designated because she acts like a female, that is, takes on the coquettish mannerisms of a woman when the expected behavior is that of the male. The behavior of the punk elicits a combination of anger and ridicule from the inmates. The tendency is to heap blame upon the punk, because the punk's "impotence" is not a constitutional failure but, rather, is due to incomplete role learning. Responsibility, therefore, is placed upon the individual. Punks are, as it were, self-proclaimed studs without substance—

unconvincing sexual deviates. The punk is despised and ridiculed by the inmates.

Whereas the punk is guilty of incomplete role learning, the "turnabout," on the other hand, claims expertise at playing both male and female roles. As a matter of fact, she not only describes herself glowingly in terms of her versatility, that is, "good either way," but stands ready to put her boasted skill to the test. Such protean versatility, however, is viewed with amused contempt by the inmates. As a prisoner put it, "There's a lot of talk, but not the right kind of talk. She should know what she is and stay that way. And we tell them, 'Get yourself together and find out what you are!' She should know what she is and stay that way."

The Alderson inmates prefer a structured situation in their prison world, and inmates playing male roles one day and female roles the next confuse the issue greatly. This is especially true for the inmate who may be planning a strategy of conquest. In addition, anything which tends to decrease the male population in the prison is apt to alarm the inmates. It is not surprising, therefore, that the turnabout is held in low esteem.

III

These social roles as distinguished and labeled by the Alderson inmates constitute the basic structure of social relationships formed as a response to the problems incidental to a prison commitment. The pains of imprisonment and their implications have already been discussed in detail, and they need not be repeated here. It was suggested, however, that the evolution of an informal social structure in the Alderson prison community represents an attempt to resist the destructive effects of imprisonment by creating a *substitute universe* within which the inmates may preserve an identity relevant to life outside the prison. The outline of this universe has been skirted from time to time in discussing the structure of the "marital" relationship and the broader kinship structure. The precise nature, however, will be examined in detail in Chapters 9 and 10. For the moment we must confine ourselves to the social roles presented here.

Perhaps the most striking feature of the social system in

the Alderson inmate community to be noted thus far is the sharpness in the definition of the roles played by the various types. This simply does not occur with quite the same rigor in the male prison communities studied to date.

In our discussion of the social roles, some comparisons with the male prison community have already been made. In addition, there are other important differences. Consistent with the cultural definition of the female as nonaggressive, the roles of violence that emerge in the male prison, namely, those of "wolf," "tough," "gorilla," "hipster," and "ball buster" are notably absent among the Alderson inmates. Also significant is the fact that a role resembling the structure of the "right guy" who is such a dominant figure in the male prison does not emerge in the female prison. Mention was made in the last chapter that concepts such as "fair play," "courage," and the like—which are consistent with the concepts of endurance, loyalty, and dignity associated with the "right guy"—are not meaningful to the female. In other words, it appears that general features of American society in connection with the cultural definition ascribed to male and female roles are imported into the prison and are reflected in the structure of social relationships formed by the inmates. Nowhere is this more dramatically revealed than in the extraordinary function of the homey role in the Alderson community, with its extended implications for the re-entry of the inmate into civil society. Acting from the same vantage point, we saw that the function of the pinner's role is to control the physical distance between inmates engaging in illicit activities and the snitcher in order to decrease for the Alderson inmates the possibility of discovery and punishment.

The number of roles clustered about homosexual behavior clearly reveals the lack of heterosexual relationships as a crucial "axis of life" for the Alderson inmates. Moreover, the distinctions made by the inmates as to motivation, role assumed, adeptness with which the assumed role is played, and so on, indicate the values and expectations of the inmates with respect to this behavior. But the rights and obligations attached to a legitimate marital relationship automatically close off much interaction among the inmates, as inmates assuming this type of relationship must account for all their contacts with members of the "opposite sex." As the inmates move closer to "legitimate" relationships in the prison, then, the refinement of roles becomes necessary to control and to account for the behavior of every inmate in the system.

Underlying cleavages and competing interests, however, constantly erupt into major breakups because of the inherent vulnerability of the dyad configuration. Thus the female prison world is notable not for struggles for power as is the case in the male prison—indeed leadership is very diffuse in the Alderson prison community—but, rather, for a shifting of marriage partners. Yet through a system of kin status, that is to say, through the dynamic mechanism of kinship—the social system of the Alderson inmates maintains its stability over time and keeps the "sex ratio" within manageable limits.

Although it is true that the interdependence of the Alderson inmates in connection with economic cooperation, emotional reciprocity, loyalty, and so on, tends to tie the inmates together *loosely* in the prison, it is the dyad configuration in the form of a marital relationship and the broader kinship structure which weave the inmates into a cohesive and meaningful social system. Indeed, kinship ties constitute the principal factor of social integration among the inmates. How intricately the kinship network interlaces the inmates into a cohesive and meaningful social system will be demonstrated in Chapters 9 and 10.

NOTES

1. Samuel Strong, "Social Types in a Minority Group," *The American Journal of Sociology*, Vol. 48, March, 1943, p. 564.

2. *Ibid.*, p. 565.

3. Sykes, *The Society of Captives, op. cit.*, Chapter 5; Clarence Schrag's social types also have their conceptual foundations in the analyis of Samuel Strong. They are described in Norman S. Hayner, "Washington State Correctional Institutions as Communities," *Social Forces*, Vol. 21, March, 1943, pp. 319–320. The differentiation of groups made by Morris Caldwell, however, is vague as to theoretical orientation. See Morris G. Caldwell, "Group Dynamics in the Prison Community," *Journal of Criminal Law, Criminology and Police Science*, Vol. 46, January-February, 1956, pp. 651–653. Other pertinent studies in this connection include: F. E. Haynes, "The Sociological Study of

the Prison Community," *The Journal of Criminal Law and Criminology,* Vol. 39, 1943–1949, pp. 432–440. Norman S. Hayner and Ellis Ash, "The Prison as a Community," *American Sociological Review,* Vol. 5, August, 1940, pp. 577–583; Hans Reimer, *op. cit.*

4. For a discussion of the social function of jealousy, see: Kingsley Davis, "Jealousy and Sexual Property," *Social Forces,* Vol. 14, March, 1936, pp. 395–405.

5. Cf. Murtagh and Harris, *op. cit.,* p. 244.

6. Sykes, *The Society of Captives, op. cit.,* p. 94.

7. Cigarettes are the most important nexus of exchange among the inmates.

CHAPTER 9 THE HOMOSEXUAL ALLIANCE AS A MARRIAGE UNIT

To the question, "What is time?" St. Augustine gives his famous answer in his *Confessions:* "If no one asks me, I know; but if I wish to explain it to someone who asks, I do not know." The Alderson inmates, however, have no difficulty in giving quick and ready answers to queries concerning the meaning and nature of time in the prison world. Indeed, the concept of time as concrete and objectified is widespread in the inmate prison culture. Time, according to the inmates, is an entity given whole to the individual by society and measured in days, weeks, months, and years. Time is an entity which stretches from the present into a distant future—a future, however, which is unattainable until the seemingly endless isolated present is somehow conquered by the prisoner. Otherwise, time can "beat," "get," or "bug" the individual—that is, the meaningless of much of prison life can result in the social and personal deterioration of the individual.[1] In order to survive in the prison world, then, time, according to the Alderson inmates, must be psychologically collapsed to the immediate present,[2] a present that places severe limits on the extent to which the inmate is psychologically bound up with events and individuals associated with the past and present in outside society. The intrusion of civil society into the prison world is incompatible with the "as if" world which the Alderson inmates have created to adjust to the pains of imprisonment.

In this chapter we begin to examine systematically the

way in which the twin features of extreme isolation and the inevitability of concrete objectified time become for the inmates determinants for social relations cast into the form of "marriage" as a major adjustment to the prison world. These features serve also as the justification for the inclusion or exclusion of elements of civil society which impinge on the process of "learning to do time," that is, the psychological suspension of self from the "free world."

II

The fundamental fact recognized by the Alderson inmates is that they must all "do time," or serve a prison sentence. Their culture places stress on the importance of doing "easy time" as the best way to serve a prison sentence. Easy time refers to the process of relating one's thoughts and energies mainly to events within the prison while serving a sentence. Inmates who are overly concerned with events in outside society and with incidents prior to incarceration are said to do "hard time." These inmates fail to adjust to prison life because they tend to maintain strong psychological ties with family and friends in the outside world. The frustration experienced by these inmates sometimes erupts in a violation of prison rules.

A few inmates maintained that hard time was their lot from the beginning of their sentence to the very day of release. Most inmates who claimed to have experienced hard time, however, found that it usually occurred during the early stages of the prison sentence, but at some point in the prison career they began to do easy time. What actually takes place in the transition from hard time to easy time is that the inmate learns with the help of sister inmates to suspend deep emotional involvement in events taking place in outside society and to live completely in the very second of the present—in the prison world of the inmates.

If the prisoner lives psychologically in both worlds—the free world and the penitentiary world—a strain is placed upon the possibility of doing easy time. The brief comments presented below were expressed by two inmates and illustrate both the rationale and the process for easy time.

The first thing that an inmate must do is to divorce her mind from outside. It's got to be a void as far as the Free World is concerned. You can't think about outside—not if you're going to do this time. It takes a while to go from one extreme to another—to go from the normal to the abnormal. It's a shock to the system. It's hard to do—to blank out everything—the ties that you have out there. It's not easy to do this. But you push them far back in your mind so you can do this time. To do successful time you must. You close out anything real—anything to do with the Free World. You face reality in the prison.

In the beginning you think about outside and shed tears. But after you're here a while you realize that it's hard to do time and you learn to shut everything out. You worry about your family, your children, mother, father, friends. But you get to the point where you shut them out, because they're *out there* doing what they want to do. There's nothing I can do to help them. No matter what happens out there, I can't do anything to help. And my tears aren't going to *help them, but they can make it hard for me to do my time.*

Although it is true that the physical removal of the inmate from the free world is made by society, the psychological "removal" or withdrawal must always be viewed as an individual accomplishment which may vary from one prisoner to another. The inmate's psychological transition of self from civil society to the prison world may be considered complete when the individual reacts neutrally to events in the outside world, even when these events concern crucial matters pertaining to close family members.

Individual personality factors and history of prior commitments undoubtedly influence the inmate's early adjustment to the inmate prison world. However, the capacity of the informal group to make its activities appear indispensable to the successful consummation of a prison sentence certainly plays a major role in inducting the prisoners into the inmate social system. And this is perhaps facilitated by the fact that few inmates have a high degree of interaction with family members or friends after incarceration.

SYMBOLS OF COMMUNICATION

The Alderson inmates are not able to resolve their sense of isolation within the formal organization; therefore they develop relationships and behavior patterns within an informal structure. The vast majority of inmates adjust to the prison world by establishing a homosexual alliance with a compatible partner as a marriage unit. The inmate culture maintains that "to play," that is, to engage in homosexuality as "duplication" of the outside world, "makes time easier," and "go by faster." Furthermore, it is widely held that "no one can do time alone." Inmates engaged in a homosexual alliance are referred to as a couple by other inmates, and the relationship is recognized in the prison as a legitimate marriage. The roles of male and female make up the homosexual alliance. This is the most important structural relationship in the informal prison world of the Alderson inmates, and many other kinship roles, as we shall see in Chapter 10, pivot about this basic dyad. Our first task, however, must be to examine the anatomy of the marriage relationship from courtship to "fall out," that is, from its inception to the parting of the ways, or divorce.

The sex identities appropriate to the prison marriage alliance are overtly assumed. Inmates assuming male roles are distinguished from those playing female roles by such symbols of communication as dress, hair style, language, and behavior patterns. As pointed out in Chapter 8, inmates assuming the female role are referred to as femmes and inmates assuming the male role are referred to as studs. When these roles are incorporated into marriage, however, a femme and stud become husband and wife to one another, and inmates use these terms to refer to each other. Some of the inmates jokingly refer to one another as "mommy" and "poppy," "my old lady," and "my old man." Occasionally, the term "friend" is used. (It will be recalled that we encountered this term in an earlier discussion of a juvenile institution for female delinquents.) Femmes sometimes refer to husbands as "aggressors." The verbal symbol which is widely used in the Alderson prison, however, and clearly distinguishes the relationship as homosexual is the term "my people." To ask an inmate whether she has "people" is to inquire whether the inmate is occupied in a homosexual relationship constituting marriage. The term is always used in the plural, although it always has a singular referent. Moreover, it refers only to one's marriage mate, and is never used to describe any other member of an inmate's prison family.

Inmates who assume a female role in a prison marriage dress in feminine attire, wear cosmetics, and play the role in the relationship often expected of the female. Inmates playing the male role, on the other hand, assume many stylized symbols of masculinity. For example, they crop their hair very short to resemble a masculine haircut, and a very few inmates sported sideburns. Their hair is worn straight, as curls are associated with femininity. Cosmetics are not worn by these inmates, nor is jewelry worn with the exception of the rings and religious medals which are sometimes exchanged between inmates at the inception of a marriage as tokens of undying love.[3]

Whenever possible, inmates assuming the male role wear slacks styled like men's trousers, that is, with a loosely fitted trouser leg. It is possible for some inmates to obtain slacks in connection with work details, and informal exchanges between inmates furnish the remainder of the stud population with slacks. Black skirts are popular for "dress" occasions, as are black vests. Moreover, the white blouses issued by the clothing room are converted by the inmates into a cultural symbol of masculinity. The collars are heavily starched and when ironed are folded lengthwise in half in order to look like the starched collar of a man's shirt. As might be expected, shoes worn by studs do not have heels; instead, they wear loafers or canvas sneakers. Masculinity is also communicated by headgear. Little caps which fit the head closely with brim worn down over the ears, knitted caps with visors, or a fedora style are popular with studs, but are not worn by femmes. Another item of clothing which designates clearly to onlookers that its wearer is playing a male role is leg covering. Studs wear their socks straight up (they do not wear nylon hose) to symbolize masculinity rather than folded over at the ankle. Some of the hand-knit styles resemble men's garter-length hose. Knee-length socks are also popular with studs. The important point here is that the socks worn by studs are never folded over at the ankle and more often than not are apt to be dark in color.

Another important way in which Alderson inmates differentiate male and female roles is in terms of the length, shape, and fit of clothing. Femmes, of course, try to make their prison garments resemble whatever is fashionable at the moment in outside society. But whatever the fashion, studs always wear skirts that are longer in length than those worn by femmes. Indeed, during a period when Parisian designers were inching women's skirts above the knee, studs in the Alderson prison— in keeping with their assumed masculine role—wore skirts approx- imately eight inches below the knee.

Differential dress for studs is intended to disguise externally the curves of the female and to achieve a flattened look; the shape of their skirts can best be described as "baggy." In addi- tion, shirts are worn over the skirt rather than tucked in and are not fitted. Some studs take in the cups of their brassieres to flatten their breasts. Other studs do not wear brassieres, but instead wear the knitted undershirts in khaki color that are issued from the clothing room, and match in color the slacks and shirts issued for many of the work details such as land- scaping, farm detail, storehouse, and so on. In addition, men's T-shirts and shorts—which are sometimes laundered at the prison for some of the hospitals in the state—are stolen by the inmates and worn by studs.

Verbal symbols of communication also distinguish the in- mates who assume male roles from femmes. When an inmate assumes a male role, a corruption of the individual's feminine name often takes place. For example, Barbara becomes Bob; Rachel, Ray; Katherine, Kelly; Mary, Marty; Lucille, Lou; and so on. If the inmate's feminine name does not lend itself readily to such corruption, then a masculine name or nickname of one's choice is adopted. In addition, the masculine pronoun is always used to refer to anyone who adopts a male role in the prison, which indicates clearly the highly institutionalized character of this cultural complex. General terms of address such as "man" or "Jack" are acceptable and quite widely used by the inmates. Terms such as "girl" or the use of the stud's feminine name, however, are taboo and inmates taking such liberties with studs are immediately corrected: "Where do you get that girl stuff? Call me ———, or don't call me at all."

Behavioral expectations of the stud's role incorporate in a general way many of the cultural expectations of the male in

American society. First, studs are expected to assume a masculine stride; mincing steps and swaying of the hips are associated with females. Secondly, studs are expected to be discreet in their talk and not indulge in wanton gossip. Third, they are expected to incorporate the traits of reliability and emotional control in their character. Injunctions to behavior are: "You should be a square shooter." "Say what you mean and mean what you say." The prerogative often claimed by women, namely, the "right to change her mind," is not part of the male role in the Alderson prison. And, finally—although the association of two women, like that between man and woman, assumes many different forms—in sexual relations the stud is expected by most femmes to assume a relatively aggressive role.

In short, in addition to assuming the external symbols of masculinity in connection with dress, hair length, and nomenclature, the inmate assuming the male role is expected to "put herself in a man's place and act like one." She is to act like a man in a world where there are no men. This point is critical. The stud must attempt to duplicate the behavior patterns of her adopted sex and make "normal" individuals of her anatomic sex feel toward her as though she truly were a male. As we saw in the previous chapter, individuals failing to meet these expectations are assigned the punk role.

Yet while this is so, a delicate equilibrium must somehow be maintained by the stud between the reality of *role innovation* in the prison world—which is legitimized by the inmate culture as necessary for nonheterosexual relations, and is, therefore, accorded high prestige—and the tendency to become carried away and enslaved with her performance of the stud character and to attempt to transcend psychologically the immutability of anatomy and biological function. We have already noted the alterations of brassieres in order to flatten breasts. In addition, some studs will "refuse to get in the kotex line," that is, refuse to ask the officer for sanitary napkins, and will order the wife to obtain them. Their pretensions in this regard sometimes take the form of fashioning crude tampons out of sanitary napkins in order to hide the menses. Moreover, they hitch up their slacks as if they were manipulating a penis. Such role-playing behavior is defined by the inmates as extreme and as outside the legitimate boundaries of prescribed "maleness."

The point is that the culture of the Alderson inmates stipulates the range of permissible innovation which is meaningful in the prison world in order to create a *substitute universe* to resist the destructive effects of imprisonment, and emphasizes the fact that *women* are assuming both roles. Under the conditions described above, then, the stud's role is viewed as an inversion, and when the opportunity presents itself, such as in the heat of argument, the inmates will shower the stud with ridicule.

Two striking variations of "maleness" which depart markedly from the "ideal type" described previously were also present at the Alderson prison, but were recognized as legitimate by the inmates. A limited number of inmates assumed the male role but did not cut their hair short. Rather they wore it brushed back and caught up at the nape of the neck with an elastic band or ribbon, or simply brushed back straight behind the ears. Many of these inmates, however, adopted the other symbols of masculinity. Secondly, a few inmates assumed all or some of the outward guises of femininity in terms of dress, length and style of hair, but acted out the behavioral expectations of the male role.

These variations may result from several factors. First, they may indicate the stage at which the male role is adopted. That is, the inmate may gradually work into the male role, and the hair cutting may be the last stage in the progress from the female to the male role. On the other hand, the reverse process also occurs, and the hair cutting for some inmates is the first step. Secondly, inmates who have short sentences sometimes prefer not to cut their hair, as they fear that upon release family members or friends may raise questions about their prison behavior. Third, inmates may not wish the officers to suspect them of homosexuality. And, finally, inmates may refuse to cut their hair because of personal preferences in the matter. Two rap buddies, for example, may decide to transform their relationship into a marriage. In arriving at a decision as to allocation of roles, the inmate who is to assume the male role may refuse to cut her hair.

By way of summary, stylized symbolic devices make it possible for the Alderson inmates to attach new meanings to a culturally defined sex *role* representation seen as a variation of a sex *type* based upon biological attributes. The institutionalized character of the differential sex roles orders the behavior of the inmates, defines the limits of permissible behavior, and regulates interaction between the inmates.

MATE SELECTION, COURTSHIP, AND MARRIAGE

With the foregoing exposition of the cultural differentiation of the sexes, it is now possible for us to proceed logically to a discussion of the mate selection process in the Alderson prison. The foundation of a lasting marriage is not religious or jural sanction but, rather, a satisfactory relationship between the two individuals involved. It is essentially a personal bond—a mutual adjustment of persons which must be accomplished in very short order, and a mutual satisfactory adjustment of roles. The goal is to enter into a homosexual alliance with a mutually compatible partner, and the sexual bond is of vital importance in this relationship.

Mate selection is based upon romantic love, and marriage is predicated upon the consent of the interested parties. All homosexual relationships are established on a voluntary basis; there was no evidence of any physical coercion such as occurs in the male prison. However, a few Alderson inmates expressed anxiety and fear in connection with homosexuality. During the month I spent observing interaction patterns in the orientation unit, for example, one youthful offender said she was "afraid" to move from the unit into a cottage because of the homosexual practices and "the way some inmates come after you." She vowed, as a consequence, that after she moved she would lock her room every night. Her fear and anxiety, however (and this seemed to be true of other inmates), stemmed from the belief that she might willingly consent to establish a homosexual relationship as a consequence of an inmate's verbal entreaties rather than from anxiety about possible physical coercion.

The usual procedure an inmate follows in laying the groundwork to "turn out" a novice is to point out the benefits to be derived from a homosexual alliance in terms of "easy time," and to ridicule the inmate if she is not willing to enter into a partnership. Occasionally, but by no means often, candy and cigarettes and the like may be plied to help matters along, but no physical coercion is used to persuade an imate.

The attitude that an inmate who is inexperienced in homosexual relations expresses with regard to this phase of prison life is extremely important in terms of the position she will acquire in the social structure—and may very well determine whether she is allocated the status of cherry, square, hip square, and so on. To express a "holier-than-thou" attitude, that is, to state or imply that homosexual behavior in the prison situation is abnormal or distasteful is reacted to with anger or strong resentment by the other inmates. The behavior expected of inmates who do not engage in homosexuality is contained in the expression: "If you don't dig 'playing'—solid, but don't rank it!"

Contacts between inmates are made wherever they have occasion to meet. As we saw in Chapter 4, the range of legitimate interaction is fairly wide because of the administrative change in connection with open campus and the liberal seating arrangements for the inmates at all scheduled activities. Although it cannot be said that marriages in the Alderson prison are made in heaven, open campus does make it possible for them to be made out on the field. Inmates meet in large groups at scheduled activities such as movies, church services, and the infrequent dances—all of which are widely exploited by the inmates as possible meeting places to meet dates, to initiate flirtations, and to carry on courtships. Moreover, it must be kept in mind that the structure of the cottage system makes for density of interaction and heightened sustained visibility among the inmates which, while it often makes it easier for the inmates to control the behavior of deviants, also facilitates contact among them in connection with homosexual activities.

It is readily apparent, then, that contact between inmates may be easily made. Moreover, symbols of masculinity and femininity clearly differentiate the studs from the femmes. The interested inmate handles the matter according to her own desires and interests on a verbal level, and very often by the use of the "kite"—prison letter between inmates.

The kite is an important means of communication between

inmates and has many functions in connection with dating, courtship, and marriage. It is widely used to express a grievance, to
explain questionable behavior, to secure a mate, and also to
retain one when the inmates involved live in separate cottages.
Kites may be handed to an inmate on the open field, on the
way to work or to the dining room, in church, may be placed
under the inmate's pillow, in the inmate's coat pocket, delivered
by an inmate go-between, placed in a magazine or in a book in
the library. In short, as one inmate put it, "Where there's a
will, there's a way." The kite may be used very early in the
inmate's prison career, for example by an inmate in the orientation unit to secure a homosexual partner before classification.
(See Appendix F for a series of such letters written by an inmate
in the orientation unit while the study was in process.)

Kites are not easy to obtain, as inmates usually destroy
letters soon after reading them. Fortunately, however (perhaps
due to the carelessness of a few inmates, and, of course, because
of prior administrative policy), I came across a few kites while
examining the inmates' case history folders. They had been
picked up by correctional officers about a year or more before
the study began and were filed in the respective writer's folders.
They are interesting documents which reveal the emotional needs
and yearnings of the inmates as well as the processes involved
in mating, and other structural features of the inmate social
system. A curious aspect is that they are often singularly inconsistent in style.

The ability to express sentiment of romantic nature in flowery
or poetic form is highly prized and rewarded by the inmates.
An inmate's lack of education or creative ability in this regard,
therefore, may place severe limitations directly on the letter
and indirectly, perhaps, on her success in securing a marriage
partner. Therefore, in order to improve a letter, sometimes a
line or two from poems appearing in women's magazines (or
books) will be borrowed by an inmate and included either
verbatim or paraphrased slightly. The result is often poignant
incongruity, as, for example, the letter addressed to "Bad Girl"
included in a later section of this chapter which is a medley of
serious grammatical errors, misspelled words, obscene expressions,

and yet which ends with the wistful, "Must I love you in vain" perfectly rendered.

A few examples of kites written by the inmates illustrating style and content appear below. They are uncorrected copies of the handwritten originals. (See Appendix G for others.) The following letter was written by an inmate with little formal education. Almost every word in the original had been erased and laboriously worked over.

Hi Angel

Just rec. your lovely kite an was more than glad to hear from you. You have been on my mind all day. sorry to hear about what happen to you last night. hope things are better now. sure miss you since you left the Hospital it hasn't been the same. baby I feel a lots better since I heard from you. if only I was with you tonight you would really know just how I feel about you. but I will tell you this much. I have felt that you were mine from the very moment our eyes met because you and I have an understanding beyond words and it take two of the same kind to make a pair. thats us. baby you know you don't have to ask if you can wright because letters from you are like manna from heaven altho I can't wright to you to often because I don't have any paper but that dont keep you from wrighting to me every day and if you do then my day would be complete knowing you cared enough to right. wrighting is slow baby because officers are regular so you dig what I mean. Well baby this is all for now take care of yourself till we meet again.

I would be the happiest person on the Res. if I only knew you would be mine only mine. I were outside this afternoon an the fresh air was wonderful. so if you happen around in the afternoon around 2 P.M. baby we can chance to talk. my roommate and I were talking about you baby wondering how you were if you were OK or not and baby the letter was a very happy surprise tonight so untill tomorrow you shall be my thoughts my dreams my very heart beat.

From your big boy

The letter below illustrates the use of formally scheduled activities by the inmates to give messages to one another.

Hello

O.K. start cursing me out. I guess you know that a dam fool is entitled to one mistake. One thing about me when I make a mistake

I make a whopper of one. Look at me now. That is one reason I am in this joint, one hugh mistake. Really I don't know what came over me. All I can say is that I must have been slightly mad. Really baby I know I have hurt you and believe me after the thought had sunk in that I had lost you I was hurt even more. I realized it at Mass Sunday. If you can possibly find it in your heart to forgive me, please do. I beg you. I know that is a lot to ask but I have to ask, because I want you more than anything. I know you are hurt and angry and I don't blame you. You have every right to be. What more can I say or do? Just tell me and I will do it. C means nothing to me and never will. I know so much more about her than I did Sat. Fickle and whatever else you care to call her. I'm telling her that it's over. All I want is you. And baby if you have copped another by now, I am sorry but there is nothing I can do because it is all my fault. I heard that you had another but I want you to tell me. If you don't sit next to me in *class* tonight I will know that you have other people. But baby I will never hurt you again. I heard you were at the storehouse this morning, but I didn't see you. I would much rather tell you all this to your face but we never have that much time together. I will really explain to you tonight if you will let me. Please think it over. All there is left for me to say now is I LOVE YOU and always will, even if you have your people by now.

Please let me know something before I go stone nuts.

YOURS

TO MINE I HOPE

Usually inmates destroy letters soon after they have read them. Carelessness, however, or perhaps the tendency to treasure letters from a lover, made possible the set of letters which follows illustrating stages of emotional involvement in a homosexual relationship.

Hello Mi Amor,

I just read your most sweet letter. I look forward to every little word that you write. Baby, I wasn't believing what I heard or I wouldn't have asked you. I was trying to ask you last night that I wanted to go home with you and if you would let me. It sure would be nice if I could. Baby, do you want me out there for real? I believe you do but what were you doing with S? I know she kites you for I read one. (Please get me straight on that little matter.) Sweetheart, I don't want anyone else but you, and I want you to feel the same. I can't play this triangle stuff and I do want you but all for my very own personal possession. Baby, you mean so much to me but don't play with me. Got to go now.

Te quira mucho por vida.

"Your Bad Girl"

Saturday Night

My Most Precious One,

Well, Baby, I just got home from the movie and I just had to write. My mind is on a lot of things right now but in every phase of thought you enter in. Baby you looked so good to me and I wanted to come to you so bad that I don't know what to do. Baby, please don't take me for a play toy. I may act young and silly at times but if I did show my true self at all times and didn't keep my guard up I would crack up. Darling, I feel so alone and lonely. Maybe I should be used to it by now but no one gets used to loneliness.

Sometimes I feel that what I am and have been searching for is something that I will never find. Just like a miner; when he thinks he's discovered gold, only to have it essayed and be told it's fool's gold. I am full of love and I want to share it but all I can find is fake love and that is no good to anyone. I want you to share it with me but I want it to be true; for love is a proud and gentle thing; a better thing to own than all of the wide impossible stars over heaven blown. I feel an inward feeling that maybe I have found it in you but I am afraid; so afraid because in my past I have thought I had found it but it was always fool's gold. Darling, if sometimes I do silly things, please understand that I'm just being careful because I don't want to be hurt again. Mi amor, te quira mucho *por vida, por vida.* If I find what I want I won't let go of it *ever.* I want to find everything in you and I can if you'll let me, Darling. I must make like the fog and drift away but like the fog I shall return. Good night my love, pleasant dreams and sleep tight, my love. You have made a green oasis in my heart but it would turn to sand if ever we should part.

Besames X X X

"Your Very Own Bad Girl"

Real Real Late at Night

I just woke up and am looking out my window wishing I could be with you. You have become an obsession with me. Night time, Noon time, Morning time, too all of these times my mind is on you. I'm going to try once more to sleep. Wish me luck!

I love you with all my heart for all my life.

"Chiquita Diablo"

Sunday Morning

Good Morning, Baby,

I just got out of this bed. When I did get to sleep last night, what dreams! I woke up once with the pillow in the middle of my bed and my little ――― upon it. Was in cold sweats. Honey, I have got to be with you and soon. I want you to hold me and run your fingers through my hair and kiss me sweet and tenderly. I dream about making love to you and it is violent and at the same time it's sweet and gentle. I don't do anything but think of you and they better move me and soon or they'll have to ship me to St. Eades. [St. Elizabeth's Hospital] Mi amor, I want you, I need you, I love you and I'm going to have you. Time for me to get a shower and get ready for Mass. Remember I love you and miss you.

Te amo mucho por vida.

Your
"Chiquita Diablo"

One reply to the above letters follows:

"My dearest Bad Girl,"

Hello Sweet heart. how my baby doing. Fine I hope. As for me I have a very bad cold. and I got your thick letter today. I couldn't answer it right away for I am always working. I am getting tired of this place. Really. And dig stop thinking that I am for someone else for I am not. understand. I AM NOT. *I am for you.* OK. And stop thinking all that ――― [obscenity] and I guss wrote my PO and try to come back to the Res. if you are not coming out. Because you are thinking up to much ―――, and the reason why I didn't go to the movie is because of this cold. and I wasn't feeling to good. how could you love me but you don't trust me. Baby have a little trust in me OK. I just knew you would come out today because They need 2 girl's now but Didn't any body come, so maby one will come. I hope so, and then you will live in my dorm. I am by my self with two Bed's in here I like it down here by myself. I am hope To Share it with you all alone you and me woulden That be nice. I have been dreaming about you also you know. thats all I do is stick to my room. or watch TV. Well Baby its time for lights out, so I close for now.

Must I love you in vain.

Always yours
Tex

Lengthy courtships are not usually carried on by the Alderson inmates. As a matter of fact, a kite stating intentions is usually favored immediately with a reply informing the inmate exactly where "he" or she stands. If the answer is affirmative, the marriage takes place immediately. No formal ceremony binds the two inmates in marriage. They simply make the decision between themselves that they will become a couple. This may vary from a simple "O.K. I'll try it," to a pledge of undying love. Sometimes the marriage is formalized by an exchange of rings or medals.[3] Occasionally when an inmate is not interested, she may reply to a kite with silence, which in matters of the heart speaks louder than words and quickly sends an inmate searching in other more willing directions for a mate.

With obvious differences, the homosexual alliance is patterned on marriage in civil society. For many inmates the femme role is an important means by which they may preserve in prison an identity which is relevant for civil society. Assumption of this role represents an attempt to seek continued fulfillment of former satisfactory roles in the prison world; it is *substitute role conformity*. For others, the role provides the individual with an opportunity to function in a role which would very likely have been assumed in civil society in a heterosexual relationship in the normal course of events. For this group of inmates, the femme role in prison may be looked upon as *substitute role experience,* as the role incorporates many of the behavioral expectations of the female in heterosexual relationships.

Except in affairs where inmates are "makin' it long distance," that is, husband and wife are living in separate cottages (and sometimes in separate cottages on different campuses), the wife is expected to do the housekeeping chores such as washing, ironing, dressmaking, and mending for both. If the inmates live in a dormitory, the wife is expected to clean the area occupied by the husband, change bed linen, and so on. And the same holds true if they occupy separate rooms. When both inmates live on separate floors in the same cottage, the wife is responsible for the stud's room if this can be managed without disciplinary action.

In addition to having housekeeping duties, the wife is expected to be well-groomed at all times, especially at public functions, so that she will not be a "drag" to her husband, that is, someone unattractive to squire about.

The stud's role incorporates many innovative features in order to complement the femme in a marriage relationship. The stud has the obligation to protect his wife against any verbal and physical assaults from all other inmates. Studs are also expected to oblige with all the courtesies expected of gentlemen, such as opening doors, and helping a lady with a wrap. In addition, studs escort their respective wives to all prison activities such as the movies, church affairs, parties, ball games, as well as to the dining hall. Husbands and wives always sit together in the cottage living room or at a scheduled activity. When they do not live in the same cottage, they arrange to meet at scheduled activities and always sit together. In this instance, whoever arrives first saves a seat for the other partner.

It is understood that the husband and wife have a reciprocal obligation so far as the expressive and sexual needs of the other are concerned. Most femmes, but not all, assume relatively consistent passive roles in sexual relations.

Alderson inmates accord the greatest prestige to couples who are observed to be "sincere." Now this term is not used by the inmates in the ordinary dictionary sense. In the argot of the inmates, "sincere" couples are those that are characterized by a principle of strict equality. These couples are said to have a "better understanding" than other couples, meaning that the relationship is not an exploitative affair, as evidenced by its democratic nature. Everything is shared equally ("fifty-fifty")—washing, ironing, other household chores, as well as commissary buying.

Sincere relationships are an ideal in the prison, but in actuality they are relatively few in number. It must be kept in mind that homosexual gratification (as well as heterosexual gratification) is a service which individuals perform for one another and which, as such, is potentially exploitable. The significance of this fact for the inmate social system is that many prison marriages are fleeting erotic attachments based upon commercial interests. An inmate may engage in a homosexual affair to solve an economic problem in the prison. Although many couples share economic responsibilities in the sense that one week the femme will do the buying and the next week the stud will reciprocate, in the majority of cases the economic function falls to the femme. Moreover, femmes usually do all the housework for both. Regardless of economic arrangements, however, when couples have a "right" or "good" understanding, it is expected that the stud will assume the role of commissary hustler to ease the economic burden when the femme has no money.

Although there is a tendency for marriage relationships to be based upon the recognition of husband and wife as companionable equals, in matters that are considered to be important the femme defers to the stud who is recognized as the head of the household and is granted the final decision. The prominent factors in the relations of most couples are demonstration of affection and love, mutual confiding, companionship, sharing of experience, loyalty, and mutual aid. Emphasis among the inmates is always upon the mutual nature of obligations, except in the case of close family members when a definite economic need exists. The relations of the inmates, even in marriage, are probably best described as a unity stemming in part from economic cooperation and from the satisfaction of psychological and physiological needs.

The inmate culture prescribes patrilocal residence. As soon as two inmates decide to become a couple, the femme initiates formal arrangements to move into the stud's cottage if she does not already live there. She moves into the cottage at the stud's invitation, and when the marriage is terminated she moves out. Until the formal arrangements for living quarters are processed, these inmates are recognized as married by the inmate community, and prison etiquette regarding social distance is observed. They meet at all functions and sit together, talk on the field, and with the help of pinners occasionally have physical contact during the long weekend. For this purpose the stud goes to the femme's cottage. "Taking care of business"—homosexual relations—requires an enormous amount of organization and is an extremely risky enterprise to carry out in another cottage. Sometimes, for example, a room on the first floor must be borrowed for this purpose. And it always entails keeping the officer occupied when the stud is entering the cottage, while the couple is occupied, and also when the stud leaves the cottage. To have successfully "copped" in another cottage, therefore, carries much prestige among the inmates, and a stud is apt to boast when it is over.

The marriage relationship provides the inmates with companionship and a feeling of belonging, meets needs for love and affection, and provides the inmates with an opportunity to express individuality in an adult role. Although the prison marriage performs these positive functions for many of the inmates, it also creates problems for other inmates when a marriage ends in divorce.

DIVORCE

In most societies ideal patterns of culture hold marriage to be a more of less permanent tie and not one to be dissolved easily at the whim of either partner. Although the ideal of marriage on a permanent basis exists among the Alderson inmates—and indeed a few couples do remain married until one of the partners is released—most couples tend to remain united for only about one to three months and then secure new partners. In short, marriage in the Alderson prison tends to be very unstable.

Although the femme expects fidelity from her mate, she understands clearly that because of the imbalanced "sex" ratio other femmes will be plying her mate with kites and verbal proposals in order to break up the marriage. Estimates of the number of inmates who are involved in homosexuality vary. Inmates who are very much involved in this phase of inmate culture place the figure at 90 or 95 percent. The associate warden (T), on the other hand, estimated that 80 percent of the inmates were involved in homosexual relations. Correctional officers tended to set the figure at 50 or 75 percent, which agrees with the usual estimates I obtained from squares. Some officers and other staff members set the figure at 100 percent. At one point in the study, I made a cottage count of inmates assuming the male role, and the studs totaled 215 inmates. The number of males in the prison tends to vary slightly from day to day depending upon inmate releases and individual role choice. And the same, of course, is true of the inmates playing the femme role. At this time, there were 336 femmes out of a total of 639 inmates. At any rate, it is apparent that femmes are competing for a scarce commodity. In a real sense, the female in the prison marriage experiences great strain, as she can easily be replaced in her husband's affections at any time with other willing femmes. "Competition," it is often said, "is very keen on the reservation." Thus, although the norm "hands off" exists in connection with prison marriages, a prettier face, more charm, undefinable magnetism, larger commissary account, and so on, are all factors which may work to put the wife on the outside. Fighting to keep what is believed to rightfully belong to an individual may occur at any time, but occurs with greater intensity in connection with one's mate. Sometimes triangular situations that lead to violence among the inmates develop. And, as we shall see in another section, femmes may retaliate after a fall out by switching from a female role to a male role in order to spare themselves the mortification of a similar experience in the future.

Although marriage is entered into voluntarily, it is usually the stud who terminates the marriage for a new partner. Femmes terminate a marriage when the stud fails to show them "respect" —especially when a husband's unfaithfulness is brought to the attention of a femme. It is noteworthy that femmes would rather be kept in the dark about a husband's unfaithful acts: "The stud should be discreet and not put it in my face." Explanations given by the inmates as to why the stud usually terminates a marriage vary depending upon which "sex" one addresses. Femmes almost without exception fall back on the popular culture ideology. Studs, on the other hand, explain it in terms of the greater discrimination of studs: "Studs know more what they want out of life. Studs quit the broads." "Once a femme gets a man, they're contented. But a stud—if they find they don't have what they want—they're willing to cut loose to find what they want."

A more plausible explanation, however, seems to lie in the composition of the inmate population, namely, the imbalanced "sex" ratio, coupled with the fact that the vast majority of the inmates are involved in homosexual behavior within or without a marriage relationship. Most of the Alderson inmates want to function in the female role. Since there are fewer studs than femmes, the former have no difficulty in securing a mate at any time. Femmes, on the other hand, must work not only to attract a stud in the first place, but also to retain a mate after marriage. Therefore, the femme tends to exercise caution about terminating a marriage without good cause.

It is understood among the inmates that "When it's over, it's over," and there is no alimony attached to the prison fall outs. Sometimes, however, a rejected and irate inmate will demand that all gifts be returned to her. The precise procedures followed by inmates to communicate divorce to a mate vary according to the quality of relations which characterized the marriage. In the rare marriages where inmates had a "good understanding," the stud will often discuss ("talk over") the situation with the femme in an attempt to maintain friendly relations after the divorce. Common explanations given are: "It couldn't be helped"; "These things happen"; "It's for the best." The point stressed is the inevitability of the event—somehow predetermined and lying outside the range of control on the part of the lovers, suggesting that the blame cannot legitimately be placed on any of the principals.

Divorce may be communicated by other direct methods. Many studs display a great deal of independence and break off relations abruptly by simply informing the wife: "I don't want to go along with the program any more," or the peremptory, "Baby, it's over!" Moreover, the stud may desert the femme by moving out of the cottage, which is public declaration that the marriage is over.

In addition to all of these direct methods by which a stud may inform a partner that a marriage is over, a stud may also inform a femme that he wishes to terminate a marriage by *inaction,* that is, by not assuming the obligations of a husband. Such behavior is meant to induce the femme to take the cue and move out of the cottage.

The failure of a stud, for example, to come to the femme's defense when derogatory remarks are made about her in the presence of the couple, is public declaration that his ardor has cooled and the marriage is over. From the femme's point of view, such behavior indicates a lack of "respect"; it is an intolerable state of affairs, and she is apt to provoke arrangements to move out of the cottage the same day. If it cannot be handled immediately, she may insist upon going to the administrative segregation unit so as to be spared the mortification of being under the same roof with the husband and, in addition, to escape the taunts and jeers of the jive bitches in the cottage.

Whether she is told by direct or indirect means, it is doubtful that a femme ever welcomes news that her marriage is over, even in instances where the stud "talks over" the situation with her. Many bitter accusations usually follow as a matter of course. Furthermore, after a divorce the femme is not only left without a mate but, in addition, she must work to obtain another—either by breaking up an established marriage; by attracting a rare unattached stud; by initiating a cherry; or by socializing a square into this phase of inmate culture. In addition, she has the option of assuming a male role herself, or may participate in another type of homosexual relationship, such as with a kick partner, or may become a chippy, and so on.

In the society of the Alderson inmates, divorce does not necessarily mean that a husband and wife become strangers to one another. Sometimes a divorce may result in the formation of a new kinship tie between inmates who have been husband and wife to one another. This point will become clearer when we discuss the kinship network. Meanwhile, we can only describe the situation under which this role change takes place. In breaking off a marriage, for example, a husband may explain: "No hard feelings, but I feel for you more like a sister," and suggest that he and his wife become brother and sister to one another. Now the establishment of kinship ties of this type serves two positive functions: First, it ensures the solidarity of the inmates and is functional for the group. And secondly, it serves as a face-saving device for the wife, as divorce does not mean complete rejection of the individual. The point needs to be made, however, that all wives are not willing to accept such a relationship, and a femme may bitterly exclaim: "I put everything I had into it, and he had the nerve to say, 'Be my sister!'" (Or "my brother" if the femme is terminating a relationship in this manner.) In such an instance, a femme may assume a stud role to show "him" she's "as good" as "he" is; or to "get back at him." We shall see in Chapter 10 that divorce may have serious repercussions for the structure of the family.

III

A society is not merely an aggregate of interacting individuals. It has a group structure which is patterned in some way. Dominant groups and subordinate groups may be found among the members. It is important to know this patterned group structure if we wish to understand the nature of a social system.

In order to increase our understanding of the structure of the Alderson inmate social system, we must now examine in greater detail the social relations among inmates. In general, it may be said that these relations have an ambivalent friendship-hostility content, although they are always expressed formally by behavior indicating personal and primary relations by the use of personal forms of address and gestures. When inmates meet or call to one another, for example, they use personal terms of address such as "baby," "honey," "hon," "darling," "sweetheart," and "doll." And they often embrace and cling to each other's hands. Yet on a covert level, as we pointed out earlier, no inmate trusts another inmate completely, and each stands ready to "get there first" if possible.

Now in the society of the Alderson inmates, the patterning of the group structure is importantly bound up with the ubiquitous dyad configurations composed of differentiated sex roles in a marriage relationship. We saw, however, that the dyad is a very unstable structure, and the social system of the Alderson inmates is characterized by a continuous shifting of marriage partners. The dissolution of one dyad evolves into one or two new dyad configurations that in turn tend to disrupt over time into other dyadic configurations which are destined for the same fate. And this process is repeated in an endless succession of dyads. In addition, the structure is further complicated by the shifting of sex roles which sometimes occurs as a result of individual choice.

How, then, does the society of Alderson inmates maintain the stability of its structure so that the members of the system may interact with one another? It is obvious that much of the interaction between the inmates is regulated and patterned by the differentiation of sex roles. And the normatively prescribed homosexual marriage as the preferred legitimate outlet for non-heterosexual gratification sharply limits the procurement and disposal of sexual gratification.

In addition, the culture of the Alderson inmates seeks to preserve the integrity of the social structure by controlling the social distance between inmates. First, the individual who exhibits instability in adopting sex roles in prison is allocated the role of turnabout and is ridiculed by the other inmates. This helps to preserve the structure of predictability, which makes possible the kinds of interaction that are important to the group, as it functions to sustain the stability of the sex ratio.

In a society where sex is made a pervasive basis of social organization, contacts between members of the opposite sex must be strictly regulated. In the Alderson prison, married inmates must justify prolonged contacts with other inmates in general and with inmates of the opposite sex whether married or single in particular. In short, interaction between inmates who are not married to one another must be confined to brief casual conversations. Failure to observe this rule is the basis for many arguments between husbands and wives. A married stud, moreover, is not expected to engage in lengthy conversations with a married femme when their respective spouses are not present. But even in the presence of the femme's husband, a stud is expected to be casual and discreet in the remarks directed to her. In addition, "dropping the belt" occurs with enough frequency so that wives are apt to become suspicious of husbands who spend a great deal of time with other studs. Similarly, studs exhibit suspicions if a wife becomes "too friendly" with another femme, as the possibility exists that one of them will become a turnabout.

Prison etiquette, then, has rules all its own to regulate the behavior of the inmates. There is, in addition, the etiquette of handling disputes between a stud and a married femme. When a stud has a grievance against another stud's wife, etiquette stipulates that the stud make a formal complaint to the femme's husband. A stud cannot address a complaint directly to a femme either verbally or by the use of physical force. It is the husband's responsibility to put an end to a wife's aberrant behavior. "It's up to the man to control the woman." However, should the husband fail to exercise the measure of control necessary in this regard, then the complaining stud has the right to take matters into his own hands, without fear of offending the femme's husband. "If he (the husband) can't control his woman, he's got no kick coming."

Thus by increasing the social distance between inmates, the culture severely limits the range of permissible interaction between the inmates. But in a society where value and esteem are placed on the ability to attract the opposite sex, solidarity among the inmates is decreased as the vast majority of the inmates are competing with one another for a scarce commodity. The social system of the inmates, therefore, is internally divided by the dyadic configurations and the competition inherent in the situation. We may state a principle simply: When the dyad is the pivotal structural element in a social system, some other structural form will be adopted by the members to facilitate social and psychological distance between members in order to preserve a community from disruption when the interdependence of the members for mutual aid and sociability requires a highly integrated group formation. We now turn our attention to an examination of the kinship network which the Alderson inmates have adopted in order to preserve the structure of the inmate social system.

NOTES

1. It has been pointed out that extreme isolation from meaningful reference groups and interaction on the level of superficiality result in serious social and personality disorders. See P. Herbert Leiderman, "Man Alone: Sensory Deprivation and Behavioral Change," *Corrective Psychiatry and Journal of Social Therapy,* Vol. 8, Second Quarter, 1962, pp. 64–74.

2. This should not be confused with Mead's *specious present* which includes both past and future in the experience of present events. George Herbert Mead, *Mind, Self, and Society,* Chicago: The University of Chicago Press, 1934, p. 176.

3. Religious medals are obtainable free of charge from the Catholic priest and circulate widely among the inmates in connection with prison marriages. In addition, a medal may be given to an inmate by another just before release as a token of good luck.

CHAPTER 10   COMMUNITY INTEGRATION THROUGH KINSHIP

It was emphasized in Chapter 9 that the dyad configuration cast in the form of a marriage alliance is the most important structural unit of the inmate social system. Indeed, the central dynamic factor operating in the inmate community is the pattern of relations between the husband and wife. The interdependence of the inmates is such, however, that a society of dyads apparently could not long endure without a connecting link to integrate these units into a system of action.

A society of dyads could conceivably function as autonomous units if it were possible for each dyad to survive in the prison as a self-sufficient system. But among the Alderson inmates, as is true of people interacting in group life everywhere, there are needs whose satisfaction requires a broader set of social relationships. Inmates need certain kinds of labor, protection, information, advice, affection, and so on from other inmates. Inmates may also need scarce goods which must be obtained from institutional stores, or clothing and other goods which may or may not be legitimately possessed by other inmates, but whose access requires the cooperation of other inmates.

Moreover, inmates are in constant competition with one another for marriage partners, because the homosexual marriage alliance is the important means of doing easy time. Without some institutional means to regulate the procurement of marriage partners as well as the social contacts of married inmates with

all other inmates, the Alderson community would be characterized by a constant "war of all against all."

We shall now show how the kinship system stabilizes the
inmate community by reconciling competing and conflicting
social motives. As we shall see, the kinship network links individuals together by convergence of interests, social and psychological needs, and sentiments. In addition, the inmate cultural
system controls and limits those conflicts between inmates which
are a result of divergent interests, social and psychological needs,
and sentiment by means of the personal selection process which
operates in the formation of kinship ties. Although spatially
separated, the cottages merge into one social unit through the
interlacing of kinship ties between the inmates. In addition,
the kinship ties span racial lines and cut across differences in
social class.

II

THE FORMATION OF KINSHIP TIES

For the vast majority of inmates, the homosexual marriage
alliance is the most important prison relationship. To preserve
relations of solidarity between the husband and wife, many kinship ties are linked up to the homosexual dyad. All married
inmates must justify to the satisfaction of everyone concerned
that no sexual involvement or attraction exists in any interaction they have with other inmates. In order to decrease
jealousy, suspicion, and misunderstanding which may arise in
connection with the contacts either partner may have with other
inmates, they form kinship links with other married or unmarried inmates with whom it becomes necessary or desirable
to have prolonged and sustained interaction. For example, two
couples living in the same cottage may play cards together each
evening. In order to define and limit the boundaries of permissible interaction between them, these inmates may form kin
relationships. Second, a married inmate who is discovered with
another inmate by a mate (or indeed any inmate who will
report to the mate) in what is perceived to be a compromising

situation, may introduce the inmate in question to her marriage partner as one in kin status to her in order to keep the marriage intact. Such an emergency situation usually results in the honoring of the kinship link.

The group structure of the Alderson inmates consists of inmates bound to one another by kinship ties; and the formation of a kinship tie to an inmate in this group structure makes it possible for an inmate to have legitimate close friendly relations with those inmates to whom she is attached in kinship bonds. For this reason, inmates with short sentences or inmates who do not wish to engage in homosexual relations may resort to kinship links in order to become members of groups. Unmarried inmates who are in constant interaction with one another stand the risk of being suspected of homosexual relations, and the culturally defined social distance consistent with homosexual alliances will be respected by other inmates in their interaction with them. As a result, some unmarried inmates may be constrained to form kinship ties. This is especially true of rap buddies who live in the same cottage and have a high degree of interaction with one another. To escape the suspicion of homosexuality, these inmates may find it necessary to define their interaction more rigidly by kinship bonds. When they do, the kinship tie becomes the ordering principle of interaction between them.

In addition to the foregoing, kinship ties may be formed by a member of a family group when any member of her family forms a marriage or other type of kinship tie with an inmate. The inmates often say that such kinship ties are made "out of respect," and usually refer to these ties as "in-law" relationships. However, if the inmate marrying into a family already stands in kin status with any member of the family, this kinship tie would still be considered legitimate for the inmates concerned and would not be in violation of the incest taboo. And, finally, kinship statuses may come about—although by this process very infrequently—as a result of rejection: such as in the case of divorce which we noted in Chapter 9, or when an inmate "hits" another, that is, proposes marriage and mutual interest does not exist. The rejecting inmate may suggest that a brother-sister relationship be assumed between them in order to soften the immediate impact of a complete rejection and to structure continued relations of solidarity between them.

In the final analysis, however, whether a kinship tie will be established in any situation depends upon the *ackowledgment* of the inmates involved. All kinship ties among the Alderson inmates are established by personal selection on a voluntary basis. An inmate may take into account such factors as the personal habits and general reputation of the inmate, as well as the social roles played by an inmate in prison. Inmates occupying roles that would conflict with the structure of reciprocal exchange of benefits characteristic of kinship relations, or that would jeopardize the stability of kinship ties or the structure of predictability among inmates in kinship status to one another, are excluded from consideration as family members. The volitional nature of kinship functions to structure the institutional means to control and limit conflicts which are a result of divergence of interests and sentiment in connection with one's mate; to sustain the inmate's structure of interaction with other inmates in situations where rejection, jealousy, or other factors may strain continued social relations; to define and limit the interaction between certain categories of inmates; and, finally, to serve the inmate's psychological and social needs.

The differentiation of sex roles is crucial, of course, as it structures at the outset many other roles which the inmate may legitimately play. The adoption by an inmate of a sex role automatically closes off some family roles, while at the same time it opens up legitimate avenues for other roles. In addition to sex, age sets some broad limits as to which role may be ascribed to (or indeed achieved by) inmates. Sex and age are the principal bases of kinship role differentiation. The assumption underlying ascription of kinship roles on the basis of age lies in the belief that broader experience and accumulated knowledge are functions of age. Hence, inmates assuming roles as mothers and fathers are older than the inmates assuming roles as siblings. Similarly, inmates in the role of grandmother are older than inmates occupying roles of mothers and fathers. Inasmuch as there are very few inmates in the upper age categories, there are few grandmothers in the Alderson prison, and there were no grandfathers, probably because inmates in the upper age bracket rarely become studs.

Despite the differentiation of age with respect to role allocation, the concept of "birth order" is not respected by the inmates. No specification in terms of sibling placement is made—either from the point of view of age, or in terms of temporal sequence in which the inmate is inducted into a prison family. Inmates who stand in sibling relationship to one another are merely brothers and sisters. An exception in a loose sense is sometimes made, however, for inmates in their teens who tend to be allocated the role of "baby of the family." When such a distinction is made, special favors are showered on the younger sibling by all members of the family.

In addition to preserving prison marriages, the linking of inmates to one another in kinship bonds provides another important function, namely, to establish *stable* groups in the prison. Kinship ties—unlike the marriage relationships which may be terminated at will—remain stable. The significance of this fact for the inmate social system (which will become clearer in later sections) is that inmates do not go about willy-nilly forming kinship links; once kinship ties are formed they are binding in terms of primary social relations and mutual aid. The kinship ties are important in the lives of the inmates because the homosexual marriage alliance—although foremost in the lives of the inmates—is a very unstable structure. The family, on the other hand, remains a stable group to which an inmate may always turn for help in connection with any problem which may arise. Although marriage partners come and go, the family, on the other hand, remains a predictable structure of social relationships.

In this connection the application of kinship concepts both as terms of reference and as terms of address symbolize the boundaries of legitimate interaction between kinsmen. (An extended treatment of the terminology of address in the Alderson prison appears in Appendix B.) The kinship concepts provide the inmate with a formal pattern of relationships and define the social distance between her and other inmates. But the content of each kinship relationship depends upon personal feelings, felt psychological and social needs, proximity of residence, and socially defined pseudo-genealogical distance. Nevertheless, the kinship concepts systematize the social contacts of the inmates and make it possible for each inmate to place other inmates in a definite relation to her—either as acknowledged kin, that is, the in-group, or as nonrelatives who make up a vast out-group which may be exploited and from which marriage partners may legitimately be drawn.

There is a set of social relationships in the family group that are recognized and are divided into roles and a content of expectations. The formation of kinship ties among the inmates tends to establish an equilibrium point between sexual relations and casual unstable and unregulated contacts. With the exception of the husband-wife relationship cast into the form of a homosexual alliance, the other roles defined in kinship terms are rendered neutralized of sexual content. This makes it possible for an inmate in a homosexual marriage to have a variety of relations with other inmates to whom she is bound up in kinship ties. Such roles as mother, father, daughter, son, brother, sister, aunt, and uncle, for example, may be enjoyed by the inmate within the limitations set by her assumed sex role.

III

We may define the prison family as a set of inmates each of whom is linked up with all or some of the other members of the family by ties of kinship, who act together in the service of common interests indicated by reciprocal rights and duties in events such as economic crises, protection against other inmates, acting in service roles for other family members, and who act as a family unit in relation to other families or isolated inmates. Furthermore, a prison family is a group of related kin linked by ties of allegiance and alliance who sometimes occupy a common household and are characterized by varying degrees of solidarity.

The Alderson inmate community may be viewed as a large network of loosely structured nuclear families, matricentric families of varying sizes,[1] and other kinship dyadic configurations or family fragments. These are linked by filaments of kinship ties to other inmates in nuclear or matricentric families and other single kinship dyadic configurations by virtue of the fact that at least one of the family members has overlapping membership in two groups.

Because the principle of personal selection operates in the formation of kinship ties, the kinship roles do not fit neatly into direct affinal relationships of husband and wife; direct relationships of descent between parents and children; and shared descent relationships among siblings. All or some of these relationships—in a pseudo-biological sense—may be present in a family, but there is no consistency in the pattern. Kinship ties are not transitive; members of the same family may be related to inmates throughout the prison who bear no kinship relation to other members of the family. In short, the volitional aspect of kinship links results in the formation of family groups of varying size and structure.

Although it is difficult to establish rigid boundaries about any prison family because of the overlapping membership which joins individual families to the larger network of kinship ties, the nuclear family, that is, parents and children (or mother and children) is recognized by the inmates as a special unit. Social relations among nuclear family members are ideally of a primary nature with corresponding rights and duties consistent with an assumed kinship role. Particularly at the point of origin, there is a strong "we-group" feeling among the members of the nuclear family. Extra-familial relations, on the other hand, are characterized by relations of a more superficial character. In other words, the Alderson inmates who are members of nuclear families make a clear distinction between family members and relatives.

Inmates do not deliberately set out to form families of any particular size. Members are added for the reasons noted earlier. Nevertheless, there is a tendency to limit the size of the prison family. Indeed, inmates requesting membership in certain prison families are often denied entry. This is due in part to the fact that inmates wish to maintain the status and prestige of belonging to an exclusive group; and, as mentioned previously, once kinship ties are formed, they are stable and are mutually binding in terms of primary social relations and mutual aid.

IV

THE SOCIAL FUNCTIONS OF KINSHIP TIES

In many respects the constellation of ties that make up the network of kinship is conditioned to a large degree by the formative principles and values that shape the family structure in the larger society from which the inmates are drawn. The analysis of family functions usually includes at least these gross categories: economic, reproductive, socialization, recreational, protective, and affectional functions. All these functions are found in the prison family with the exception of the reproductive function. Because of the unisexual character of the inmate group the reproduction of members for the inmate society is not a function of the prison family. In a real sense, "reproduction" of new members depends upon a prison commitment—an act which is independent of the activity of the members of any prison family. Except in a symbolic sense, there are no "births" in the prison. However, it is possible to conceive of inmate commitments to the prison as "births" for the inmate social system, and in the same way, inmate releases to civil society may be looked upon as "deaths."

We have already discussed relations between husbands and wives in Chapter 9, and need not review them here. Now we turn to the social relations which obtain between inmates occupying kinship roles other than marriage. The social relations between all inmates who are members of families are made up of respect, affection, and mutual identification. One of the significant characteristics of the social relations of family members is that of social equality except in situations in which parents must exercise the duties and obligations of the parental role. The norm governing the relations of parents and children is that children owe their parents respect and parents have the right to expect children to obey them.

One of the important duties of parents is to socialize children to act in the role of inmate. The socialization function of parents does not extend to the orientation of children to proper modes of behavior for civil society. Parents socialize their children to present themselves to staff members in a conventional manner so as to secure an early parole release and not "lose days." (In one sense, all inmates who are acknowledged kin to one another perform this socialization function.) The following are maxims frequently used by parents to orient a child's behavior to inmate cultural standards and, also, to reinforce inmate norms when the necessity arises:

Keep your nose clean and stay out of trouble.

The officers are on one side and the inmates on the other and never the two shall meet. You say to them what you don't care that they know. They've got the keys. They've got a job to do. They lock doors and unlock them. They go home. They don't really care about us as people.

I tell them all like I told Betty (one of her daughters) : "There's no point in trying to fight these people. They wear the keys and you've got no win. When the ax goes down, it chops clean. No matter what happens, you're always wrong."

Give respect to an officer. Get in line when the bell rings and don't be caught in a room with a girl. Do your assignments and keep your room clean. And keep your mouth shut.

In addition to providing orienting principles to the prison staff, parents advise their children that a certain social distance should be maintained between them and inmates who are not bound up to them in kinship ties. This is stressed for general social intercourse, but parents also discourage their children from accepting aid from inmates who are not related to them so as not to incur obligations.

Don't put your business in the streets. Don't tell all the inmates your business, but act hep. You should be discreet about important matters.

Don't ask anyone for any favors and don't do anyone any favors. If you need anything, ask a member of the family. One of us should have it, and if we don't, we'll try to get it or do without. If you can't contact a member of the family and you need something immediately, use discretion that the inmate won't exploit you and always pay back immediately.

An important element in the relations of members of a group is in terms of rights and duties. Where there are rights and duties, there are corresponding rules that persons should behave in certain ways. These may be positive, prescribing actions to be performed, or they may be negative, imposing the avoidance of certain acts. Prison parents not only expect that they should be obeyed, but they expect their children to come to them with their problems; moreover, parents believe they have a corresponding duty to advise them in connection with these problems and, further, that their advice should be heeded. Parents also believe that they have the right (other close family members also claim this privilege) to voice opinions about the selection of mates. They consider it an obligation to voice objections when they feel that it is in the best interests of a child; that is, that the inmate under consideration as a potential mate is undesirable either from the point of view of character, personal habits, or the social roles played by the inmate. Parents are especially diligent in exercising this right in connection with the marriage proposals received by daughters, although their advice is not always followed. A daughter relates her experience:

(I told my father) I received a kite from —— in 22. And he said, "If I didn't have your interest at heart, I'd tell you to go ahead and come what may—and me and your mother would still stick by you. But I've been here on the Res a long time and I don't feel that this person would be good for you." And I asked him, "Why?" and he said, "The main reason is the broad is real old—old enough to be your grandmother, and she's always flagging young girls. Maybe if you and she got together, she'd be all right with you. I don't know." So I did—I went ahead and tried it out. And a few days after that the broad sent me a long commissary list, and I knew what Poppy was talking about.

The advice given by parents in connection with homosexuality is consistent with the norm prescribing legitimate marriage between inmates as the preferred sexual outlet.

Sandy comes to me for advice mostly about studs that kite her. She'll get a kite and she'll come to me and ask me, "Pop, should I write?" And I tell her, "Yes, if the guy means what he says and isn't jivey." I tell her, it's not right to go whoring around. "Pick one guy and stick to him, but don't go whoring around."

It will be recalled that homosexuality for the vast majority of inmates is the important means of doing "easy time" in the prison. However, when inmates are under a period of observation and study at the Alderson prison, parents sometimes advise these inmates not to become involved in a homosexual relationship, but rather to wait until the observation period is completed. Then if it becomes necessary for the inmate to remain in the prison, parents usually advise children to "pick one and settle down" and not to "chippy around." In short, children are admonished to establish a legitimate marriage alliance.

In addition, a rare parent will sometimes advise first offenders who have short sentences not to become involved in homosexuality during their incarceration. One inmate related that her father (who was a lesbian) gave the following advice to her and to her prison sister:

> She told us that she had lived that way for a long time, but there was no reason for us to get involved. We didn't know anything about it and she said there was no point in us getting into it. She didn't like to see anyone not in it get started. She said we were young and would be going home soon. So she advised us to just do our time and go home. She said, "I don't want to see you in it."

While parents expect obedience and respect from their children, children expect parents to satisfy their social, expressive, and protective needs:

> To help me all they can.
> Give me advice and instruct me how to handle problems that come up.
> Stick by me right or wrong.
> Talk to me when I'm blue.

Inmates take all kinds of emotional problems to parents and other kinsmen rather than to staff members. The meaning of the prison family for the inmates is revealed in the following excerpts from interviews:

> They talk to me and console me in moments of tension. They advise me for my childish ideas. They don't down me. Whatever I do, they listen. We talk it out.

> If things didn't work out right on the job, I'd come home and I wouldn't feel good. They would come to my room and talk to me and I'd feel much better. It's nice to know that if you have a problem that you can't talk to your PO about—a problem with your "people," or in your job—'cause your PO's not interested anyway, it's nice to be

able to go home and talk it over with someone who's close to you like a mother and father would be in the free world and talk it over with them. And you know they'll give you the best of advice.

We get material security from the institution—bed, room, food. Love and understanding and companionship is from the family. We turn to each other—more so, I suppose, because the staff isn't really interested in you as a person.

In addition to the emotional support provided by the family, protection of its members from the general population is another important function as it adds to the security and well-being of the inmate. As one inmate put it: "If an inmate feels like saying anything to you, they'll think twice because they know they have to say it to the whole family. It's not just to one person, but to the whole family." Obviously, the larger the size of the family to which the inmate belongs, the more protection she has against other inmates.

Apart from the direct cooperative effort expended by the members of a family for the protection of its members, each member has an obligation to provide informal reciprocal help in economic goods and services for the benefit of other family members. Family members provide mutual aid to one another in the sharing of contraband and commissary. They borrow one another's clothing. All relatives are potentially exploitative in this regard. In some families, anything that any member of the family has may be borrowed by other members. Other inmates draw the line, however, when it comes to a treasured item that cannot be replaced if lost, stolen, or destroyed. In an interview, an inmate who had several relatives throughout the prison made the following comment which reveals clearly the rights and obligations of family members in this regard:

If they need any help, I tell them to come to me before they go to someone else. If they need something to wear, I say, "Come to me first before you go to someone else." If he goes to someone else, they'll say, "The mother —— only comes when he needs something." But I expect him to come to me because I'm his brother.

As in the male prison, the negative sanctions available to the Alderson prison administrator are few. And those that are available, such as the removal of commissary or cigarette privileges, are mitigated by the cooperative structure of kinship ties. Negative sanctions of this nature imposed by the staff are not felt to be depriving by inmates in prison families, as no inmate who has kinship ties "goes without" when such privileges are removed. Even when a member of the family is removed to the seclusion unit, inmates somehow manage to get cigarettes to her. In such emergencies, however, it should be noted that she is apt to receive cooperation from close family members with whom interaction is more dense.

The Alderson inmates claim that it is possible to obtain anything on the reservation if one belongs to a family where a member is in the right position to get it. No single inmate, however, has access to *all* scarce goods and services, nor is the narrow nuclear family in a position to provide its members with all scarce goods and services. Cooperation from other inmates is absolutely essential. Obviously inmates placed in positions where they can function in the role of connect or booster are valuable family members. In point of fact, however, whatever an inmate's work assignment, upon request from a family member she is expected to assume the role of connect or booster in whatever capacity she functions—whether in the kitchen, dressmaking department, storehouse, and so on. Therefore, the additional kinship ties made by individual members are functional for all family members, as they widen the size of the group which may be exploited to provide scarce goods, information, and other services.

Because homosexuality plays a prominent role in the lives of most prisoners, family members tend to allocate the role of pinner to one another. Understandably, inmates are apt to entrust this important task to relatives rather than to other inmates. Parents often pin for children (when they live in the same cottage) and children return the favor. This is one reason why an inmate tends to establish new kinship ties soon after she moves to a new cottage. The interdependence of the inmates requires the cooperation of other inmates in order to carry out their activities successfully. In the words of an inmate:

Even if you wanted to go it alone, it's almost impossible to do. The situation is such that you need the help of other inmates. For example, if you're makin' it with someone, you need a pinner. This means initiating the aid of a third party—maybe more. And you might be called up to help two other people in the same situation . . . The way pinning works is this—maybe I've got two friends who are involved with each other. O.K., well I'll go into the office and keep the officer busy for an hour talking about a problem I have or I make one up. She can't be in two places at one time, so usually this is a safe procedure. Or a girl will stand at the foot of the stairs with a tin can in her hands. If the officer or a person known to be a snitcher goes up the stairs, she drops the can, or she whistles loudly. These signals are understood.

If the inmates are using a room on the second floor of the cottage, it becomes necessary to take added precautions when the inmates are at large. Therefore, one or two inmates are placed at the head of the stairs who stand ready to run and open the inmate's door at the sound of the signals. The reason for this is that the din created by the inmates' voices and the radio is such that signals made by the dropping of a tin can, loud whistling, or singing, would not be heard easily on the second floor. In short, the cooperation of other inmates is necessary.

The cohesion of family members is further facilitated by the fact that they tend to do many things of a recreational nature together. In the cottages one can see the family groups sitting together in the living room watching television or playing cards. Whenever possible, these inmates also attend scheduled functions together, such as movies, dances, and ball games. Inmates who are tied by kinship links but do not live in the same cottage meet at these functions and sit together. Moreover, close family members celebrate each other's birthdays with gifts and birthday cards, and other relatives tend to be remembered at Christmas.

The willingness on the part of family members to listen, advise, and counsel one another on problems, be they real or imagined, sets off this small nucleus of inmates as individuals who are "sincere," "who take an interest"—and functions in a large sense to nullify the negative effects of the woman-to-woman popular culture. Furthermore, relating economic, service, socialization, affective, supportive, and protective functions to members of the family serves to create an exclusive group—excluding both staff members and other inmates. This increases the interaction among kin members as well as the interdependence of these inmates upon one another, thus sustaining relations of solidarity among the members of the family group.

This is not to say, however, that all is bliss within any prison family circle. Arguments and fights abound: inmates may feel that other members are taking advantage of them economically, or that they are not living up to their obligations in other areas. In addition, the divorce of a family member may create discord among the members of a family, particularly if other members are bound up in "respect" or other kinship links to the inmate who is being displaced. Under any of these circumstances, relations within the family may be strained. Nevertheless, the kinship ties (other than marriage) remain stable, although the nature of the social relations obtaining between inmates in kinship status may be strained for a time.

The stability of kinship ties is further facilitated by incest regulations. The Alderson inmates have placed rigid boundaries around those social categories which lie outside the range of legitimate sexual exploitation, so as not to disturb intrafamilial harmony and cooperation.

Marriage is not permitted between inmates who stand to one another in an acknowledged kinship relation. And this category includes "respect" relationships as well. Homosexual relations between inmates who stand in kinship relationship are considered misconduct and are classified as incestuous behavior. The important point is that the restriction includes everyone within the inmate's field of social relationships that she *acknowledges* as kin. Kinship thus becomes a device for openly declaring one or more persons sexually and maritally out of bounds.

The inmate community ridicules inmates who marry individuals to whom they stand in kinship relation. To illustrate the values of the inmates in this regard: One inmate assuming the role of father confided to me that her daughter had suggested that they assume a homosexual marriage when the inmate who was respectively wife and mother to them was released. The father patiently explained that, "It couldn't be—it wasn't right." And no amount of pleading on the part of the daughter could sway the father. Another inmate, during a discussion of her family, said that she was physically attracted to her father and the thought of transforming their relationship to one of husband and wife had occurred to her a number of times. When asked if she had broached the subject to her father, she replied that she had not because she feared it might strain their relationship severely. Moreover, to accuse inmates in kinship status of homosexual relations has been known to lead to violence if the accusing inmate does not retract the charge.

Although the husband-wife relationship may be transformed into a brother-sister relationship as a result of divorce to sustain continued relations of solidarity between them, it is considered shameful for the reverse process to occur. Divorced inmates who transform their relationship to one of sibling status have been known to resume a marriage relationship at a later point in time; this does not occur frequently, and when it does the inmates joke about it and treat it with amusement. However, it is not considered shameful because their first kinship tie was that of marriage.

As in every society, incest occurs in the Alderson inmate community. Nevertheless it is an infrequent phenomenon. During my field work, I knew of only one case of incest, and this occurred between an uncle and niece. The habits, attitudes, and organization of civil society with respect to incest are carried over into the prison world and provide internal barriers to incest for all but a very few inmates. Once the relationship between inmates is socially defined as one of kinship, incest is incompatible with the cooperative and affective structure of the prison family.

V

The informal family group structure has important consequences for the type of leadership and power structure which emerges among the Alderson inmates. Leadership is widely diffused because it is inextricably bound up with the prison family structure. Leadership is defined here as a social process in which a person (or persons) organizes and directs the interests and activities of a person, or group, or persons, through securing and maintaining their more or less voluntary approval of the goals of the community.

The extent to which any inmate can exercise control or influence another inmate depends largely upon the family role that the inmate assumes. As is now apparent to the reader, the parents (or parent) have a large measure of power and influence in the nuclear family. Authority is largely and importantly vested in the parental role. When the members of a family all live in the same cottage, the parents are the undisputed leaders of the group, but each family member has much to say about the behavior of other family members. However, a decrease in interaction between parents and other family members tends to decrease the authority of the parents. Children tend to form new kinship ties after moving to another cottage, and these kinship bonds become the important ones while the inmate lives there.

Any family member, however, may exercise influence over another member in some circumstances. A parent, for instance, may allocate functions of authority to one of her children concerning another child whose behavior warrants closer supervision —that is, who may "lose days." Although aunts and uncles (and most grandmothers) usually act as buffers between children and parents, it is also possible for these inmates to have considerable influence over any member of the family. When authority is legitimately delegated to an "older" inmate in the family, other family members accept criticism from her with much grace, as they feel she is "taking an interest" and "doing it for their own good."

Apart from the authority vested in the parental role, each stud in the prison is a leader of sorts. As soon as a femme forms a marriage alliance, the leadership role of her parents (or other family members) is immediately diluted and passes over to her husband. Femmes obtain approval from their studs about the most trivial matters. Certainly it is inconceivable that a femme would take any action of an important nature without obtaining approval from her husband.

The structures of family, marriage, and kinship are functionally interrelated to foster integration of the inmate social system by reconciling competing and conflicting social motives. But by forming exclusive family groups and by relating all meaningful interaction and functions to those inmates who are linked by kinship bonds, the Alderson inmates have in effect created a social structure which deters the possibility of a leadership emerging that could unite the many prison families. Causes which would require a united inmate body are not likely to meet with success in the Alderson inmate community. *Paradoxically, the kinship network which integrates the inmates by intimate social bonds and serves to maintain the internal equilibrium of the inmate social system is the very structure which also functions to keep the inmates forever divided into small family units.*

VI

Having made these general remarks, I now wish to direct attention to examples of prison families. The role structure of two family groups will be discussed, and features of role change will be pointed out to illustrate how the internal structure of a prison family may change over time as a result of cottage moves, sex role change, marriage, and inmate releases. These families have been selected for illustration because they have several features which distinguish them from families in civil society. At the same time, the other characteristics of these family groups are typical of all other prison families.

It was possible to obtain data on a number of prison families; the number of inmates included in these prison families total two hundred and seven inmates and span all the residential units. With the exception of sixteen inmates, they all link up in kinship ties in an interlacing network of kinship relationships.[2] Because this kinship role structure includes a large proportion of the inmate population, numbers instead of names have been assigned to the inmates in order to ensure their anonymity. (See Figure 2 and Figure 3.)

FAMILY WITH PARENTS LINKED BY SIBLING TIES

The inmate kinship network is a composite structure made up of many nuclear families, matricentric families, and family fragments or kinship role syndromes. The inmate family groups vary in size from two members to as many as fifteen members. The family group that social scientists refer to as the nuclear family is based upon criteria of sex and generation and consists of eight roles: husband, wife, father, mother, son, daughter, brother, and sister. Some family groups in the Alderson prison exhibit all of these roles.

One family group at the prison, however, was unique in that the parents were not married to one another; instead their relationship was that of siblings. The role structure is charted in Figure 2. Inmates may form kinship ties anywhere in the prison. This family had its initial beginning a few months before the study began in the orientation unit with Inmates 183, 20, 83, and 186. It will be noted that Inmates 183 and 20 are brother and sister to one another, yet they are parents to Inmates 83 and 186. The structuring of the sibling relationship between the parents is largely due to the fact that Inmate 183 is influenced by religious principles regarding homosexual behavior, although she is by no means a square in the eyes of the inmates.[3] The sex role of Inmate 20 was determined by the fact that she is a lesbian and assumes a male role in homosexual relations.

Alderson prison families are not increased by births nor are they decreased by deaths.[4] Rather they grow in size by *accretion* and are decreased by the release of family members from the prison. Hence prison families vary in size from one time period to another. The family under discussion, for example, began to add to its membership while the four members were still in the orientation unit. The father, Inmate 20, saw Inmate 185 walking by the orientation building, was physically attracted to her, made the inquiries pertinent to such interest, and before Inmate 20 had moved from the orientation unit arrangements had been completed between them for a marriage alliance. Before this relationship could be assumed, however, Inmate 185 had to divorce her marriage partner; furthermore, she had to "drop the belt," that is, switch from a male sex role to a female sex role in order to marry Inmate 20.

It is pertinent to ask whether Inmate 20's marriage changed the structure of the family. Interestingly, it did not. Inmate 183 continued to function in the role of mother—which we would expect because of the principle of personal selection in the formation of kinship ties. Indeed, although Inmate 185 was usually present when problems of the family were discussed by Inmates 20, 183, 83, and 186, she did not figure importantly

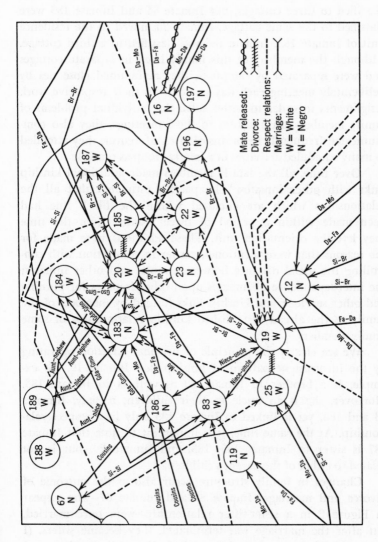

FIGURE 2 FAMILY WITH PARENTS LINKED BY SIBLING TIES

in these discussions. Her presence was due to the fact that she was a relative marked by respect.

After the orientation period of these inmates, they were classified to three cottages, but Inmate 83 and Inmate 183 were classified to the same cottage. Inmate 20 moved to the residence unit of Inmate 185. Inmate 186 was classified to a third cottage. Although the members of this family lived in separate cottages and were separated by campuses, they maintained close ties by deliberately meeting each day en route to their respective work assignments in order to better solve the individual problems of family members. In addition to these meetings, they also communicated frequently by means of kites. Moreover, they attended as many scheduled activities in a family group as possible.

Over time, all the family members made additional kinship links with other inmates. The parents estimated that all the relationships which are enclosed within the black line had been made within a period of three months from the time they left the orientation unit. These additions were made for the reasons that were mentioned earlier in connection with controlling the social distance between couples and other inmates; the interdependence of inmates upon other inmates for pinning and other services; and kinship links formed by members of the family to the already established kinship relationships of some family members.

We see clearly the principle of personal selection operating by the inconsistent pattern of kinship ties. Inmate 19, for example, is a brother to Inmate 20 as well as to Inmate 183. Moreover, she is an uncle to their children, namely, Inmates 83 and 186, yet is linked to Inmate 185 only in a respect relationship. At the same time, it is important to note that Inmate 187 is sister to Inmates 185, 183, and Inmate 20, but is not related to either of the parent's children.

Changes in family structure occur also as the outcome of divorce and marriage. Inmate 83 and Inmate 67—who appear in Figure 2 in a sister-sister relationship—were once married, but after the marriage was terminated, they became sisters. (I have simplified the chart by not including this marriage and divorce, as it occurred long before the study began.) Usually a brother-sister relationship is the outcome of divorce, but Inmate

67 "dropped the belt" to marry a stud, which explains the homologous sex kin relationship at the termination of marriage between Inmates 67 and 83.

Approximately one year after the nuclear family began, Inmate 83 switched from the female to the male role and married Inmate 119. All the inmates appearing in Figure 2 who were in kinship status vis-à-vis Inmate 83, with the exception of Inmates 187 and 186, were still at the prison when this change in sex role took place. Presumably, a change in sex role for a member of the family would affect the structure of the family. In this particular group, all members of the family acknowledged the change in sex role—and made the necessary adjustments as far as kinship ties were concerned—with the exception of the mother. Inmate 183 continued to acknowledge Inmate 83 as a daughter. (The reason for this may be because Inmate 183 has a daughter of approximately the same age in civil society, and this relationship may represent *substitute role comformity* for her in the prison setting.) The upshot of this was that Inmate 83 continued in the role of daughter in her interactions with Inmate 183, but acted out the role of male in other relationships. It is rare for an inmate to function in two sex roles. When a change in sex role takes place for one of the family members, other relatives acknowledge it and make the necessary adjustments. It is accepted as one of the facts of prison life. A change in sex role does not alter the fact that inmates tied in kinship links still desire the benefits which accrue from membership in a family group. Hence kinship ties among the Alderson inmates tend to be very stable. Once a kinship tie is formed between inmates, it usually lasts throughout the inmate's prison career, despite the fact that the inmate may change her sex role. And as we shall see in the next example, changes in residential arrangements result in decreased interaction and may affect the nature of social relations between inmates linked in kinship bonds; nevertheless, the kinship tie is still acknowledged.

A few comments should be made about the fall out between Inmate 20 and Inmate 185 which appears in Figure 2. This marriage actually lasted for over a year, which would clearly classify it as a sincere relationship in the eyes of the inmates. About one month before Inmate 185 was to be released from the prison, Inmate 20 divorced Inmate 185 to marry Inmate 16. How do members of a family react to divorce? Does divorce change the structure of the family? Reactions tend to vary from one family to another depending upon the nature of the social relations obtaining among the inmates. The social relations of the members of this prison family were warm and close. It was a tightly knit group. Therefore, Inmate 20 discussed the impending divorce with all the family members and requested that they accept Inmate 16 as a member of the family. Inmate 83 exhibited little reaction to the divorce, as she acknowledged Inmate 185 only in a loose respect sense "because of Papa ——." From her point of view, the family only consisted "really" of Inmates 20, 183, 186, and 83. (Inmate 186 had been released from the prison.) However, all other inmates who were tied in respect and other kinship ties to Inmate 185 bitterly resented the divorce and opposed it. They refused to accept Inmate 16 as a member of the family. Furthermore they pointed out that Inmate 185 would be released in a month's time and such action was unthinkable. Inmate 183 pointed out that she had "done time" with Inmate 16 in another institution: that Inmate 16 was "cheap and common," that Inmate 20 "was too good for her," that she wasn't the "type" to include as "family."

The marriage relationship, however, is foremost for the vast majority of inmates, and the opposition of family members usually does not have sufficient strength to prevent a change of marriage partners. Inmate 20 summed it up in this way:

They (the family) resent —— (Inmate 16) and my breaking up, but these things happen. I talked to all of them. I said, "Look, I'm grown and family relations can only go so far. If you brought a donkey home, I'd love it, and my feelings for *you* wouldn't change!" They'll get over it. (*short pause*) They'll get over it. It'll take a little time.

As soon as the fall out was final, Inmate 185 moved out of Inmate 20's cottage, and the entire family ostracized Inmates 20 and 16. For a time the relations of the family with these inmates were strained. Yet by the time the study ended, all the family members with the exception of Inmate 183 had attached themselves to Inmate 16 by respect relationships. This marriage broadened the structure of the family group under discussion.

We see clearly by the filaments of kinship linkage trailing away from Inmate 16 how the marriage of two inmates can link up a number of inmates by the overlapping membership of an inmate in two family structures.

A few other comments about the structure of this family must be made as they were characteristic of many other prison families. This family group is not only racially integrated, but it also spans several cottages. For example, Inmates 20, 185, 23, 196, 22, and 197 lived in the same cottage. On the same campus, but in different cottages, lived Inmates 19, 25, and 187. These inmates were joined at a later time by Inmate 183, who had been classified to the other campus out of orientation. For a time, Inmates 183 and 83 lived in the same cottage, but Inmate 83 moved to Inmate 67's cottage when these inmates became married. This move was consistent with the cultural prescription that the femme moves to the stud's cottage. Inmate 184, who acted in the role of grandmother to the members of the nuclear family (and served as a court of final appeal for the parents when they felt they could not cope with their children's problems), lived on the same campus as most of the family members did, but in a different cottage. Note that Inmate 184 is simply "grandmother" to all members of the nuclear family. No distinction is made between the parents and children. In sum, it is easily possible for these inmates to have intimate and frequent interaction and to provide one another with services when the need arises.

FAMILY WITHOUT IN-LAW RELATIONSHIPS

All families that contain couples do not necessarily acknowledge respect or in-law kinship ties. The evidence suggests that when the group is small and is isolated from other inmates, the bonds of kinship formed by the inmates are those of the primary family for *all* inmates. No distinctions are made for marriage partners. This would suggest that the greater the social and physical distance of the group from other individuals, the more intimate, dense, and interdependent the interaction. Hence the kinship relationships are defined more closely in order to preserve the stability and structure of the family.

A family made up only of nuclear kinship ties is shown in Figure 3. This family lived in the dairy cottage about a mile from the main reservation. The inmates assigned to this cottage all work at the dairy. If their work assignment is changed, they must move to the main reservation.

In Figure 3, we see that Inmates 26 and 27 are the parents in this family and they are linked by a marriage tie. Inmates 143 and 44 are also linked by marriage. For the present discussion we ignore the divorce between these inmates (indicated by the lines cutting through the horizontal bar) which occurred at a later time. Another couple is made up of Inmate 45 and Inmate 46. As is apparent from the chart, no in-law relationships are observed in this family. The ties are all those of the nuclear family, with no distinctions made for marriage partners. Inmate 28 is a son to Inmates 26 and 27, and stands in sibling relationships to the other inmates [5]—again, all ties of the nuclear family.

We saw in the preceding example that the structure of a family may be changed by divorce or sex role change. In addition, the departure of inmates from the family circle resulting from cottage moves and prison releases also importantly influences the social relationships among family members and the structure of the family unit. The family under discussion, for example, continued as a stable structure for several months until Inmate 27, the father, was released from the prison. The departure of this inmate, however, precipitated a number of further changes in the structure of the family. Shortly after Inmate 27 was released, Inmate 26, the mother, moved to the main reservation because of a change in work assignment. Shortly thereafter, Inmate 28 moved to the same cottage as her mother. The other family members, however, remained behind.

After Inmate 26 moved to the main reservation, she acquired a number of other kinship ties at different points in time—in her words, "a new family." The kinship links formed by Inmate 26 after the cottage move are shown in Figure 3 by the trailing lines. Inmate 28 formed her own independent ties with other inmates, but over time these were linked up to Inmate 26. The reasons for the formation of kinship links have been dealt with in detail earlier, and they need not be repeated here. As stated previously, once kinship ties (apart from those of

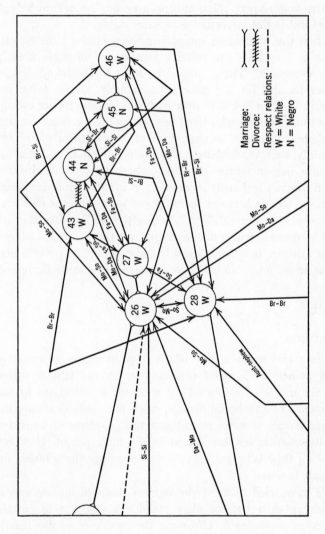

FIGURE 3   FAMILY WITHOUT IN-LAW RELATIONSHIPS

marriage) are formed they are rarely terminated. Adjustments are made for changes in sex role structure, but the kinship link is still acknowledged. Divorce may strain the relations in a family, and respect relationships may not be acknowledged, but the kinship link nevertheless remains stable.

When the immediate interdependence of the inmates who are kin is decreased, the relative importance of these kinship ties is decreased. Thus, although Inmate 26 acknowledged "another family" on the reservation, namely, at the dairy, her important kinship ties were now with the inmates in her cottage unit or those inmates who lived in cottages on the same campus. Nevertheless, meetings between Inmate 26 and members of her first family were marked by a display of affection and the use of kinship nomenclature. However, when the physical distance between inmates is sharply increased and interaction is decreased, the social relations between them appear to take on the character and tone of "distant relatives." Actually, such inmates are still bound by mutual bonds of sentiment and the reciprocal obligations of kinship, but the leadership function of the parents may decrease when interaction between inmates is sharply decreased.

VII

CONCLUSION

The social spheres into which kinship enters as an articulating principle of social organization in the female prison world are inextricably bound up with the deprivations of imprisonment. The informal system which has evolved among the Alderson female inmates to mitigate the problems of imprisonment, however, is notably absent in the male prison. How can we explain this? Why are kinship and marriage the solution for the female inmates?

We have tried to show throughout that the inmate society and culture exist because they provide a solution to certain problems of adjustment. However, the problems of the female and male inmates arise out of very different circumstances—the differences in the cultural definitions ascribed to their respective roles as male or female. As a result, male and female prisoners seek different solutions in the prison world. They seek solutions that will not endanger their identification as essentially male or female, and that are consistent with their sex role and the distinctive patterns of behavior attached to it.

In the beginning of this study, we pointed out that cultural expectations of male and female roles in American society are seen to differentiate along several crucial axes. The cultural definition of the female role in American society is oriented to that of wife and mother. The male, however, is expected to prepare for an occupational role, and his prestige rank is established by the nature of his life work. From an early age, the male is oriented *outward* to the market place, to the world of affairs rather than to the home. The life goal of the female, however, is achieved through marriage and child-rearing. From an early age, the female is oriented *inward* to the home, and it is in the role of wife and mother that she derives prestige and status. Indeed the status, security, and self-image of the American female depends in large measure upon the kinds of relationships she establishes with the opposite sex.

The family group in the female prison is singularly suited to meet the internalized cultural expectations of the female role. It serves the social, psychological, and physiological needs of the female inmates. These interrelated needs arise mainly from three sources:

1. The individual's dependence and status needs based upon cultural expectations of the female role.

2. The individual's needs which arise from residing within the prison; and the inability of the formal organization to supply the female inmate's need for emotional reciprocity.

3. Needs related to the individual's personality.

The complex series of social relationships formed on the basis of marriage and kinship make it possible for the female inmates to engage in a wide range of satisfying relations. Indeed, the prison world of the Alderson inmates is a functional *substitute* to resolve the female's sense of isolation within the formal organization. The prison homosexual marriage alliance and the larger informal family groupings provide structures wherein the female inmate's needs may find fulfillment and expression during the period of incarceration. Kinship and marriage ties make it possible for the inmates to ascribe and achieve social statuses and personalities in the prison other than that of inmate which are consistent with the cultural expectations of the female role in American society.

The cultural orientation of males, however, precludes legitimate marriage and family groupings as a feasible alternative solution for the male prisoners, as the serious adoption of a female role is contrary to the definition of the male role as masculine. It is noteworthy that in the male prison the fags and punks are both held in derision by the vast majority of male inmates, as it is felt that they have sacrificed their manhood, but the homosexuality of wolves is looked upon as a temporary adjustment to sexual tensions generated by the prison setting. The absence of sentiment and the aggressive behavior of the wolf is consistent with the cultural definition of the masculine role, and thus homosexuality in the prison loses the taint of femininity that male homosexuality tends to carry in civil society. In addition, the cultural orientation of the male role with respect to demonstrations of affection toward another member of the same sex clearly precludes the adoption of legitimate feminine roles by male inmates in informal kinship groupings such as those found among the female inmates. The ease with which women may demonstrate affection, both verbally and physically, toward members of the same sex perhaps may provide a *predisposition* to widespread homosexuality and its ready acceptance under the extreme conditions of isolation in the prison setting. This fact alone however is not enough to account for the emergence of the female inmate social system.

The remarkable difference in *structural form* between the female prison system and that which emerges in the adult male prison suggests that functional theory does not provide an adequate explanation of the genesis of inmate prison culture. The interpretation given for the emergence of the inmate social system in the male prison by current functional theory asserts that inmate society assumes its form in the male prison because it reflects a response to the *conditions* of imprisonment: It is a response to the deprivations of imprisonment.[6]

Yet as we have seen, although the deprivations of imprisonment are present in the Alderson prison and are felt keenly by the female inmates, the typical inmate cultural system which emerges in the male prison is not present in the Alderson female prison. Hence the differences in structural form found in the female and male prison communities are inadequately explained by current functional theory as solely a response to the deprivations of imprisonment.

The deprivations of imprisonment may provide necessary conditions for the emergence of an inmate system, but our findings clearly indicate that the deprivations of imprisonment in themselves are not sufficient to account for the form that the inmate social structure assumes in the male and female prison communities. Rather, general features of American society with respect to the cultural definition and content of male and female roles are brought into the prison setting and function to determine the direction and focus of the inmate cultural systems.

These general features are those concerned with first, the orientation of life goals for males and females; second, cultural definitions with respect to dimensions of passivity and aggression; third, acceptability of public expressions of affection displayed toward a member of the same sex; and finally, perception of the same sex with respect to what I have called the popular culture. If my analysis is sound, it would seem that there is greater unity between the inner and outer worlds than has heretofore been thought. Greater understanding of the prison communities, then, may best be accomplished by focusing attention on the relationship of the external and internal cultures rather than by trying to understand the prison as an institution isolated from the larger society.

NOTES

1. A family rarely begins as a "patricentric" family. Two inmates assuming male roles usually become brothers.

2. It is extremely difficult to say whether nor not these inmates are actually isolates. Other data seem to point out that some inmates form rudimentary kinship ties such as a sister-sister relationship at the beginning of their prison career—often in the orientation unit. Over time, however, as inmates make new acquaintances they tend to form

additional kinship ties with other inmates which link them to the larger kinship structure. It may be that I simply did not obtain the information that would have linked them to the larger kinship structure. Perhaps they had a single link, and the inmate was released; or perhaps no link exists.

3. A short time before the study ended, however, Inmate 183 participated for the first time in a homosexual relationship. She assumed the stud role.

4. Deaths do occur at the prison, but they are so rare that they do not warrant serious consideration in this context.

5. It was not until Inmate 28 moved to the main campus that she became linked up in a marriage tie.

6. It should be pointed out that Irwin and Cressey have advanced the thesis that there are three subcultures in the prison that reflect the presence of different types of prisoners. These differences presumably are a reflection of the values and attitudes particular inmates bring into the prison and are related to latent identities. See John Irwin and Donald R. Cressey, "Thieves, Convicts, and the Inmate Culture," *Social Problems,* Vol. 10, Fall, 1962, pp. 142–155. Similarly, Schrag attempts to account for inmate deviants with respect to internalization of inmate culture and support of the inmate code in terms of their pre-prison characteristics and identities. See Clarence Schrag, "Some Foundations of a Theory of Correction," in Donald R. Cressey, Editor, *The Prison: Studies in Institutional Organization and Change,* New York: Holt, Rinehart and Winston, 1961, pp. 309–357. Schrag's analysis, however, remains unclear, for at one point he comments: "Juxtaposed with the official organization of the prison is an unofficial social system originating within the institution and regulating inmate conduct with respect to focal issues, such as length of sentence, relations among prisoners, contacts with staff members and other civilians, food, sex, and health, among other things." (p. 342) This suggests that all inmates face a number of common problems of adjustment as a result of incarceration and that social organization develops to provide solutions. Moreover, Roebuck has pointed out that Irwin and Cressey do not demonstrate that their three subculture groups share learned behaviors which are common and peculiar to them in or out of prison. See Julian Roebuck, "A Critique of 'Thieves, Convicts, and the Inmate Culture,'" *Social Problems,* Vol. 11, Fall, 1963, pp. 193–200. Nevertheless, these scholars have called attention to the important thesis that the behavior patterning of inmates may be influenced by social identities and cultural backgrounds.

APPENDIX A THE METHOD OF THE STUDY

To analyze a community as a system of roles and functions is by no means an easy task. For the careful observer, the continuity of events is the important aspect. It is necessary, therefore, to examine the structure over a considerable length of time. The data for this study were gathered over a period of one year from July, 1962, to July, 1963.

For the theoretical reasons pointed out in Chapter 1, the study constituted a frank recognition of the necessity to investigate the social situation of the female prison as an exploratory effort. It seemed apparent that what was needed in investigating the women's prison—at this stage of our knowledge—was flexibility of approach and extensive study of the social structure. It appeared more fruitful to conduct an exploratory or formulative study in order to formulate specifically the content of the inmate value system and the over-all organization of the prison.

In this connection, I think it important to call attention to the rationale which invariably guides exploratory studies. Whether or not a researcher proceeds from a set of interrelated hypotheses depends upon the nature of the problem and the extent to which the problem area has been empirically studied. In view of the lack of available data, to have begun the study with a set of interrelated hypotheses would have been understandably premature: For without some knowledge of the scope of the area, of the major social variables influencing the inmate social system, any hypotheses set forth would be trivial. Moreover, the precise testing of hypotheses generally presumes that the researcher knows the relevant variables under investigation, since without this knowledge it would be difficult to establish adequate experimental controls.

This is by no means to say, however, that a carefully thought-out study does not have definitely formulated objectives in the absence of hypotheses which are formulated at the outset. These concerns have been stated in Chapter 1 and need not be repeated here. In terms of the goals of the research, however, they rest upon the following assumptions:

1. A study of a small community will provide an opportunity for better understanding of how men live in all groups, regardless of time or place.

2. Careful observation by a researcher who enters the group naturally without disrupting its usual behavior patterns and who carries on these observations systematically over a period of time yields the most accurate data.

3. The meaningfulness of prison life and its consequences upon inmates and staff members cannot be revealed by examination of the formal structure of the objectives of a penal system.

4. There exists in the female institution, by inference from the study of male institutions, an informal pattern of life.

5. It is possible to compare the findings of both female and male prison structures and to establish social and personal types of behavior sequences and processes.

II

To increase the depth and scope of his understanding of the social unit under examination, it is necessary that the scientist utilize whatever techniques may be empirically appropriate. Records, for example, yield useful information about the formal rules of an organization and the sociological characteristics of the population. On the other hand, if one wishes to obtain information about beliefs and attitudes, the questionnaire is an appropriate method. For the study of behavior in natural settings, participant observation, or participant-as-observer as it is sometimes called, is particularly appropriate as a method of data collection.

The participant-as-observer method is especially appropriate in exploratory studies because it affords the greatest opportunity to discover what things are of importance to the people being studied and to follow up the interconnections of these phenomena. It allows the researcher to revise and reformulate the models which develop out of the data collection by furnishing instances of phenomena which are not included initially, and compels the scientist to search the field for further evidence on new problems. The most important sources of data collection in connection with the inmate social system were obtained by this method. It would have been impossible to uncover the content of the female inmate social system otherwise.

The task the researcher set is as follows: first, to gather data by participating in the daily life of the group, by personal observation of the inmates as they participated in formal inmate activities. To this end, I observed the inmates at their work assignments, attended vocational and avocational classes, group counseling sessions, academic education classes, and visited the orientation unit. I went to the movies which were held for the inmates, dances, baseball games, religious services, and all other formally scheduled functions for inmates to see what situations the inmates met and how they behaved in them for the purposes of assessing the meaning of these activities for the formal and informal organization. At all inmate functions, I sat with the inmates. In addition, I engaged in personal observation of informal interaction patterns in the cottage units and on the grounds. Casual and unstructured conversations were the sources of data collection to discover the interpretation of the events observed and the value structure of the group.

The researcher's aim, then, was to study and record social data in the field as comprehensively as possible, exploring each significant and related fact as it was uncovered. In each situation, therefore, even in the case of what appeared to be a familiar situation, the observer asked: What meaning does the observed group attach to it? The reason underlying this approach is important and should not be overlooked. It is essential that the meaning and the consequences of the phenomena in the life of the inmates be understood in order to gain insight into the following: First, the nature of the cultural experiences and activities of the group; second, the meaning of these experiences and the social values attached to them; and finally, the informal social system which is a result of group experience.

The sociological characteristics of the inmate population were obtained by an examination of the record files of 653 inmates who were confined at the same time.

The third segment of data were obtained by informal interviews with correctional officers, other staff members, and prison administrators. In addition, a questionnaire was administered to the correctional officers in small group sessions over a period of one week at the end of the study to obtain data on the sociological characteristics of the correctional officers and perceptions of their role functions.

III

A number of scholars in the field have given their attention to the difficulty of obtaining data in penal institutions from inmates and to the importance of maintaining one's neutrality. To eliminate possible identification with the staff, the researcher did not live on the institution grounds. However, I visited the physical plant daily from the beginning of the day's activities to the end of the day, or from about eight o'clock in the morning to approximately ten o'clock in the evening. During the first six months of the study I was at the prison almost every day of the week. However, I made a special effort during this period to make my behavior unpredictable both to inmates and staff. From time to time, I would arrive at odd hours, or leave the prison during the day for an hour or so, in order to dissociate my role from that of the inmates and staff. Insofar as it was possible for me to do so without actually living in a cottage, I tried to approximate the living existence of the inmate.

The study was introduced to the staff and inmates by a memorandum signed by the warden of the prison. The memorandum was addressed to both staff members and inmates and stated that the investigator was a social scientist from Northwestern University, and would be at the prison for a year for the purpose of making a scientific study of "institutional living." (I had chosen this term as it was vague and broad enough to include all things.) The cooperation of staff and inmates was urged and the confidentiality of all interviews was stressed. A copy of the memorandum was given to each staff member, and one copy was placed on each of the cottage bulletin boards.

As far as the staff is concerned, this method of introducing the study posed no problems, and informal conversations with staff members sufficed to answer any questions staff members had regarding the study.

After a couple of days at the prison, however, I discovered that inmates rarely read notices placed on the cottage bulletin boards. Matters which are considered to be important by the administration are read aloud to the inmates by the correctional officers. Therefore, I abandoned my original plan of spending the entire first week or two in the Record Office reading each inmate's case history and collecting data on the sociological characteristics of the inmate population, and instead proceeded to introduce the study personally to the inmate body. Hence the better part of the first two weeks was spent walking about the prison grounds, joining groups of inmates on the field, in front of the cottages, or on the cottage porches. I would begin, "Hello, we haven't met . . ." The inmates raised no objections when they were asked if I might join them, but they were extremely suspicious of my presence at the prison. Everyone's presence in the prison structure must be justified—one is either part of the staff or part of the inmate body. And the researcher in the prison setting is neither fish nor fowl.

Visitors from the outside world are rare. Individuals visiting inmates are brought directly to the visiting room by car from the gate, and they leave the same way; therefore, the general inmate body does not see them. Other visitors are escorted through the garment shop, vocational building and school building, certain cottages by the warden or associate warden. They do not, however, walk freely about the prison grounds talking to the inmates.

The researcher's role required clarification. All the inmates I met during the first week raised these questions without exception: "Where do you live?" "Do you live on the reservation?" I explained that I lived "in town." If they had any doubts (and some inmates did), it soon became apparent to the inmates that I did not live on the institutional grounds. Had I done so, there is no doubt that it would seriously have hampered the study, as it would have identified me with the staff.

The next questions which seemed to be of vital concern to the inmates were how I entered the prison and who was paying for the research. "How come they let you in?" "Other people have tried to get in here and couldn't." "Who's paying for all this?" "Where's the money coming from?" "Are you a reporter?" "Are you from the FBI?" I assured the inmates that I was not a reporter, nor was I from the FBI. I explained that I was a sociologist; university affiliation and sponsorship and the scientific nature of the study were stressed. All this, however, still tended to leave the inmates skeptical, and they said they would have to take my word for it. "How do we know you're not lying?" they insisted. There are no quick and ready answers to such objections, and I found myself simply repeating the same statements which had made the inmates skeptical in the first place. After this, I began to carry with me the Northwestern University Dental School Bulletin which listed me as a lecturer in sociology. While faculty listing did not, of course, "prove" my identity, I found it helpful and to be sufficient evidence for most inmates during this early and crucial stage of the research. The researcher's role-playing in the research setting is important for the kinds of responses he is able to obtain. Equally important, however, is the role which is assigned to the researcher by the informant; and this role will be based largely upon the informant's conception of the researcher's group affiliations. University affiliation and sponsorship gave the research a neutral character.

The inmates often asked what "good" the study would do. To the original classification of the study as one concerned with "institutional living," I added verbally that the purpose was to "help women in trouble everywhere." However, it was emphasized that participation in the research would in no way mitigate the inmate's sentence, nor would it increase her chances for parole. It was made clear that the inmate would not receive any direct benefit from the study. At the same time, however, it was pointed out that participation would not be harmful to the inmate. In all instances, the scientific nature of the research was emphasized.

Approximately one to three hours were usually spent with each group of inmates or isolated inmates in idle and friendly conversation about general prison life. During the first three weeks, I met about one-fourth of the inmates in this way. Care was taken not to raise questions about the inmate's informal structure, although the inmates introduced many issues and topics which they discussed among themselves and which provided many clues and orientation for later interviews. When I left each group (or inmate) I thanked them for talking with me and asked if I might come to visit them in their cottage units sometime during the year. I had expected some refusals; none of the inmates refused, although a few inmates said that I could come but that they had "nothing to say." During the entire year, one recently committed inmate refused the observer an interview and this was about four months before the study ended.

Looking back, I think this time was very well spent. At the outset, attention was directed solely to developing rapport with the inmates. I did not pressure them with questions, and I began to establish very early a viable place for myself in the prison. As a result, I was not unduly tested. However, I was put through a few trials during the first two months, particularly in connection with contraband which inmates claimed (whether true or not I do not know) they had hidden somewhere in their rooms. Inmates stole food and pots of coffee from the dining room in my presence, and made certain that they called it to my attention in some way. After I was accepted by the inmates, however, my presence was ignored in the same way that the presence of an inmate known to be loyal to the inmate group would be ignored.

During this early period, two inmates asked me to do them "favors." One inmate asked me to mail a letter to her husband, as she claimed she had not received any mail from him and she was certain her mail was not "going out." I refused politely and firmly, but in no uncertain terms, and said that the only material I took out of the prison was material for my research and that I would bring nothing into the prison. A short time after this, another inmate asked me if I would bring her in a certain magazine. She received the identical explanation I had given the other inmate. Neither inmate showed any resentment. After this I never received any requests for "favors."

Inmates also tested me in the beginning concerning the confidentiality of the responses. They would say, "I suppose the other inmates have told you this"; "I saw you talking to —— the other day. Did she say . . . ?" and "Have the other girls told you the same thing?" To questions of this nature, I gave the stock answer: "All interviews are confidential."

When I interviewed inmates for the first time, I always prefaced each session with remarks about the scientific nature of the study and the confidentiality of the interview, and also stressed the fact that the inmate's participation was voluntary. In connection with the latter, it was pointed out that it was the inmate's privilege to refuse to answer any questions which might be directed at her. This clearly established that the researcher did not stand in an authoritarian position to the inmates and eliminated serious questions of reliability and validity in connection with responses. In the early interviews there was a reluctance on the part of some inmates, or an expressed preference not to answer questions, particularly in connection with their homosexual activities. In these instances, I immediately dropped the subject and made no attempt to elicit responses to the original questions. The same inmate, however, was interviewed one or two more times at a later date.

When inmates made statements about prison life, I asked them to describe a situation which was related to the point under discussion, but asked them not to mention names—either those of the staff or inmates. Inmates were often eager to mention names of the staff; when they did, I reminded them that it was not necessary to mention names. This procedure did much to eliminate fear on the part of the inmates that anyone would be reported and that I was "checking up" on any particular inmates.

After three months at the prison, my prefatory remarks, namely, that the inmate's participation was voluntary and that the inmate was free to refuse to answer questions were waved aside with: "It's O.K., you can ask." "I heard you don't say anything." "Inmate —— said if you had told what she said, she'd be up in seclusion," and the like. The crucial factor in prison research is the investigator's daily conduct.

After approximately four months at the prison, old timers would describe me to new inmates, "She's no cop. You can answer her questions." Another index of my acceptability was that whenever I joined groups of inmates, they ignored my presence except for a greeting and continued with their conversations in my presence. However, when inmates who were of questionable loyalty (or strangers) approached, the inmates would halt the conversation with such phrases as: "cool it," "later for it," "this one's got nose trouble," "watch this snitcher." Furthermore, if the inmate was so rash as to raise any questions relating to inmate life or any particular inmate, she was silenced with, "That's a penitentiary question." In addition, whenever I appeared in any part of the cottages or elsewhere in the prison where inmates were functioning in the role of pinner or booster, they went about their affairs and ignored my presence. Inmates who were fortunate enough to have contraband coffee would often enjoy this in my presence while I visited in their rooms. And inmates would often stop me on the grounds and ask when I was coming to see them. Or inmates might come to the cottage window as I was walking by and say, "How come you haven't come to see us lately?"

My role as participant-as-observer at all inmate activities and in the cottage units made it possible for me to get to know all the inmates who were at the prison when the study began and many of the inmates who were committed during the course of the year as well.

The interviewing did not interfere with prison routine. Inmates were not called off the job to talk to me. I made myself available to the inmates on their own time and at their convenience when they were not on the job. All inmates were interviewed on their free time during the day, in the evening, or on weekends. Sometimes I arrived at a cottage for a scheduled interview only to discover that the inmate had had a "bad day." At such times I had to forget the purpose of the research, and simply listened to the inmate's gripes for as long as she wished—this meant until she had talked herself out, and sometimes this took as long as two hours. This kind of event can be something of an inconvenience in research. Yet I learned early in the field work that an observer cannot stop the flow of conversation, even when the observer is not interested or when the conversation is not relevant. For to do so would have been interpreted as "not being interested" in the inmates "as people." This meant, of course, that I had to talk to the inmate again. In such instances, I scheduled another interview a week or two later—hoping that the situation had clarified itself.

My willingness to listen to the inmates about any of their problems and ailments won me the reputation in the eyes of the inmates as someone "sincere," "pretty understanding," and "easy to talk to." Inmates looked forward to my visits and when I left they invariably said I could "come anytime to talk." In this way perhaps I was useful to the inmates. That is, some of them may have looked upon me as a "visitor" they otherwise would not have had during their incarceration. Apart from this, however, I did nothing for the inmates. I did not carry messages from one inmate to another, although I was sometimes asked to do so in the beginning. Nor did I deliver any packages from one inmate to another, although staff members sometimes cooperated in this way. My reason for this was that I wanted to dissociate myself from existing roles in the prison and, furthermore, I did not want to risk the possibility that a message might get distorted and I might find myself part of an inmate squabble.

Throughout the time the study was in process, I sustained my own role in the prison as one which was quite one-sided, namely, that of an observer of "institutional living." Although I did not carry messages from one inmate to another, if an inmate mentioned to me that another inmate in a certain cottage wanted to talk to me, I made it a point to look up the inmate that very day and made an appointment for an interview at her convenience.

While the above may all seem pretty straightforward, I did make mistakes. For obvious reasons, in the beginning of the study I did not understand fully the informal social system of the inmates. In my evening interviews, which were held in the cottages early in the study, I sometimes overstayed my welcome. I recall vividly interviewing a very articulate and cooperative inmate with whom I had spoken on several occasions, and I was eager to complete the interview that evening. During the evening, an inmate opened the door and excused herself three times. Finally, she walked into the room, threw her commissary bag on the bed and exclaimed: "It's nine o'clock!" I learned tactfully to terminate my interviews in the evening for appropriate inmates at eight-thirty so that I would not interfere with their informal activities.

Conversations with inmates were held, of course, anywhere in the cottages, but the majority of the extended interviews were held in the inmate's room. During the early interviews, sometimes an inmate would open the door and quickly excuse herself saying that she didn't know I was there. When I knew the inmates better, I realized that those who usually interrupted the early interviews were femmes, and I had been interviewing their respective studs. But this kind of interruption did not occur often after the first ten weeks. Inmates who lived in dormitories were interviewed in the dormitory if privacy was guaranteed, or in another inmate's room who had granted permission that her room could be used, or on the grounds if weather and season permitted.

I took notes in the inmate's presence in these sessions. If an inmate showed a reluctance to have her statements recorded (and some inmates did in the beginning) I said that I wouldn't take notes if she preferred that I didn't, or that she could see my notes before I left. In the few cases that inmates refused to have their statements recorded, I simply put the notebook in my handbag and wrote up the notes from memory at home if I was leaving the prison immediately, or made notes in the ladies' room shortly thereafter.

IV

As must now be apparent, I not only spent a good deal of time in the cottages in connection with the interviewing, but also joined inmates in the living room, in the laundry room, in the hall, and in the dormitories, as well as just casually visited with inmates who might call to me from their rooms. Such free and easy coming and going in the cottages presented an important problem in connection with my interaction with correctional officers, as well as with other staff personnel.

An important decision which I had to make at the outset was how I would present myself to the staff in the presence of the inmates. Several factors had to be taken into account. In the first place, I did not want my presence to be anxiety-provoking for the correctional officers, although it was obvious that it was in the beginning. In the early days of the study, my presence in the cottages was clearly disturbing to the officers. When I entered a cottage, the officers made apologies, "You're coming to a dirty cottage"; "It's not always like this"; "The girls aren't always so noisy." After a few weeks, however, when the officers realized that I did not report *them* any more than I did the inmates, this never occurred. Secondly, I needed the cooperation of the staff to carry out successfully my research. And, finally, it was extremely important that I have the confidence and trust of the inmate body.

As far as my behavior toward the staff was concerned, I followed this procedure consistently: Whenever I was with an inmate, I greeted any staff member that went by whether or not the inmate did. If I was seated in front of a cottage and a staff member drove by in a car, I waved to her by way of greeting whether or not the inmate did. Whenever I entered a cottage I made my presence known to the officer. Upon entering, I spoke to any inmate who happened to be in sight, stuck my head in the office and greeted the officer. In the evening the door was locked; since I had no keys, the officer had to open the door, which solved the problem. We simply exchanged a few neutral pleasantries and then I went about my business. When I left a cottage, I always said goodby to the officer and thanked her. If the officer was on the second floor when I arrived, I stayed in the hall talking with the inmates until she appeared. When she came downstairs, I greeted her and continued talking to the inmates for fifteen minutes or so and then proceeded with whatever I had planned. Very often the inmate with whom I had scheduled an interview would be waiting in the hall for me at the scheduled time. Before going to her room, I would say simply, "I just want to say 'Hello' to the officer," and then we would go to her room. None of the officers escorted me to the inmate's quarters unless the inmate was locked in. I simply looked at name plates until I found the inmate I wanted. I would knock at the door and wait for the inmate to open it. And very often, inmates gave me directions.

Did these brief encounters with the officers in the cottages have any effect in gaining the confidence of the inmates? My conversations with the officers in the cottage units were always brief, courteous, and made in the presence of the inmates. My consistency and openness in approach was obvious to the inmates, and none of them ever questioned these brief encounters with the officers in the cottages. In a real sense, I was merely giving the officers the kind of "respect" that inmates understood. Moreover, whenever I had conversations with inmates, either in the cottages or elsewhere in the prison, and a staff member approached, I always pointedly halted the conversation until the officer was out of earshot.

Now while my contacts with the correctional officers were confined to casual greetings in the cottages, I had many opportunities to have casual conversations with the officers as well as with prison administrators and staff members, in other parts of the prison and at staff meetings. There were casual encounters with staff personnel in town, in the laundromat, in the local restaurant, in the post office, on the main street, and in their homes. Sometimes I visited the lieutenants' office in the evening and chatted with whoever happened to be on duty, or chatted with the officer on duty in the control center. In addition, I joined officers in the officers' lounge and I occasionally ate in the staff dining-room. Whenever I did, I made it a special point to sit at a different table each time. In addition, I sometimes walked to the prison; staff members would always stop and ask me if I wanted a lift to the prison. In the evening, staff members would often drive me home. All of these encounters and meetings provided an excellent opportunity to obtain valuable data for the study. Thus, during the first six months I had gained not only the confidence of the inmates, but also the confidence of the vast majority of the staff on an informal basis. At no time, however, did I intimate to the members of the staff that my casual conversations with them, whether they took place in town, on the grounds, or in a staff member's home, would all be carefully recorded.

APPENDIX B GLOSSARY OF PRISON TERMS

The words and phrases below may be looked upon as an inmate's working vocabulary. The meaning of these terms is generally known by the inmates. However, all these terms are not unique to the female prison; a few are also used in the male prison and in other subcultures.

Act. To deceive through pretense in order to gain one's wants.

Around, to have been. To be sophisticated and knowledgeable in the ways of the underworld.

Ass Breaker. A bitter disappointment; a slave driver; a strict disciplinarian.

Bad. Anything good or fine.

Ball Breaker. Any discouraging thing.

Bang. Sexual intercourse; injection of a drug; any thrill or "kick."

Balling. Petting, necking, or having sexual intercourse.

Ballplayer. Anyone capable of being bribed or influenced into criminal activity.

Bat, to go to. To do one's utmost to help a friend; to go to the limit.

Beat. To steal from a victim or to rob a place; to avoid punishment of any kind. In connection with time: to cause to become mentally defective, highly neurotic, or severely depressed.

Beat a Rap. To avoid a prison sentence.

Be Cool. Warning to be careful; to exercise caution.

Beef. To whine; to complain; to inform.

Beefing. The act of complaining.

Behind That. As a consequence of; because of, or as a result of.

Belt. To attack physically.

Benny. Overcoat.

Big House. A penitentiary.

Blast. A good time.

Blow. To lose; to flee; to move on; to tell any individual "where to get off."

Blow Away. To silence by forceful argument; to talk belligerently.

Blow One's Top. To lose one's sanity; suffer a nervous attack.

Blow Snow. Sniff cocaine.

Board, the. The parole board.

Board To Get Your Ass. Disciplinary court in prison; adjustment board.

Boost. To steal.

Booster. A shoplifter; anyone who steals.

Boss Understanding. Describes relationship between two inmates carrying on a homosexual affair; to have "boss understanding" is to have no conflict; a sincere relationship; a good understanding.

Bounce. To cash, as a bad check.

Bouncer. A bad check.

Box. A hi-fi unit.

Box. Vagina.

Bread Basket. Stomach.

Broad. Any female, woman, girl.

Bucket Brigade. Inmates carrying night jars to and from their rooms.

Bug. To commit to an insane asylum; to cause to become mentally defective, highly neurotic, or severely depressed; to bother or annoy an individual.

Bug House. An institution for the mentally insane or for mentally defective delinquents.

Build Up. To inspire confidence in an individual, especially in a prospective homosexual partner.

Bull Dyker. A lesbian.

Bum Rap. An unjust charge.

Bum Steer. A false or misleading piece of information.

Burn. To cook.

Burn Up. To arouse one's anger.

Business, taking care of. Homosexual act.

Busted. To be arrested or convicted; to be reported for violation of prison rules by an informer; to be caught with any contraband or a kite.

Butcher. A prison doctor.

C. Cocaine.

C and M. A mixture of cocaine and morphine.

C-Joint. A place where cocaine is sold to addicts.

C-User. A cocaine addict.

Can. Jail, prison, or reformatory.

Cap. To notice; to call attention to.

Cap That. To improve upon anything; to do it one better.

Case, don't get on your. Request not to render a long involved explanation; stick to the point.

Cash Register. Vagina.

Charity Goods. A promiscuous woman, but one who does not practice prostitution.

Cheaters. Eyeglasses.

Check Out. To find out what something is about; to obtain details on anything of interest.

Cherry. A virgin as far as homosexual relations are concerned; any person inexperienced in underworld activities.

Chicono. Spanish person.

Choppers. Teeth.

Chuckin'. Overeating due to curing oneself of drug addiction.

Clean. To be dressed up; to look attractive.

Clean Oneself Up. Prison inmate who has assumed male role in homosexual relations recaptures femininity before release by assuming guises of femininity; may or may not drop homosexual partner.

Coke. Cocaine.

Coked Up. Under the influence of cocaine; under the influence of cocaine and morphine.

Cokey. A user of cocaine; a drug addict.

Cold-blooded. Inmate who has no feeling or compassion for others.

Cold Blow. A shock or disappointment of any kind.

Con. A convict; anyone with five numbers.

Con. To swindle.

Connection. Any inmate or staff member through whom contraband or stolen goods may be obtained, favors received, or rules circumvented.

Contraband. Any illegal materials.

Cool It. To be on the alert; to change the subject or to stop talking.

Cop. Correctional officer; any prison official or employee; any police officer.

Cop. To steal; homosexual act.

Cop an Attitude. To become angry over something or someone.

Cop a Plea. To bargain for and plead guilty to a lesser crime than that charged in the indictment in order to escape the punishment attached to the higher plea.

Cop Out. To back down under pressure from an aggressive stand; to confess to any illegal act.

Cotton. Thread.

Couple. Two women in a homosexual relationship as husband and wife.

Course, to have had. To have heard enough; to have understood meaning.

Cow Juice. Milk.

Crack, in a. In a hopeless position; checkmated.

Crap. Anything contemptible; lies; nonsense.

Crazy. Anything that is well-liked; something agreeable; may refer to persons, places, or things.

Cubes. Morphine tablets.

Cut. A share; an order to go (anywhere).

Daisy Chain. A group performance by homosexuals of diversified sexual activity.

Dear John. Goodbye letter written to husband or sweetheart.

Degree. (used figuratively) The underworld knowledge obtained in a prison or reformatory.

Deuce. Two-year sentence.

Dex. Dexedrine.

Dig. To understand; to call attention to; listen.

Don't Feel a Thing. Literally, don't care; not affected in any way; to be insensible.

Dope. Narcotics.

Do Time. To serve a prison sentence.

Douce Bag. An inmate who is so loose morally as to be the eager subject of anyone's advances.

Dozens. Vulgar and profane epithets with regard to one's mother; questioning one's parentage.

Drag. Anything or anybody annoying, dull, or unattractive.

Drop the Belt. To switch from a male role to a female role.

Dump. Inmates' term of contempt for prison.

Eat One's Heart Out. Intense suffering.

Equalizer. Any weapon, knife, scissors, razor, etc. used in fights or crimes of violence.

Fag. A male homosexual.

Fairy. A male homosexual.

Fay Broad. A white inmate; especially one who seeks the company of Negroes.

Fix. A single narcotic shot; a contract or agreement secured through bribery.

Flag. To give a signal of any kind; to warn of impending danger.

Flagging. Older inmate attempting to involve youthful inmate in homosexuality.

Flick. A movie.

Flip One's Lid. To become insane while serving a prison sentence; to become "stir crazy."

Found a Home. To find prison life congenial; "never had it so good."

Free World. Community outside the prison gates.

Get. To cause to become mentally defective, highly neurotic, or severely depressed.

Get a Load Of. To listen closely; to watch attentively; to make oneself aware of someone or something.

Get to Steppin'. Order to start walking, i.e., move away or to begin something.

Get Up. The day of release.

Gig. A job.

Good People. Any loyal member of the inmate community; an inmate who can be trusted.

Go Upside Your Head. Warning that inmate will use physical violence.

Grapevine. Underworld system of communication.

Grey Broad. White woman.

Gun. The penis; to have sexual intercourse.

H. Heroin.

H-Joint. A place where heroin is sold to addicts.

Habit. Addiction to narcotics.

Hand Job. Digital stimulation of the genitals.

Happy Dust. Cocaine.

Head Shrinker. A psychiatrist.

Heart. Courage; nerve; foolhardiness.

Heat, the. Any policeman, correctional officer, or prison member.

Heel Up. To arm oneself; especially to arm oneself with a razor.

Hep. To have underworld knowledge; to be sophisticated in the ways of the underworld and prison inmate activities.

High. State of exhilaration, elation, or stimulation caused by the influence of drugs.

Hip. See *Hep.*

Hit. To make a proposal of homosexual marriage.

Hit the Fence. To escape; to run away.

Hole. A seclusion cell in prison.

Holier-than-thou. An inmate who implies or states that homosexual behavior in prison is abnormal or distasteful.

Hooch. Alcoholic beverage made by prison inmates.

Hooked. To become addicted to drugs.

Hooker. A prostitute.

Hophead. A drug addict.

Horse. Heroin.

Hot. Anything illegally made or stolen.

Hot Seat. The electric chair.

House. A room in a prison cottage; a house of prostitution.

House Mother. The madam of a house of prostitution.

Hung Up. To admire, like, or love someone or something.

Hustle. To seek out clients for purposes of prostitution; to prostitute; to steal.

Hustler. A prostitute; a professional thief.

Hypo. Syringe and needle used for injecting narcotics.

In. In prison; to be entitled to share in contraband; to be included in illegal activities of the inmates.

In a Bad Way. To have problems of one kind or another.

In the Life. Any criminal business or occupation.

In the Streets. Community outside prison gates.

Inmate Payroll. Officers capable of being bribed or influenced by inmates to do special favors; i.e., take out letters, bring in contraband, etc.

Jag. Drug habit.

Jams. To listen to music.

Jive. Any tale that is false; so contrived as to be unbelievable; any verbal account that is not acceptable.

Joint. A marijuana cigarette; penis; prison.

Juicehead. An alcoholic; anyone who drinks excessively.

Junk. Drugs; narcotics.

Junk, on the. To be currently addicted to the use of narcotics.

Junked Up. To be under the influence of narcotics.

Junker. A narcotic addict.

Junkey. A drug addict.

Keep Straight. To keep business affairs on the "up and up," i.e., all exchanges are to be transacted immediately and on the spot; no installment plan buying.

Kick. Any thrill or excitement; to cure oneself of addiction to narcotics.

Kill It. To complete a task of any kind.

Kissin'. To state that everything is going well; individual has no complaints.

Kite. An uncensored note or letter passed between inmates.

Knock It Out. To complete a task.

Knock Off. Suggestion to stop activity or conversation.

Knock Off a Piece. To have sexual intercourse.

Larceny-hearted. Untrustworthy; dishonest.

Later For It. Postponement of any matter which cannot be handled immediately; to forget.

Lay. Act of sexual intercourse; a prostitute; any loose woman.

Legit. In accordance with prison regulations; within the law.

Lid. A hat.

Line. Manner of talk which is persuasive but insincere.

Loaded. Drunk from alcoholic beverage.

Long-handled Spoon, to feed with. To maintain physical and social distance from informers and prison staff.

Lush. A female alcoholic.

M. Morphine.

Main-Line. A vein.

Make Bush. To escape from prison.

Makin' It. Two inmates carrying on a homosexual marriage.

Max. Maximum term.

Mellow. Anything pleasant or good; any situation that is compatible with one's interests.

Moss. Hair.

Mouthpiece. A lawyer.

Moxie. Nerve; courage; effrontery.

My People. Partner in a homosexual relationship.

My Stick. What one knows best to do; anything one prefers to do.

Never Had It So Good. (used contemptuously) To be more comfortable in prison than in free society; to find prison life congenial.

Nice People. Anyone that is liked or admired; anyone reliable, faithful, trustworthy.

Nickle. A five-year prison sentence.

Nothin' Happening There. Individual has no involvement in a homosexual affair.

Off the Wall Jive. Any conversation which is not based upon facts; anything untrue.

Pan. Prison or penitentiary.

Panning. General derogatory gossip about an inmate when she is not present.

Pants. A male.

Paper Hanger. One who passes or issues worthless checks.

Party. The act of homosexual or heterosexual experience.

Peddler. A seller of drugs; a prostitute.

Penitentiary Darby. Gossip which circulates about the prison.

Phony. Anything hypocritical; a pretender.

Pick Up On That. To look at or notice an individual or thing.

Pin. The act of an inmate in the role of lookout.

Play. Homosexuality.

Play Straight. Heterosexual relations; a nonperverted sexual act.

Police. Police; correctional officers or any prison official or staff member.

Pot. Marijuana.

Pros. A prostitute; to practice prostitution.

Pull One's Coat. To call attention to something that has taken place, or is taking place.

Pull Time. To serve a prison sentence.

Pusher. An individual who is a supplier of narcotics to drug addicts.

Pussy. Vagina.

Put Down. To belittle; to derogate.

Put the Finger On. To inform against something or someone.

Queer. An individual who engaged in homosexuality outside prison, especially a male.

Raid. A search by prison staff members.

Rap. A conviction.

Rat. A snitcher; a stool pigeon; an informer.

Read. To lessen or belittle by speaking derogatively of an individual.

Really. Precisely; exactly.

Red Devil. Seconal.

Reefer. A cigarette containing marijuana.

Rep. Reputation.

Ride. Trip to seclusion; to agitate; persecute; to have sexual intercourse.

Roomie. Any inmate in a dormitory.

Run Down. To give a complete and accurate account.

Scarf. Oral stimulation of the genitalia.

Set-up Job. Discovery of contraband because an inmate informed prison officials of its whereabouts; a frame-up.

Shades. Sunglasses.

Shakedown. A complete search of room, dormitory or cottage premises for contraband, weapons, etc.

Shipment. A transfer of convicts from one prison to another.

Shitlist. A blacklist; a list of persons under disfavor, censure, suspicion.

Shiv. A razor or knife.

Short, to be. Nearing the end of one's prison sentence.

Short-timer. Inmate whose sentence is approaching expiration.

Shot. A dose of narcotics.

Snap. Anything easy; a quick decision.

Snap Broad. A woman who is said to know what she is talking about.

Snatch. Vagina.

Sniff. Process of taking a powdered drug by inhalation.

Snitch House. Honor cottage.

Snitcher. An informer; a stool pigeon.

Snow. Cocaine or heroin.

Snowstorm, caught in. Under the influence of morphine, cocaine, or heroin.

Solid. To agree with what is being said; dependable; all right.

Something Else. Any extraordinary person, place or thing; may be used in a complimentary or insulting sense depending upon the context.

Sounds. Music.

Sour Paper. Forged checks.

Spiel. Conversation.

Spike. Needle syringe.

Split. A share of stolen goods.

Split. To go immediately.

Split Tail. Female; girl; broad.

Square. Accidental criminal; individual who earns living by conventional and legitimate means.

Square Business. Anything believable, true, factual.

Stash. Any contraband; any hidden goods; a hiding place for contraband; to conceal contraband.

Stomps. Shoes.

Stone Cop. A correctional officer (or other prison staff member) who abides strictly by the rules and meets out punishment on a standard disposition basis; any prison staff member who cannot be bribed or intimidated.

Stone Thing. Anything which is unchanging; routine.

Stoolie. An informer.

Streets, in the. The world outside the prison gate.

Stretch. A term served in prison.

Stroke. A rule.

Strung Up. To care a great deal about someone or something.

Stuff. Any drug.

Sucker. Anyone who can be taken; a gullible fool.

Suede. A colored inmate; usually suede broad.

Swag. Stolen goods or loot; contraband.

Swinging. Anything good, fine, or agreeable; may refer to persons, places, or things.

Talking. Refers to someone engaged in a homosexual act.

Terrible Blow. A severe emotional shock; any bitter disappointment.

Thing. The penis.

Threads. Prison issue of clothing.

Tight. A homosexual marriage.

Time. A prison sentence.

Trick Baby. A child borne by a prostitute.

Turned Out. To be initiated into homosexual practices.

Turnkey. A correctional officer.

Walking Time. The unexpired portion of a sentence which remains when a prisoner is released on parole or good time.

Wax. Record.

Wee-Wee. A male.

Weed. Marijuana.

Weed Benders. West Virginia correctional officers.

Weeds. Cigarettes.

Whip. A request to give information; to get rid of; to allocate.

Whip Game. To take advantage of; to "play for a sucker"; to put on the sucker list.

Whizz Bang. A potent mixture of cocaine and morphine; any potent drug mixture.

Whorehouse. A prison cottage where all inmates are paired off in homosexual couples.

Wise Up. To become alert to what's going on; to become "hep."

Yellow Jack. Usually Nembutal, but may refer to any sedative or hypnotic.

APPENDIX C THE TERMINOLOGY
OF KINSHIP

The terms for the categories into which the inmates classified the inmates that were acknowledged as standing in kinship relation to them are presented below. This listing is exhaustive of all the kinship terms that were used by the inmates while the study was in process. Inasmuch as personal selection plays a major role in the formation of kinship ties other relationships may, of course, be acknowledged at another point in time.

Mother	Aunt
Father	Niece
Son	Grandmother
Daughter	Granddaughter
Brother	Grandson
Sister	Great Grandmother
Uncle	Cousin
Nephew	

The most frequently occurring roles among the inmates are those of mother, father, son, daughter, husband, wife, brother, sister, aunt, and uncle. Brother-sister relationships tend to be discouraged as the inmates believe it to be a dangerous relationship and easily transformed into marriage.

The kinship terms are used by the Alderson inmates both as terms of reference and as terms of address. More often, however, inmates use colloquial or diminutive forms of the categories to address one another.

A child addresses an inmate to whom she refers as "my father," as "pop," "pa," "papa," or "poppy," and occasionally as "dad." The term "daddy" is rarely used, however, as stud broads are referred to as 'daddys." A child addresses an inmate whom she refers to as "my mother" as "mom" and "ma." Sometimes "mama" is used, and on rare occasions the term "mommy" is used to address a prison mother. The latter, however, is not used often because of its use in connection with femmes. The terms "mother," "father," "daddy," and "dad" are not used often to address parents. Instead the colloquial and folksy expressions are commonly used. As reference terms, however, "mother" and "father" are always used by an inmate to describe the inmates who are her parents.

A parent addresses a daughter by name except in certain situations which require emotional support or the implementation of disciplinary measures—in which case she may say "my daughter" or "my child." She refers to her as "my daughter" when speaking to other inmates. A parent addresses a son by name, but quite often uses the term "son." The term "son" is also used in connection with a son-in-law as a term of address. It was also observed that a few parents used the term "my kid" to refer to a child.

Inmates who are sisters to one another address each other as "sis" and "sister"—but the latter is used less frequently. These same terms are used in connection with respect relationships made with a brother's wife which are the equivalent of "sister-in-law." A brother's wife, however, is never addressed as "sister-in-law," although the term is used as a reference term. A brother addresses a sister as "sis" or "sister."

Brothers address one another as "bro" (bûr). Sisters also address brothers by this term. In the early stages of my field work, the use of this term was a source of great confusion, as it seemed to me that everyone who assumed a male role was addressed as "bro." It was only after I began to gather data systematically on the kinship network that this apparent confusion resolved itself. Stud broads also address one another as "bro," but they are not in a sociological relationship to one another as brothers. Primary meanings and sentiment are attached to words employed in kinship relations when a sociological relationship exists between the individuals occupying kinship roles. The term "bro" is also used by inmates when they address a sister's husband, thereby acknowledging the respect relationship between them.

When an inmate describes a mother's brother or father's brother, she used the term "uncle," if she acknowledges the relationship. The term "uncle" is not used often as a form of address; rather, the diminutive "unc" is used, as well as the inmate's name. In connection with a mother's sister or father's sister, the term "aunt" is used as a reference term. As a special mark of courtesy, the kinship term is sometimes used to address her, but usually an aunt is addressed by name.

Inmates occupying the roles of aunts and uncles address inmates they acknowledge as nieces and nephews by name, but refer to them when speaking to other inmates as "my niece" or "my nephew."

There are very few kinship ties marked off by the term "cousins" among the Alderson inmates. In the few families that it appeared, it was a sort of gross status, clearly implying that the inmates who were cousins to the members of the family were one step removed from being strangers to them. In one family, for example, I learned that this relationship was formed because the family members would not accept these inmates—who had incidentally requested membership—in a closer kinship tie. Inmates standing in a cousin relationship address each other by the term "cous" (cŭz), but frequently use given names.

There are few grandmothers in the kinship structure of the inmates and there were no grandfathers while I was at the prison. This is undoubtedly due to the fact that kinship roles tend to be ascribed on the basis of age and the role of grandmother is allocated to the inmate who is quite advanced in years. This role tends to mark off from homosexual relations the inmate who assumes this status. Similarly, older inmates do not become studs, which explains the absence of grandfathers. (There is a saying among the Alderson inmates that the only individuals in the prison who do not eventually become involved in homosexuality are those that "no one wants" because of their extreme unattractiveness, or those that are "so old" that they are undesirable as sexual partners.)

Inmates who do have grandmothers usually address them by name, but use "grandmother" as a term of reference. Occasionally, an inmate will use the term "granny" as a mark of courtesy in addressing her. Grandmothers address granddaughters by their name, but use the term "granddaughter" when referring to the inmate. It is rare that a grandmother addresses an inmate as "granddaughter." One inmate who claimed both a grandmother and great-grandmother addressed them both in the same manner, that is, consistent with the nomenclature applied to grandmothers in the prison. The inmate in the role of great-grandmother addressed her great-granddaughter by name. When each referred to the other, however, the "genealogical" distance was respected with the appropriate nomenclature.

Although the kinship concepts are known, all inmates at one time or another address kin by name regardless of the kinship tie. Kinship terms are not used consistently. Sometimes this is due to the presence of staff members, although some officers are aware of, and indeed acknowledge, the putative kinship ties between inmates. To cite one example, an officer was overheard by the observer to say to a prison "mother," "O.K. Ma, get your kids and let's go to supper." Nuclear family members tend to use kinship terms often when they address one another. When asking for favors of any kind, however, all inmates tend to preface their requests with the appropriate kinship term—a reminder of the primary nature of kinship ties.

Remove bedspread and fold in creases when you sit or lie on bed. Place on back of chair.

Read attached "SMOKING REGULATIONS" carefully and follow instructions. They are for the protection of you and the other women.

DAILY ROOM CARE

Daily room care must be completed before breakfast.
  A. Make bed.
  B. Wipe off screen, outer window sill, and outerparts of toilet †
      with damp cloth.
  C. Wipe up floor daily with damp cloth. Move furniture and get
      dust from corner. Do not use broom or mop.

Two cloths are hanging on the bottom rod of the foot of the bed. (1) for use on screen, outer parts of toilet and floor; (2) for all white woodwork, bed cabinet and dresser. Wash cloths after using and spread out on bottom rod at foot of bed where they are to be kept when not in use.

GENERAL

Stationery—You will be provided with stationery if you wish to write to
      your family.
Personal Clothing—The personal articles you brought with you will be
      packaged by you and the officer at a later date.
Medical Attention—You will be seen by a doctor and dentist very
      soon. If an emergency arises, however, notify an officer on duty,
      or after "lights off" turn on your room light.

ORIENTATION ROOM TRAINING INSTRUCTIONS

  1. Read the rules and regulations concerning visiting, general infor-
     mation, and correspondence.

* Issued in the orientation unit.
† Some rooms in the orientation unit have toilets.

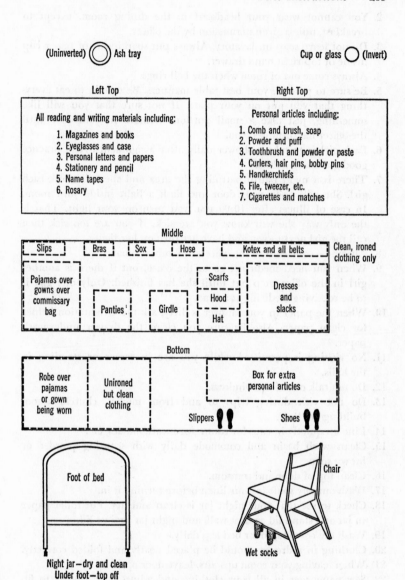

(Uninverted) ⦿ Ash tray   Cup or glass ◯ (Invert)

Left Top

All reading and writing materials including:

1. Magazines and books
2. Eyeglasses and case
3. Personal letters and papers
4. Stationery and pencil
5. Name tapes
6. Rosary

Right Top

Personal articles including:

1. Comb and brush, soap
2. Powder and puff
3. Toothbrush and powder or paste
4. Curlers, hair pins, bobby pins
5. Handkerchiefs
6. File, tweezer, etc.
7. Cigarettes and matches

Middle

Slips | Bras | Sox | Hose | Kotex and all belts — Clean, ironed clothing only

Pajamas over gowns over commissary bag | Panties | Girdle | Scarfs / Hood / Hat | Dresses and slacks

Bottom

Robe over pajamas or gown being worn | Unironed but clean clothing | Box for extra personal articles

Slippers   Shoes

Foot of bed   Chair

Wet socks

Night jar—dry and clean
Under foot—top off

FIGURE 4.   DRAWER ARRANGEMENT

2. You cannot wear your headscarf to the dining room, except to breakfast, unless given permission by the officer.

3. Do not leave soap on lavatory. Always put soap inside of paper cup inside of top right hand drawer.

4. Always come out of room when the bell rings.

5. Be sure to practice your best table manners. Be certain to eat everything that you put on your plate. If not sure that you will like something, just take a small portion. Remain in your seat until the officer has dismissed you.

6. Each girl is to take a shower daily after assignments. Also practice good grooming habits.

7. There is a night patrol patroling the area and she will check each girl. She will open your door and flash a light inside your room. In case of illness after 10:00 P.M. you turn on your light. That is the only way she will know you are sick. If you are too sick then call the girl next to you and have her turn on her light.

8. Always be courteous to the officers and other inmates.

9. When you need medicine, go to the office, but if there is another girl in the office, step out until she has finished. Only one girl is to be receiving medicine at a time.

10. When the paper in your drawer is dirty, ask the Orientation helper for clean paper. Also be sure you clean the drawer underneath paper.

11. No visiting is permitted while you are in rooms or standing in the halls.

12. Do not talk out of the windows.

13. Do not visit during trips to and from movies, church, school building or clinic.

14. Line up quietly in twos for count, for meals, movies, etc.

15. Clean wash basin and commode daily with scouring powder or brown soap.

16. Clean top of door and transom.

17. Wash out any spots in your linen before turning it in.

18. Check to see that your night jar is clean and dry. Put toilet paper in jar and stand lid against wall, and night jar against lid.

19. Wash the coasters under bed legs daily.

20. Clothing in a dresser should be placed neatly and folded correctly.

21. When leaving your room upstairs, leave door open.

22. Sew name tags in all your clothing and adjust your clothes to fit.

23. Each girl is to wrap used sanitary napkins in toilet tissue and put in container for these in toilet room.

APPENDIX E CLOTHING: STANDARD OUTFIT ORIGINAL ISSUE *

3 dresses or 2 dresses and 1 pair slacks
3 slips
3 brassieres
3 pairs of panties
3 pairs of anklets (or long stockings)
2 pairs of shoes
1 pair of rubbers or
1 pair of overshoes
3 pair bedroom slippers
3 nightgowns (or two pairs of pajamas—2nd one gown if preferred)
1 housecoat
1 jacket (short)
1 coat (full length or three-quarter length)
1 hood (wool)
1 rain cap or 1 rain scarf
1 head scarf
3 handkerchiefs
1 belt (dress)
1 belt (sanitary)
1 commissary bag
3 safety pins
1 shower cap
10 buttons for dresses
1 whiskbroom
1 hairbrush
1 testament
1 laundry bag

* Issued to the inmate while in orientation status.

CLOTHING ISSUE—WORK ASSIGNMENTS

Dressmaking and Arts: 4 dresses

Farm:

Dairy
- 8 white slacks
- 8 blouses
- 4 dairy coats
- 3 hair nets
- 3 pair winter underwear (shirts and pants)
- 3 pair wool socks
- 1 pair work gloves
- 1 heavy jacket

Farm Group
- 8 pairs slacks
- 8 blouses (3 should be heavy)
- 3 pair winter underwear (shirts and pants)
- 1 heavy jacket
- 3 pair wool socks
- 1 pair work gloves

Garden Group
- 8 pairs slacks
- 8 blouses (3 should be heavy)
- 3 pair winter underwear (shirts and pants)
- 1 heavy jacket
- 1 pair wool socks
- 1 pair work gloves

Hospital:

Office   4 dresses

Attendants
- 6 dresses (Indian head—yellow)
- 6 white aprons and bibs

Custodian: 4 pairs slacks (May have 4 dresses in place of slacks and blouses)
4 blouses

Commissary: 2 pair slacks (May have all dresses)
- 2 blouses
- 2 dresses

Culinary:

Bakery
- 5 kitchen caps
- 8 white uniforms
- 3 hair nets

Cottage Kitchens
and Dining Rooms
- 8 white uniforms
- 5 kitchen caps
- 5 dining room caps

	10 dining room aprons
	3 hair nets
Orientation Unit	5 kitchen caps
	8 white uniforms
	3 hair nets
Staff Food Service	
(Kitchen)	5 dining room caps
	5 kitchen caps
	8 white uniforms
	3 hair nets
	10 dining room aprons
Staff Dining Room	8 uniforms (special)
	3 hair nets
	5 dining room caps
	10 dining room aprons

Industries:

Laundry	3 gray uniforms
	1 dress
Garment Shop	4 dresses

Offices: 4 dresses

Paint Group: 8 pair slacks
8 blouses

School:

Regular	4 dresses
Custodian	4 pair slacks (May have all dresses)
	4 blouses

Storehouse:

Butcher Shop	8 white slacks
	8 white blouses
Office	4 dresses
Other	4 pair slacks
	4 blouses

Warden's Residence: 8 uniforms special trim
5 aprons special trim
5 caps special trim
3 hair nets

Weaving: 4 dresses

APPENDIX F EXAMPLES OF PRISON LETTERS

The letters below were written by an inmate in the orientation unit while the study was in process. They were given to the observer by the inmate to whom they were addressed. The order in which they appear was suggested by the content of the letters, but it cannot be verified that they were written in that order. They are uncorrected copies of the handwritten originals. The inmate to whom the letters are addressed is 29 years of age and the writer is 19 years of age.

Hi Rag Muffin;

Thats your nickname you know. A Little Sweet Rag Muffin. I really enjoyed your letter. I was sorry you were cold. You need something to keep you warm!

You'll have to excuse this papper it's all I could find this morning.

You can't argue with me. I still know which cottage I want, and I know the Prettyest girl around, and the sweetest, I was hoping I would see you this morning.

You better than coffe you know for waking up. "To me." Say I'm a poet; how about that. Well at least I try. If you want me to I'll write you one. Let me know in your next letter.

I'm not going to the (Dairy) I'll try for something else. Maby the fix it shop.

Wish you were over here, it's lonely.

We're having a meeting at 9 o'clock this morning, so I'll close for now. Write soon. Stay sweet.

Love always
Lee

Hi; Rag Muffin;

You waved at me this afternoon, so I figured it was safe to write, even after telling you how I felt.

I watched by the window tonight after you left work, but the bell rang, and I missed you, but I'll try again.

Don't guess you noticed, but I'm on a diet, "a needed one". I've lost 5 pounds, I'm real proud of myself.

Yes, I will see you Sunday in Mass.

My room mate is a sleep. We can't even talk to each other. She is Mexican, I can't speak Spanish, and she knows very little English.

I wrote you a poem. I'll put it on the last page.

I'm lonely. Sure wish you were here to keep me company.

I'm praying they put me where I want to be. Maby I'll be lucky and they will, if they don't I may develop a complex and go mad on them.

You know I always thought that know one could get any emotion out of me anymore, but I bet if I didn't see you in the mornings I would be *awful hard* to get along with.

I wish I could see you —— (illegible), but it's entirely too cold for you to be outside. I don't want *Baby* "that's you" to get cold. I'll write you a note Saturday night and try to give it to you after Mass. O. K.

You know you sure look cute down there going back and forth from one door to the other. I see you but lots of time you don't see me.

I have pretty good eyes, even from the other end of the Hall, when I want to see something. Lord I want out of orientation. I love your hair the way it is, but you know yourself you wouldn't look right with hair like mine. I don't or wouldn't order you not to have it cut, but I will say this. It's beautiful the way it is. I don't have the right to order you, but I can put in a little request "can't I."

Well I shall put the *poem* on papper, it's been following me all day.

"I love you"—Lee

The Shawdows fall, and I can but dream
But sometimes so real they all seem
That I can fill your lips and see your face.
But I reach and you disappear, without a trace.
But the time will come and soon I pray.
That I'll have dreams and it will be day
And my dearest that will show
That your not a dream and will not go.

To be with you and I with you,
Threw skies of stars and skies of blue
And I'll be then forever dreaming of you.

Loveing you "Lee"

Dear Rag Muffin;

It's light o'clock but I thought I would turn in and write you.
You know, just from the mail I know your a very sweet person.
But I'm wondering, I've never ask you before, but do you want me to
move into the cottage. I want to if I can, but not if you don't want me to.

As I said first impressions mean a lot to me and just from seeing
you and writing you, I've become very fond of you. Maby I shouldn't
be writing that, but I don't lie eather. I'm a very serious sort of
person, even tho you wouldn't know it by looking at me.

I don't misbehave if I have someone who cares, I guess it's the
mother complex. It may sound crazy but, I've always stuck to one person.
I've never went with anyone under 34 years of age. Really I haven't
been around too much. I guess you proberly think I'm nuts after
reading this, but it's the truth, and you wanted to know about me. I
know I can trust you. I trust very few people. I've never written to
anyone before telling them anything about myself.

I guess you would say I'm lonely, or crazy, but the reason the
real reason I'm writeing you, is because I care about you. Believe it
or not, Its you, I think of you at night and can't wait until morning
to see you. I guess I had better close before you get sick of reading
this. Well anyway, I've written a little poem. *Please don't laugh at me.*
If you don't want me to write then I wont.

Love
Lee

(IF)

If you will give your heart to me, only me
I will always treat it tenderly,
Like an angles.
And if you can somehow find the time
Then I will surely find the ryme
To make our hearts combine
Like running Roses.
I guess I shouldn't say!
That our twining lives are gay,
But that way we will stay
Forever.

So just me the chance
Just a second glace
And I would love you
As a Princess.

Lee

Sunday Night;

My dearest Rag Muffin;

I love you, and I'm very lonely tonight. I really believe I would jumpt out the window if I could *except for one reason*. You! I'll get to see you tomorrow. You can't know what that means to me.

I don't show my nerves much, but this place is bugging me, it's funny but when your here in the day it doesn't. But at night I keep looking down their, and knowing your not their.

I think your Janet is a very attractive person, much more than myself, of course.

I'm jelouse, but I can't blame you for loveing her. I proberly can never mean ½ as much to you, as she does. But Honey I won't hurt you, and I wont run around. As I said you don't have to love me, just let me love you—that can't be too much. My emotions are not like anyones, I love you, and I sincerely mean it. You keep saying I can't, but I can and do.

All I've ever really wanted in my life was someone I could love, who wouldn't reject my love.

You looked so pretty today, as you always do.

I'll write you a poem tomorrow, my stomach is cutting up on me a little tonight. "Good Old Osker" Oh! Thats my ulcer.

Today was the First time in seven years I went to Mass. I made myself a promise not ever to go again, but you see I did. Just like the poems. Now see who's changeing.

I'll see you in church Wed. night O.K. I know you don't like the Prod. church, but I don't either. I just want to see you. I'll sit on the otside if I possibly can. No possibly can, *I will sit on the end*. I guess the movie will be Fri. after next. I'll go to it to. Anything to be near you.

Well darling, I'll close. Write soon. I Love You.

Love

Lee

XXPS. Please stay warm. I don't want you catching an old cold. Unless I can catch one to. O. K. Sorry about the papper, its all I could find.

Love You!

My Dearest One;

I have come from church, and could think of nothing more pleasant to do here, than to write you.

Rag Muffin, talking sincerely, you know I cut up a lot, but there is only one person I am interested in. I don't jump from person to person. I have as I know you have, been hurt in the past. I know it sounds crazy, so I'm crazy, but I'm falling very hard for you, and I wanted to know how you fill.

You proberly not like me, for in many ways I'm strange. I know you at least like me, or you wouldn't write. I'm just wondering if you have any others. You are very attractive, and I hope our writing isn't just something to pass the time. I know it isn't for me.

As I said I'm crazy and I have no right to fill the way I do about you. But I do. You proberly think that what I'm writering is just a line, but it isn't. I *swear* it.

You have been honest with me in the past, and I fill I must be honest with you. I worked one day in staff, and a girl there I guess became attracted to me. I liked her, but only as a friend, but I don't beleave she took it that way. I received a note from her tonight. I was very happy because I thought it was from you, but then I noticed the handwriting wasn't yours. I'm sorry she was mistake about my intentions, I gave her no reason to be. But I thought she or someone might mention it to you, and I wanted you to know that my only thoughts are *yours*.

I am sending you the note, which I hope you will destroy. For I surely don't want it, and I don't think you do. But I felt I must tell you, so if someone else informed you, you wouldn't think of me as playing both ends against the middle.

If my fellings for you are getting stronger than you would like them to be, Please inform me, I don't want to be hurt. I know by now, you must share my thought that I surely must be crazy.

Receiving mail from you is all I really think of these days (except for you yourself).

Perhaps I'm being foolish, and you are laughing at me, But I can hope and pray that you aren't. But I felt I should be frank, no matter what, for beleave it or not I'm neither a cheat nor a lier.

Did you like the little poem it was ment for you. Well it's almost time to put the lights out now, so have sweet dreams. I know I shall for I will dream of *you*. Write tomorrow night after you get this. I will see you in Mass Sunday. I will write as often as possible, it isn't easy to get these to you, as you know to.

So I will close. Please don't think me to forward. I just wanted

you to know my true fillings, for it has been quiet a while sience I
have dared to have them.

With my Love
Lee

(Below is the kite written by the inmate referred to in the preceding
letter.)

Hi there honey,

   While sitting here thinking of no one but you I through it would
be a pleasure to let you hear from me at the present time darling.
I am glad that you took me under consideration. I relize that you
care a lot for me sweetheart.

I am also glad that you have been thinking of me darling. Sweetheart
do you have any other peoples beside me if so please let me know
because I really don't want to get hurt and I don't want you to be hurt.
Darling I will walk with you, if roads are dark or fair only place your
hand in mine.

Just trust in me for I will not fail you. for I will help you day by day
sweetheart.

Love alway
Your friend

(On the reverse side of the above letter, the following explanation
was written):

I don't know what the girls going to Staff have told her, but I haven't
written her. So some smart person must be telling her I said I was
thinking of her, and no telling what else. She seems to be a nice
person, but I don't want her to get the wrong idea.

Lee

My Dearest Rag Muffin; I LOVE YOU!

   I only talked to them, because you said you wouldn't come to
the window. I know you were watching today. I'm sorry I mean it.
It won't happen again. Honey I forgot that you could be busted for
comeing to the window. I wouldn't want to be the cause of that. But
in a way, it made me fill good, to know you cared enough to come
and cuss me out.

   Forgive "Baby" will you? Or have I lost that title. I hope not.
Rag Muffin I wouldn't change my choise for anyone. So please

don't be real mad at me. O.K. I saw (you) a couple of times today, but you didn't see me.

My Honey has a temper doesn't she? Well if you want to beat me when I get out, you can. I told you that before.

Did you like the poem? Wrote it for you you know.

I hope your not going to drop me, and quit writing. I never thought you would get real mad. Please forgive me. You know or should know, I'm your boy! I am in here, and I will be when I get out.

I would have liked to have seen the funeral, I guess I may get to see one anyway. *My own.*

If you will forgive me this time I won't ever ever do it again. But I was only talking. I wasn't trying to flirt with her.

My stomach hurts! Serves me right. Seriously I do have an ulcer. Good old osker.

I see you at church tomorrow night. Please try to sit by me. I'll try to get the place I had in the movie. I don't think were going to get to go to the Catholic service Thurs. Mrs. Z (officer) said she didn't believe we would. Really and truly I don't have a religion. I gave it up when I was 12, the only reason I'm going is to see you. I found a little poem I thought you would like. So I'm sending it to you. I wish I could see you tonight! I would take you in my arms, and hold you, and tell you how much I love you. For I do, Very Very much.

I won't even speak to anyone if you say so. Now that I had my fun, I've been worried sick that you would stop likeing me. I fill just about O high.

You proberly won't believe me; but it's 7:00 and I'm in my room, just so I can write you.

If I were to lose you because of my acting smart today, I would never forgive myself.

It's raining out tonight, and that makes me even lonelyier for you.

Honey I love you, I love you more everday. Please don't say I don't. When I get out of here I will treat you like a *queen*. No a God.

I'll write you tomorrow to and give it to you tomorrow night.

Margaret is going to give me a note tomorrow morning, for you to give to Reb, hope you don't mind.

The trouble with me is when I fall in love I get real emotional. I worry about everything I do, afraid to make the other party mad. You might have noticed it.

I also have an inferiority complex that wont quit. I took eight thorazines a day at the —— Reformatory for girls and campozines when they didn't have the other.

I guess I sound like a big Baby tonight, but I just want you to forgive me.

The rain falls softly past my window
And your so close yet so far it seems
I cannot reach out and hold you
I must be satisfied with dreams
Please forgive me if I falter, for I am but a human to.
But if I hurt you my darling, it now hurts me more than it hurts you!
I will my dearest in the future, take from you all doubt.
And any worries that you have, will soon I hope be left out.

So now I end the poem, the one that my heart has made ryme.
But one little thing before I do dear,
I'll love you until the end of time.

There now that is the way I fill tonight. Well my Love I will close. Please write. Stay sweet as you always are.

I Love You
Lee

May Good keep you safe and free from harm
Change not one feature of your face nor your charm
Just let you remain the way that you are
As sweet as a rose and lovely as a star.

P.S. I've got —— embroidered on my handkerchiefs.

Dearest Rag Muffin; I Love You!

I read your note and reread it, honey Please forgive me for being so foolish. I don't even know anyone in 26. They called me, I didn't call them.

Would you like me if know one else did? Your still the only one out their.

Honey; I still want the upper campus, and the same cottage. I'm still in hope you want me their to.

I've been wandering around all day. Very lonely and very ashamed. Trying to think of something to say, to make you forgive me, all I can say is I'm sorry.

I wasn't cold to you when you were across the road. The Police was standing in the hall.

Do you want me to write you? Or are you threw with me? I want to, but I wont, if you don't want me to anymore.

I was very hurt to; I thought you trusted me. I told you I love you and I do. I'll wait until I hear from you, No; I'll write tonight. I hope you will to.

Love
Lee

I saw you in the hall just now; I was signaling; I was trying to ask you if *you* wanted to hang me.

Love you Lee

Hi; Rag Muffin I Love You

I just talked to you; Honey I've said I'm sorry, what else can I say. Your tearing me up inside. Killing me would be a better word.

Alice said you weren't angry. D.D. says you said you were going to kill me. Honey your doing that, if you want to beat hell out of me O.K. But I'll still love you.

I told you you were the one I wanted, why can't you believe me. As I said I'm also a very nervous person, and it's all I could do today to keep from I don't know what.

Please write tonight; *P l e a s e* I love you: I've stuck to myself today, trying to see you from the hall, but you wouldn't even look at me.

What do you want me to do, tell me and I'll do it. Even if it's suicide. If thats what you want. I love you. I mean it. If I've lost you, then I'm giveing up. I've never been able to love anyone and really have them love me in return. I see no real use in even trying when I don't have anyone who will be proud of me for things I do.

See you tonight in church and tomorrow morning. I also hope you'll go to the movie Fri. after next. Will you.

Love you
Lee

Dearest Rag Muffin; I Love You!

I'm glad you aren't angry with me any more, it's a load off my mind.

You won't belive me, but I've been so nervous all day, that I'm sick. "Aren't you ashamed." I know, it does serve me right.

You were alful pretty in church tonight. But I almost fell threw the floor when you came in. What were you trying do do "scare me to death." Mrs. Breen said I was cutting up in church. "Shame on me," and Mrs. Cody said she was supposed to sit where I was. All the girls thought it was funny because I told her, I didn't want to move.

I got a letter from mother and my sis today, everything is O.K. with them.

You didn't write me for church. Punishing me?

I hope some different Police are on tomorrow afternoon. I sure would like to stand in the hall without being threatened with a six o'clock lock. One of these days they'll proberly do it to.

I have to wash tomorrow, ha will try to anyway.

If the bell or something doesn't stop me, I'll see you when you go back to work after dinner tomorrow and when you leave work tomorrow evening.

I was waiting for you at noon, for you to come back. But they called us in the living room.

"Poor Baby" Doesn't have any mail to read tonight.

I liked the way you had your handkerchief especially the lettering. Mine are pretty to. Only I can't write as I said. But their real pretty on the handkerchief.

I bet everyone sure thinks I work on that hall of mine a lot.

Well Honey I'll close. I'll write you a poem tomorrow O.K. I'll be thinking of you all day tomorrow, and dreaming of you tonight as usual.

Loveing You
Lee

The following are additional examples of letters written by the inmates to one another. They were filed in the inmates' case history folders. They are uncorrected copies of the handwritten originals.

My One and Only

"You have kisses sweeter than wine." I love you very much darling. Now and always. Sweet, I told you a lie today and its biting my conscience. I am not 33 but almost as bad. Really only 31. There now I feel better. Angel I had said I wouldn't ask you any questions until you were ready to tell me but the time has come and I have to know these things. Please answer me and tell me the truth. Isn't there a man out there waiting for you? Husband or not? I have heard both ways. If it doesn't make any difference to you it doesn't to me either but still want to know.

Honey why must you taunt me the short time we have together? You play around and it drives me mad. Today I could have screamed. Baby I just don't play with people as you do. Not for a minute could I kiss someone like you do. Please my love no more teasing. Don't you know that you are my life? You can tear me up so easy. And sometimes seem to take a lot of pleasure doing it. I love you little one too much. More than I've ever loved anyone before and never again. Only you have possession of my heart. You're the one that found the tiny hole in my heart and moved in and now occupy it completely. Over the years I have always maintained a barrier but along came you and it crumbled to dust. Darling you can either make or break me whichever is your desire.

Everytime I think of you now I feel the thrill and the sweetness of your kiss. Sweetheart, love! There isn't room in my mind to think of anything else but you, you, you. Every minute of everyday is centered on you and your happiness. For as long as you want me it will always be you above all else. And every day that we are apart I'll spend trying to bring you home to me. When you do get home you'll have everything you want. I will see to that first. One day our day will come when all this is over and I'll do my best to make you happier than you've ever been. It's all up to you. If you're positively sure that you love me and will when you're free, I'll be there waiting for you. There are so many things I want you to tell me. Please tell me honey. All please.

Baby from now on you will read all my incoming and outgoing mail. Then you'll know I'm not telling you any lies. There isn't anyone I give a snap for except you. You will probably get one letter Tues. OK?

Oh sweet I wish you were with me now. I want to hold you close and tell you how much I love to turn out the lights and snuggle up real tight and listen to the rain (later) coming down. I would be perfectly content. You'll never know how much I love you and want you. Many long nights I lay awake day dreaming of you. I even hate to talk to these people around me because it interrupts my thoughts of you. Oh my darling how I love you. So much, so much. Please love me too. Not just words but your heart. Please? If anything were to happen to you now it would end all purpose of life for me. Everything I say or have ever said I mean. From the depths of my soul. God knows I don't lie to you ever. He knows all and I would be committing an unforgiveable sin saying this is it if it were untrue. All of my life, I'll give you all my love. Be sure of your heart my love before I go. I am never far from you at any time. For mentally I'm with you always wanting to comfort you in your time of need. Giving you all my love and understanding and anything else you want or need. My darling it's time to say goodnite for now. I will say my prayers and then dream of you the whole night thru. Please dream of me a little sweetheart. I'll love you always.

Your wife always,

Goodmorning Sweet

Alright baby, we'll do it your way. No more explanations will I ask you. All this could have been avoided if you had run it down in the beginning. So now we'll start anew. OK?

Baby here's a tho't for you to remember and get it straight. I'm not one of these juveniles. I've been farther around the proverbial pot looking for the handle than 99% of these broads have been around

their own hometown. Altho I've done many things with a big variety
of people this is one phase of life in which I am a virgin. This is
the thing for you to remember. I am not ashamed of a thing I've
done nor will I ever be. If we're here or in the ground it's all the
same to me. There is no way that I'd be ashamed of living with
you so that's that. You can be assured that if we are still in agreement
at the end of my time, I'll be an Ave M when you hit there. If at
some time after I'm gone you should change your mind you can let
your friends know and I'll get the message. I'll be checking with
them every so often. I intend to do some traveling. In fact it will
probably be forced. This man of mine as you call him doesn't lose
very easy and has said the only way I'll get away from him is in a
box . . .

Try to be a good baby and I'll see you for sure on Sunday
morning. I'll sit on the side you sat on alone. I love you baby now
and always. More tonight.

Yours
Mac

Hi Marlene

I know you would have liked to kill me yesterday in the Library
but you couldn't hurt me any worse than you already have. But you
see Marlene words mean a lot to me. I take everything serious. I can't
talk to you. It wouldn't do either you or I a bit of good. You
probably wouldn't listen anyway. I'm sorry it has to be this way. I
still mean everything I've ever told you. I'll always love you. I could
never love another as I love you. I know now that I have never
meant anything to you, just another woman to hurt. Believe me, you
have hurt me more than you'll ever know. Why did I have to be
you're victim. You couldn't possibly have loved me. When you love
someone you can't forget as easily as you have. It just isn't love.

(unsigned)

Howdy

This is in a hurry so overlook all mistakes. I have been working
like a dam mule this morning and just found time to kite you. A
says she saw you this morning. I started to go on the truck this
morning but I had to get ready for the ——— (not legible). So here I
am. By the way did you get the kite I wrote yesterday? I did my
best to explain. Didn't do such a good job did I? I will never do it

again. I will be looking forward to seeing you in *Church* tonight. Please be there. I will be very disappointed if you aren't there. Will see you.

FROM ME TO YOU

Hi Baby

Listen I just wanted to tell you that I'm thinking of you. Baby, you really don't know How much it Hurts me to be away from you all day Long. Oh yes!! Sweetheart, I'm going to be good just for *you*. Baby, I might not show you How much I love you, But only God knows what I feel for you, only He knows How much *I Love you*. Sweetheart, like I tole you before there is no one Here in this *place* that could take your place, and as you already know I don't belong *to* nobody, But to Helen —— and that's you Baby.

Look Baby, do something for me okay? trust me please okay and I will do the same, from now on I'm going to trust you and if you do something wrong please tell me before anybody else comes and tells what you done okay? I will give you my word I will tell you if I do something *wrong*. Baby, Let me say this once more before I close, I Love you Helen I really do Love you with all my *Heart, body* and *soul* and *mind*. Well Sweet think, I'll say good night for now so please be good for your Momie that Love's you very *much* with all of Her Heart.

"Love"
Your very "own"

"I will be missing" you
something *terrible*.
You will be on my mind no matter where I will *be*.

Hi Again Sweet Dragon,

I was going to write this last night but then decided not to with my being to evil after flick. What took you off so deep in wonderland during the flick? I'm just wondering because I surely didn't have the warmth of your big longing eyes on me at all. Instead they were lingering on someone else. In fact I don't believe you even noticed my being at the flick at all. Did you? Yes I guess you could say that jealousy does have the best of me after all. Although I was happy for the few kisses you blew my way, I was still disappointed on the other hand. Well I guess that's enough for the jealousy kick. Honey I want to thank you for being so honest and truthful with me about writing to this other broad, which I had a little talk to last night about you. Yes, it was all good from both sides. (Smile) Although the truth may hurt and a lie make you feel good, I was very glad it was the truth. I do wish it wasn't true of you writing to this other broad cause I really dig you very down deep I do. But on the other hand there isn't anything I can do except wait for better days in the future. Honey, do you think I am making a big fool out of myself? That's one thing I don't want to do. I've never made a fool of myself in my life and I sure as hell don't want to start now. I've played too many games in life to be torn into now.

(unsigned)

BIBLIOGRAPHY

Addition, Henrietta, "Institutional Treatment of Women Offenders," *National Proceedings of Prison Association Journal*, 3, January 1957, pp. 21–30.

American Women, Report of the President's Commission on the Status of Women 1963, Washington, D.C.: U.S. Government Printing Office.

Barnes, Harry Elmer and Negley K. Teeters, *New Horizons in Criminology*, Englewood Cliffs, N.J.: Prentice-Hall, Inc., 1959.

Barringer, Emily D. et al., "Minimum Standards for the Prevention and Treatment of Venereal Diseases in Correctional Institutions," *National Committee on Prisons and Prison Labor*, New York, 1929.

Bishop, Cecil, *Women and Crime*, London: Chatto and Windus Ltd., 1931.

Booth, Maud Ballington, "The Shadow of Prison," *Proceedings of the 58th Congress of the American Prison Association*, 1928, pp. 201–206.

Brockway, Zebulon R., "American Reformatory Prison System," *American Journal of Sociology*, 15, 1910, pp. 454–477.

Bryan, Helen, *Inside*, Boston: Houghton Mifflin Company, 1953.

Burleigh, Edith M., "New Use of a Clinic in a Woman's Reformatory," *Survey*, 31, 1913, p. 155.

Burnham, Creighton, *Born Innocent*, Englewood Cliffs, N.J.: Prentice-Hall, Inc., 1958.

Caldwell, Morris G., "Group Dynamics in the Prison Community," *Journal of Criminal Law, Criminology and Police Science*, 46, January-February 1956, pp. 648–657.

Children's Bureau, *Statistics on Public Institutions for Delinquent Children*, 1956, Washington, D.C.: U.S. Department of Health, Education, and Welfare.

Clemmer, Donald, *The Prison Community*, New York: Holt, Rinehart and Winston, Inc., 1958 (Reissue of the 1940 Edition).

Codding, J. K., et al., "Recreation for Women Prisoners," *Proceedings of the American Prison Association*, 1912, pp. 312–328.

Coggeshall, Janie M. and Alice D. Menken, "A Woman's Reformatory in the Making, Minimum Standards," *Journal of Criminal Law and Criminology*, 23, January-February 1933, pp. 819–828.

Cooley, Charles H., *Social Organization*, New York: Charles Scribner's Sons, 1913.

Cressey, Donald R., Editor, *The Prison: Studies in Institutional Organization and Change*, New York: Holt, Rinehart and Winston, Inc., 1961.

Davis, Katherine Bement, "The Laboratory and the Women's Reformatory," *Proceedings of the American Prison Association*, 1920, pp. 105–108.

Davis, Kingsley, "Jealousy and Sexual Property," *Social Forces*, 14, 1936, pp. 395–405.

De Beauvoir, Simone, *The Second Sex*, Translated and Edited by H. M. Parshley, New York: Alfred A. Knopf, Inc., 1953.

Dewees, Mary, "The Training of the Delinquent Woman," *Proceedings of the American Prison Association*, 1922, pp. 82–90.

Falconer, Martha P., "Reformatory Treatment of Women," *Proceedings National Conference of Charities and Corrections*, 1919, pp. 253–256.

Festinger, Leon, Stanley Schachter, and Kurt Back, *Social Pressures in Informal Groups: A Study of a Housing Project*, New York: Harper and Brothers, 1959.

Firth, Raymond and Judith Djamour, "Kinship in South Borough," in Raymond Firth, Editor, *Two Studies of Kinship in London*, University of London: The Athlone Press, 1956.

Ford, Charles A., "Homosexual Practices of Institutionalized Females," *Journal of Abnormal and Social Psychology*, 23, January-March 1929, pp. 442–449.

Glueck, Sheldon and Eleanor Glueck, *Five Hundred Criminal Careers*, New York: Alfred A. Knopf, Inc., 1930.

——, *Five Hundred Delinquent Women*, New York: Alfred A. Knopf, Inc., 1934.

Goffman, Erving, "On the Characteristics of Total Institutions: Staff-Inmate Relations," in Donald R. Cressey, Editor, *The Prison, Studies in Institutional Organization and Change*, New York: Holt, Rinehart and Winston, Inc., 1961.

——, *Asylums*, Garden City, New York: Doubleday and Company, Inc., 1961.

Gouldner, Alvin W., "Organizational Analysis," in Robert K. Merton, et al., Editors, *Sociology Today*, New York: Basic Books, Inc., 1959.

Gouldner, Alvin W., "Reciprocity and Autonomy in Functional Theory," in L. Gross, Editor, *Symposium on Social Theory*, Evanston, Ill.: Row, Peterson and Company, 1959.

Greer, Scott, *Social Organization*, New York: Random House, Inc., 1955.

Harper, Ida, "The Role of the 'Fringer' in a State Prison for Women," *Social Forces*, 31, 1952, pp. 53–60.

Harris, Mary B., *I Knew Them In Prison*, New York: The Viking Press, Inc., 1936.

Hayes, Rutherford B., Address: *Proceedings of the National Prison Congress*, Atlanta, Georgia, 1886, pp. 43–46.

Hayner, Norman S., "Washington State Correctional Institutions as Communities," *Social Forces*, 21, 1943, pp. 316–322.

Hayner, Norman S. and Ellis Ash, "The Prison as a Community," *American Sociological Review*, 5, August 1940, pp. 577–583.

Haynes, F. E., "The Sociological Study of the Prison Community," *The Journal of Criminal Law and Criminology*, 39, 1948–1949, pp. 432–440.

Henry, Jules, *Culture Against Man*, New York: Random House, Inc., 1963.

Hodder, Jessie D., "The Treatment of Delinquent Women," *Proceedings of the American Prison Association*, 1919, pp. 212–223.

Homans, George C., *The Human Group*, New York: Harcourt, Brace and Company, 1950.

Irwin, John and Donald R. Cressey, "Thieves, Convicts, and the Inmate Culture," *Social Problems*, 10, Fall 1962, pp. 142–155.

Keely, Sara F., "The Organization and Discipline of the Indiana Women's Prison," *Proceedings of the Annual Congress of the National Prison Association*, 1898, pp. 275–284.

Kellogg, Virginia, "Inside Women's Prisons," *Colliers*, 125, No. 22, June 3, 1950, pp. 15, 37–41.

Kellor, Frances A., "Criminal Sociology—Criminality Among Women," *Arena*, 23, 1900, pp. 516–524.

——, "Psychological and Environmental Study of Women Criminals," *The American Journal of Sociology*, 5, 1900, pp. 527–543.

Kosofsky, Sidney and Albert Ellis, "Illegal Communication Among Institutionalized Female Delinquents," *The Journal of Social Psychology*, 48, August 1958, pp. 155–160.

Leiderman, P. Herbert, "Man Alone: Sensory Deprivation and Behavioral Change," *Corrective Psychiatry and Journal of Social Therapy,* 8, Second Quarter, 1962.

Lekkerkerker, Eugenia C., *Reformatories for Women in the United States,* Batavia: J. B. Wolters, 1931.

Loveland, Frank, "Classification in the Prison System," in Paul W. Tappan, Editor, *Contemporary Correction,* New York: McGraw-Hill Book Company, Inc., 1951.

MacIver, Robert M., *Society,* New York: Farrar and Rinehart, 1937.

McManus, Virginia, *Not For Love,* New York: G. P. Putnam's Sons, 1960.

Malinowski, Bronislaw, *Crime and Custom in Savage Society,* New York: Harcourt, Brace and Company, 1932.

Mead, George Herbert, *Mind, Self and Society,* Chicago: The University of Chicago Press, 1934.

Merton, Robert K., *Social Theory and Social Structure,* Glencoe: The Free Press, 1957.

Murtagh, John M. and Sara Harris, *Cast the First Stone,* New York: Cardinal, 1958.

O'Hare, Kate, *In Prison,* New York: Alfred A. Knopf, Inc., 1923.

Otis, Margaret, "A Perversion Not Commonly Noted," *Journal of Abnormal Psychology,* 8, June-July 1913, pp. 113–116.

Parsons, Talcott, "Age and Sex in the Social Structure of the United States," *American Sociological Review,* 7, October 1942, pp. 604–616.

———, *The Social System,* Glencoe: The Free Press, 1951.

Pollak, Otto, *The Criminality of Women,* New York: A. S. Barnes and Company, Inc., 1950.

Polsky, Howard W., *Cottage Six,* New York: Russell Sage Foundation, 1962.

Potter, Ellen C., "Problems of Women in Penal and Correctional Institutions," *Journal of Criminal Law and Criminology,* 25, May-June 1934, pp. 65–75.

Redfield, Margaret Park, "The American Family: Consensus and Freedom," *The American Journal of Sociology,* 52, November 1946, pp. 175–183.

Riemer, Hans, "Socialization in the Prison Community," *Proceedings of the American Prison Association,* 1937, pp. 151–155.

Roebuck, Julian, "A Critique of 'Thieves, Convicts, and the Inmate Culture,'" *Social Problems,* 11, Fall 1963, pp. 193–200.

Rogers, Helen W., "A Digest of Laws Establishing Reformatories for Women," *Journal of Criminal Law and Criminology,* 13, November 1922, pp. 328–437.

Rogers, Helen W., "A History of the Movement to Establish a State Reformatory for Women in Connecticut," *Journal of Criminal Law and Criminology*, 19, February 1929, pp. 518–541.

Schafer, Stephan, "On the Proportions of the Criminality of Women," *Journal of Criminal Law and Criminology*, 39, May-June 1948, pp. 77–78.

Schrag, Clarence, "Some Foundations for a Theory of Correction," in Donald R. Cressey, Editor, *The Prison: Studies in Institutional Organization and Change*, New York: Holt, Rinehart and Winston, 1961, pp. 309–357.

Selznick, Philip, "Foundations of the Theory of Organization," *American Sociological Review*, 13, February 1948, pp. 25–35.

Shepard, Dean and Eugene Zemans, *Prison Babies*, Chicago: John Howard Association, 1950.

Shih, Kuo-Heng, *China Enters the Machine Age*, Cambridge: Harvard University Press, 1944.

Strong, Samuel M., "Social Types in a Minority Group," *The American Journal of Sociology*, 48, March 1943, pp. 563–573.

Sullivan, Katherine, *Girls on Parole*, Cambridge: Houghton Mifflin Company, 1956.

Sutherland, Edwin and Donald R. Cressey, *Principles of Criminology*, New York: J. B. Lippincott Company, Sixth Edition, 1960.

Sykes, Gresham M., *The Society of Captives: A Study of a Maximum Security Prison*, Princeton: Princeton University Press, 1958.

T'ien, Ju-K'ang, "Female Labor in a Cotton Mill," in Kuo-Heng Shih, *China Enters the Machine Age*, Cambridge: Harvard University Press, 1944, pp. 178–195.

Ward, David A., and Gene G. Kassebaum, "Lesbian Liaisons," *Transaction*, 1, January 1964.

——, "Homosexuality: A Mode of Adaptation in a Prison for Women," *Social Problems*, 12, Fall 1964, pp. 159–177.

Wheeler, Stanton, "Social Organization in a Correctional Community," Unpublished Ph.D. Dissertation, University of Washington, 1958.

——, "Socialization in Correctional Communities," *American Sociological Review*, 26, October 1961, pp. 696–712.

Whitehead, Alfred North, *Science and the Modern World*, New York: New American Library, 1925.

Whyte, William H., Jr., *The Organization Man*, Garden City, New York: Doubleday and Company, Inc., 1956.

Williams, Lorraine O., "Short-term Treatment of Women: An Experiment," *Federal Probation*, 21, September 1957, pp. 42–51.

Williams, Robin J., Jr., *American Society*, New York: Alfred A. Knopf, Inc., Revised Edition, 1960.

INDEX

241

Date Due

MAY 24			
NO 7 '67			
MY 20 '69			
NO 1 3 '69			
NO 3 0 '70			
AP 25 '72			
MY 1 '72			
MAY 6 '74			
OCT 23 '75			
NO 1 8 '78			
NO 1 8 '78			
NOV 1 1 1981			
APR. 1 8 1984			
NOV. 0 8 2004			